KNOWLEDGE
AND
AUTHORITY
in the
Psychoanalytic
Relationship

CURRENTS
IN THE QUARTERLY

A Book Series
edited by Sander M. Abend, M.D.

Published continuously since 1932, *The Psychoanalytic Quarterly* is one of the oldest psychoanalytic publications in the United States. Free of ties to any school, institute, or organization, the editors have, over the years, maintained an independent spirit that has allowed for the publication of thoughtful, insightful, and often controversial papers from a wide range of psychoanalytic perspectives. Now in this series, *Currents in the Quarterly*, a group of its most distinguished editors brings together classic and new papers devoted to topics that continue to spark interest and debate in the field today.

Volume 1: The Place of Reality in Psychoanalytic Theory and Technique
Sander Abend, Jacob Arlow, Dale Boesky, and Owen Renik, editors

Volume 2: Knowledge and Authority in the Psychoanalytic Relationship
Owen Renik, editor

KNOWLEDGE AND AUTHORITY

in the Psychoanalytic Relationship

Owen Renik, Editor

JASON ARONSON INC.
Northvale, New Jersey
London

The material in this volume was originally published in *The Psychoanalytic Quarterly*, Vol. 65, No. 1, 1996, and is reprinted by permission.

This book was printed and bound by Book-mart Press of North Bergen, NJ.

Library of Congress Cataloging-in-Publication Data

Knowledge and authority in the psychoanalytic relationship / Owen
  Renik, editor.
    p.   cm.
    "The material in this volume was originally published in The
  psychoanalytic quarterly. vol. 65, no. 1, 1996"—T.p. verso.
    Includes bibliographical references and index.
    ISBN 0–7657–0139–1 (alk. paper)
    1. Psychoanalysis.   2. Authority.   3. Knowledge, Theory of.
  4. Psychotherapist and patient.   I. Renik, Owen.
    [DNLM: 1. Professional-Patient Relations.   2. Psychoanalytic
  Therapy—methods.   3. Psychoanalysis.   4. Authoritarianism.
  5. Psychoanalytic Theory.   Not Acquired / WM 62 K73 1998]
  RC506.K59   1998
  616.89'17—DC21
  DNLM/DLC   ˙
  for Library of Congress   97–29287

Printed in the United States of America on acid-free paper. For information and cata-
log write to Jason Aronson Inc., 230 Livingston Street, Northvale, NJ 07647-1726. Or
visit our website: http://www.aronson.com

CONTENTS

PREFACE

What is the nature of the understanding arrived at through clinical psychoanalysis? What kinds of expertise can legitimately be claimed by analyst and analysand? These are questions fundamental to much of what is being currently discussed at the forefront of psychoanalytic theory-building. Accordingly, the editors of *The Psychoanalytic Quarterly* have decided to devote a special issue to "Knowledge and Authority in the Psychoanalytic Relationship."

Our strategy has been to invite contributions from a group of preeminent psychoanalytic investigators who in their work have dealt implicitly with issues of knowledge and authority, but have never focused on them explicitly. In this way, we tried to avoid rounding up the usual suspects—analysts whose views on our topic are already well known. We are excited about the results: discussion from a multiplicity of points of view that is in itself instructive. Various aspects of knowledge and authority in the analytic relationship are examined, but in every instance the ideas offered are experience-near and have obvious implications for the treatment situation. This clinical orientation is in keeping with *The Quarterly's* focus on the interests and concerns of the analytic practitioner.

We will let the papers speak for themselves. Larry Friedman has given us a shrewd, thoughtful, and comprehensive overview; readers can either begin with this commentary, using it as a kind of annotated table of contents, or can save it for retrospective reflection, according to taste. We hope you will find, as we do, that this issue of *The Quarterly* offers an exciting, wide-ranging look at contemporary psychoanalytic thinking about the crucial subject of knowledge and authority in the psychoanalytic relationship.

OWEN RENIK, M.D.

OVERVIEW

Lawrence Friedman, M.D.

THE TWO MEANINGS OF AUTHORITY

Psychoanalysts have usually maintained that patients are struggling with obscure problems that become easier to resolve as the analyst points out their elements. At first, the social and scientific community asked whether analysts really knew what those elements were; that was the challenge that most concerned analysts at the dawn of their profession. But even then the issue of proof intersected with the issue of technique, for instance, in the accusation that results were produced by suggestion: Did the conduct of treatment persuade the patient to confirm what his analyst already "knew"? Did the analyst's *knowledge* seem to be authoritative just because he had *exercised* authority in the relationship?

As analysts became less interested in (and perhaps less hopeful about) establishing the truth of their findings in the scientific community, they became more interested in the authority invested in them or withheld by their patients. What claims are they making on their patients? How do they want patients to regard them? Why should they expect to be seen that way? And (more recently) is it possible to defend those claims? These technical questions have become increasingly insistent.

As is well known, Freud believed that the analyst has the

authority of a beloved parent. That sort of authority reflects a relationship. Of course the other kind of authority—possession of knowledge—always meant factual rightness for Freud.

For the most part, Freud saw even the relationship type of authority as a vehicle for conveying authoritative facts. But analysts shortly expanded the mission of the relationship, expecting now to be seen as *moral* authorities. There was a belief that the analyst's ego ideal is contagious (Sachs, 1925), his superego a model for the patient (Alexander, 1925; Strachey, 1934). This was to be no ordinary moral authority. It was a peculiarly—I should say uniquely—specialized authority, because it governed only mental regulation and left the patient in full charge of his life. To buttress both the moral authority and also its very strict limitation, the analyst was enjoined to be impartial in conflict and secretive about his person.

Many analysts have come to regard this as too exalted a posture. They urge colleagues to climb down from their pedestals. It is more realistic, they argue, to recognize the common, fallible humanity of analyst and patient. But in this volume (especially in the contributions of McLaughlin, Hoffman, and Bollas) we see a further twist in the plot. We are told that in order to be truly humble analysts will have have to admit that, no matter how ordinary they feel, their words will always carry moral authority—an implied "ought" or a "better way." Try as he might to free himself, the analyst is chained to his pedestal. If he doesn't realize that, he won't be prompted to counterbalance his power (McLaughlin) or take advantage of it (Hoffman). For these authors, arrogance amounts to speaking from the pedestal while pretending to be unlocatable. It is true that in this modern version, the venerable superego manipulation has a more tragic feel to it: the analyst's power is viewed wryly rather than complacently, and McLaughlin sees in it a touch of unavoidable bullying that deserves the rebellion it encounters. Yet, once again the analyst is back on his pedestal, in the relationship sense if not in the knowledge sense.

Readers may be surprised by this turn of the historic wheel. What they are watching, I suggest, is an effort to rethink the two kinds of authority and the nature of their interaction in the light of challenges to both of them. This volume moves back and forth between them: authority as authoritativeness, and authority as a personal relationship.

We all know that interpersonal relationships can be marked by the exercise or absence of authority. But these social roles also express individual mentalities, and Kernberg reminds us that an analyst says something about himself by exercising or not exercising authority and by manifesting or not manifesting an authoritative attitude. When it comes to behavior, it is just as expressive of the analyst's attitude to refuse an authoritative role as it is to luxuriate in it. The refusal may show, for instance, the analyst's fear of his sadism or erotic interest. An analyst who accepts demotion from authority may be masochistically submitting to his patient's pathology. Finding a kindness where McLaughlin sees a hurt, Kernberg observes that an authoritative manner may reassure the patient of the analyst's indestructability.

Brenner concentrates on the other kind of authority— authoritativeness in knowledge. He reasons that, because the analyst has less at stake (and the benefit of training and a completed analysis), he can see things more clearly than the patient. Whether or not the patient *regards* him as an authority, he is positioned to be relatively authoritative as a knower. Hoffman and McLaughlin doubt that. They think that analytic detachment only or mainly serves to make analysts *seem* to be authorities. In other words, analysts are authorities as *actors* far more than as knowers. We may compare this with the contribution of Bollas. He sets out to study the analyst's authority-as-a-role, but finds that the role includes maternal, paternal, and oedipal modes of *cognition*. His formulation blends knowledge and action: the analyst possesses a defining and containing power that cannot be split into role authority on the one hand, and knowledgeable authoritativeness on the other, just as it makes no sense to ask whether, in a primary sense, our parents really were authorities or just seemed to be. Perhaps the word "raising" (as in raising a child) expresses this no-man's-land in which someone (or some part of the mind) simultaneously mediates and defines the world, constrains and promotes growth. Bollas's mother- , father- , and oedipal-modes are modes of cognition *and* of relationship; they are defining influences (performatives, in the words of John Austin and Leston Havens)—ways of both knowing and doing—that are exercised by the analyst toward his patient and then within the patient's mind (as Loewald has also described). And we find in the paper by Hanly that analysts of both sexes are well supplied with all these modes of moral feeling and influence.

THE EMPHASIS ON AUTHORITY AS A ROLE

Despite the many differences in these papers one notes agreement with Freud's old maxim: Patients are not required to be credulous. The analyst does not *try* to be seen as an authority. But though the analyst does not demand respect, one gathers from most of these papers that he is entitled to assume as a baseline that his authority will ordinarily be accepted for cognitive and/or dynamic ("good") reasons that are universal, and can confine his curiosity to those instances where patients do *not* accept it, for symptomatic ("bad") reasons that are idiosyncratic, if not to the patient, then to the analytic dyad.

Is that presumptuous? The justification might be that, without an expectable baseline of what is "due" the analyst, there could be no departure to jolt his curiosity. (He would certainly not be able to make the assessments of sadism and avoidance to which Kernberg refers.) Gestures can only be evaluated against a background of norms. But surely convenience alone would not account for such diverse contributors agreeing that patients' rejection of authority is more remarkable than their acceptance of it. The more compelling reason for the agreement may have to do with recent concepts of authority. The majority here locates the analyst's authority in his procedure rather than in his knowledge. And procedure is something that presumably certifies itself to the patient by its aptness. Procedural authority is the sort of authority that a patient will genuinely accept only when and because it vindicates itself. (Does that make the patient the ultimate authority as witness?) Seen in that light, absolute incredulity would mean that something was wrong with the operation. Schafer works that out in detail here.

This is worth pondering, especially since the casual reader might miss the new emphasis on the authority of procedure. With the conspicuous exception of Brenner and Kernberg, it is not advertised as authority because the idea of authority grates on the modern nerve. Indeed, what pervades these papers is skepticism about the analyst's knowledge, as in McLaughlin's modesty, Chodorow's debunking of psychogenic formulas, Hoffman's denial that the analyst can possibly know the contexts that give meaning to his actions, Elliott and Spezzano's de-idealization of coherence, and Mayer's (opposite) de-idealization of analytic (in the literal sense) understanding, in favor of holistic apprehension. But this humbling of the analyst's claim to causal knowledge simply shifts the emphasis from authority, defined as expert knowledge, to authority as a relationship role, spelled out in the design of treatment.

Schafer gives us a clue to where authority will be found in the modern paradigm. Such qualities as the analyst's sophisticated open-mindedness and genuine non-exploitiveness are recognized by patients not primarily as a persuasive style, but as part of the very "rightness" of what is heard. In treatment, Schafer tells us, the interpersonal purpose of a judgment can undercut its accuracy, and, conversely, the accuracy of a judgment (its cognitive authority) can be rendered irrelevant (non-authoritative in action) by the patient's imputing to it a noxious purpose, or framing it as a sign of an undesirable attitude. This might imply that in psychoanalytic treatment right meaning and right action are not different things; if it comes across as the wrong interpersonal action, it can't be the right interpretation.

Following out that line of thought, analysts might start to think of personal knowledge (of oneself or others) as a matter of attitudes. (That is one way of describing Schafer's work on narratives.) But if knowledge-authority lies in an attitude, what can we possibly mean by an accurate attitude? (Substituting "usefulness" for "accuracy" won't buy much time.)

INTERMINGLING KNOWLEDGE-AUTHORITY AND ROLE-AUTHORITY

Authority as rightness and authority as influence remain separate definitions of authority. But the reader of this volume will be struck by how much the question of rightness and the question of influence are fused in recent years. What accounts for that? This volume suggests that it is because of a contemporary interest in the way meaning is formed. We find that many authors no longer believe that there is a difference between defining meaning and influencing meaning. We read again and again that meaning is "co-created" in the very process of trying to nail it down. Authors are impressed by the ambiguity of meaning, its pluripotentiality, the possibility that it could develop just as well in many different directions, depending on how one interacts with it.

Innovations are not always as new as they seem, but this one certainly seems to move psychoanalysis in an untraditional direction. That is not to say that the subject of creativity is foreign to analytic theory. The bibliographies in this volume reflect a rich legacy of theory dealing with playfulness, imagination, and invention. But many of the contributors here are vastly more inclined than their predecessors to think of every clinical encounter as an example of creativity. Many of them ask us to move away from a deterministic outlook with its reassuring causal chains. They talk of *discontinuity, fragmentation,* and unpredictability (Elliott and Spezzano), and *relativity* to perspective (Schafer), openness to *inexplicable* communication (Mayer). I think the real pivot in the dialogue is the idea of *novelty*—the unpredictable outcome of an encounter. Inquiry into a patient's meaning is regarded as trail-blazing rather than path-hunting. There is a certain arbitrariness to the outcome.

If the clinical encounter were really as emergent as that, the knowing kind of authority would find scant employment. Authoritative knowledge seems to require a more static subject than is allowed by some of our contributors who believe that, before the treatment moment, there is nothing (prefigured) upon which authority could be exercised. (I am exaggerating somewhat for schematic purpose.)

Here we should note that this epistemological agnosticism is loosely—but only loosely—associated with a nondogmatic approach to patients. Much of the earnestness of anti-authority analysts is fueled by their conviction that the analytic virtues of modesty, flexibility, tentativeness, sensitivity, open-mindedness, and the readiness to accept correction from patients stand in need of encouragement (McLaughlin; Schafer). But it is important to remember that those virtues are only encouraged by, and are not bound to, the belief that meaning is unpredictably created at the moment by the interaction of analyst and patient. It is perfectly possible for an analyst to believe that there is a knowable truth in front of him, which, alas, he will never reach. It is even possible for such a truth-seeking analyst to feel helpless without his patient's "instruction." And, on the other hand, it is equally possible for an epistemologically skeptical analyst to dogmatically overrule every attempt to find a truth. Arrogance is the trait of a person, not the property of a theory.

AUTHORITY AS KNOWLEDGEABILITY

What carries us beyond the question of the analyst's modesty is the more radical question of whether a hidden meaning is known even to the Eye of God. If it is, then perhaps some piece of it might also be known to the eye of the analyst. If it is not—if there is no already-given predisposition from which momentary developments are lawfully elicited—then the analyst's "co-creation" of meaning is, indeed, an adventure of a vastly different sort than we have imagined. That different sort of adventure, inspired by current philosophical trends, is what we see described, for example, in the papers of Elliott and Spezzano, and Mayer, who think that the unpredictability of the development of a meaning is not merely the result of our limitations as knowers, but is due to its intrinsic undetermination. Their views may be contrasted with that of Chodorow, a more moderate skeptic, who allows a determinate truth to the analytic encounter over which analysts can obtain some measure of authority by studying the general *forms* of human problems and transformation of meaning as they are regularly developed, for example, in infancy. What Chodorow doubts is not regularity per se, but that old, authoritative, high-resolution, X-ray vision of biographical etiology that analysts have been known to claim.

Readers will be less troubled by the emphasis on the analyst's uncertainty, which was always acknowledged to some degree, than by the new doubts about factuality itself. And that, in turn, will be disturbing, I predict, not because an ambiguous world is unfamiliar. (Toilers in the mind business are used to that.) It will be disturbing because it is hard to imagine how an analyst would work who no longer believes he is hunting for something that is already there to be discovered. For instance, Hanly observes that the strongest pillar of an analyst's authority has always been his dedication to objective truth. It is that dedication that prevents him from pulling rank on patients or engaging in other personal manipulations. If there is no objective truth to be known, what self-discipline will take its place?

We are often told that mutual reflection can replace the hunt for truth. For instance, it is plausibly pointed out that mutual reflection on how patient and analyst perceive each other will be enlightening. But that seems to be a hunt for an objective truth (about the relationship)—a hunt that has, perhaps, a bit less confidence and a lot less focus than the old psychoanalytic project. (Brenner argues that a professional activity needs a sharper focus than that, and he states his focus plainly.)

Some suggest that we might replace the hunt for truth with a project of dislocating patterns; if we undermine a patient's passive acceptance of his accustomed perceptions, that will make them free, even if neither we nor God has a truer perception to offer. This is the view of Elliott and Spezzano. Hoffman, too, thinks that dislocation is a useful goal, but he cautions that it is no more possible to challenge a viewpoint neutrally than it is to describe it neutrally. According to Hoffman, when we intervene or react in any manner, we are always trying to turn the patient one way or another, though if we are aware of that fact we may be able to detach ourselves from our pushing long enough to reflect with the patient upon our mutual structuring maneuvers.

PRACTICAL TIPS FROM THE SKEPTICS

In the wake of these skeptical critiques of authority (in both knowledge and relationship forms) comes a familiar, practical sermon: it is a plea for freer action on the part of the analyst.

We are told to be less official, more spontaneous, less calculating, more advisory, less secretive, more personal, more daring and adventuresome. Elliott and Spezzano believe that the analyst should be more imaginative and less didactic. McLaughlin cedes some of his own intent and power to the patient so that a more equitable balance may be achieved. Hoffman argues, in effect, that since we are always "body-Englishing" patients toward one goal or another, we might as well use our leverage visibly to advise on important issues, rather than denying our half-hidden judgments and pretending to be merely seeking understanding, while real-life opportunities slip away. Hoffman believes that it is less manipulative to do our advocating openly even if the analyst's opinion will always carry preternatural authority.

But why, we may wonder, would analysts who know that they don't know be freer in their behavior for that reason? Why not more restrained? Uncertainty doesn't usually tempt people to greater freedom. The argument seems to be that analysts walk carefully in order to stay with what they know (or to conceal their ignorance), and if they realize that the game is already lost, they will have less reason to be inhibited. That way, at least, they won't be adding an idealizing myth to the general confusion. But if we were completely uncertain about outcomes and sequences and had no good ideas about states of mind, it would be as senseless to act as to refrain from acting. An "um-hm" would do as well as anything. Happily, none of our contributors suggests that we are so lost. For all the talk of non-linearity, non-causality, unpredictability, and emergent meaning, their programs, like every treatment recommendation, reflect an understanding of how people usually behave and react. Our contributors have at least as reliable an anticipation of how patients will respond as we all have about people in our ordinary life, where we usually act with whatever circumspection the situation requires.

If, on the other hand, the problem is merely that the analyst doesn't know with certainty what the patient is experiencing, or what he has contributed to the experience, why wouldn't he try to standardize his behavior as far as possible to make the job easier? Even without pretending to obliterate one's influence or predict one's impact, it is not wholly senseless to try to keep the static down. The modern psychoanalyst is realistically (and uncomfortably) aware that he transmits a host of subtle, unintended, and ultimately unforeseeable messages, and he may even acknowledge that some large configuration of the treatment relationship hovers just outside his vision. But he is also not likely to forget his first lessons: life teaches quite small children that they have some control over what they communicate, and even infants learn to anticipate their gaze-partner's reactions. Nobody advocates a blank screen neutrality in marriage, but no sensible spouse ignores prudent caution.

Brenner draws attention to the evident but often overlooked fact that no matter how vigorously the modern analyst disclaims authoritative knowledge, every therapist without exception offers himself as an expert on how therapy should be conducted, which is a tacit claim to knowledge about the mind and its afflictions. This is the functional authority that Kernberg refers to in his contribution. Authorship of treatment implies authority about mental processes and illness. None of our contributors is derelict in this respect. There is not a wild analyst in the bunch. Each has an idea of how the mind works, and an image of pathology.

But if they are not telling us that we must act more recklessly because we don't know what we're doing, then what *are* the skeptics telling us about treatment? They all have their individual messages, of course. Chodorow recommends a focus on the here-and-now, Hoffman suggests that we reveal our stand on some current life decisions, Mayer urges receptiveness to unusual modes of awareness, Elliott and Spezzano look for a more eccentric and playful program, McLaughlin helps the patient redress and therapeutic imbalance. But most general-

ly, I think, what the skeptics are telling us is that patients suffer
from a disturbance of meaning-making, and that meanings
have an emergent aspect that will be better encouraged if we
stop making a fetish of the regularities that are also present—
if we play down rather than play up such authoritative knowledge and authority role as we have. It may even be that the
skeptics, while hardly knowing it, are telling us that we will
exercise *more* authoritative power to compel progress if we
make our knowledge-type-of-authority harder to find and our
relationship-type-of-authority harder to pin down.

This is an empirical question. It is for the profession as a
whole to judge the cost and benefit of these recommendations,
and these may not always be obvious. For example, when analysts decide how much of their inner response to conceal, they
are at the same time deciding what sort of concealing *intention* to *reveal*. In other words, they are declaring how sociable
they are going to be. This open declaration of intention is
important in its own right. On that subject it matters little
whether an analyst actually succeeds in concealing what he
said he would conceal, or revealing what he said he would
reveal; he is casting himself in a more or a less socially recog-
nizable role and asking for a more or less defined relationship.
Thus, if an analyst should decide to make a larger gesture of
openness, he will not only be sharing information about himself, he will also be making a different declaration of sociabili-
ty. The empirical question has to do with what is gained and
lost by altering the ambiguity of the analyst's *intention,* and by
promising a relationship that is less strange than the one that
has generally characterized analytic treatment.

Finally, we may ask ourselves what general concern animates
this volume as a whole. I think it is a new fascination with the
elusiveness of humanly relevant, value-laden reality. That is
what seems to inspire much of this re-evaluation of authority.
Relationship-type (role) authority exists inside a frame of
social meaning, and factual authority (in psychoanalysis) pro-

nounces upon a set of social (rather than physical) meanings, such as superiority, mistrust, loyalty, shamefulness, envy, desirability, goodness and badness, affiliation, obligation, motheringness, fatheringness, and so on. And yet it is not clear what it would signify for social meanings to be objective, that is, to exist anywhere outside the head of each participant. Furthermore, the role-authority that analysts experience in directing treatment is based on the claim that they understand how the mind works, and yet the working of the mind consists of movements and transformation of the same hard-to-define, social, value-laden, humanly relevant meanings. If we have not decided what the difference is between idiosyncratic and objective views of social reality, we can expect disagreement as to where and if there is authority about these matters.

It is a problem that the sociologists ran into long ago. For instance, Karl Mannheim (1936) searched hard for an objective sociopolitical reality that would be independent of the sociologist's bias (his knowledge-authority), and could therefore serve as a platform for legitimate social planning (role-authority). Related efforts by hermeneuticists are cited in the present volume. A more specific part of the task has been subcontracted to psychoanalysis: psychoanalysis must decide what, if anything, certifies a given subjective, biographically saturated meaning, to be a more accurate perception of common human reality. If we can find no distinction in principle between social reality and anybody's view of it—if it all turns out to be just a matter of alternative subjectivities—we will incline toward the corresponding view of authority (in both of its senses). If, on the other hand, we conclude that there is such a thing as an objectively justified subjective awareness, in other words, a realistic way of integrating one's subjectivity with a common, human world, we are likely to look differently on authority.

Meanwhile, this very uncertainty has trained our attention on the immediate process of experiencing. Psychoanalysis has historically studied the deep wellsprings of meaning, and has catalogued the spectrum of well-formed meanings and unformed meanings, but (at least after the fading of the topographic model, and with a few notable exceptions) it has tended to leave to phenomenologists and existentialists the task of exploring the fluid development of momentary meaning, the relationship of that meaning to the less defined matrix from which it has just emerged, and the continuous, elusive slide of the moment's meaning into something slightly different in the next moment—in sort, the general office of novelty, with all of the monumental questions that attend that mysterium. It is worth a good deal of theoretical strain to have that subject brought before us.

REFERENCES

ALEXANDER, F. (1925). A metapsychological description of the process of cure. *Int. J. Psychoanal.*, 6:13-44.
Mannheim, K. (1936). *Ideology and Utopia. An Introduction to the Sociology of Knowledge.* London: Routledge & Kegan Paul.
Sachs, H. (1925). Metapsychological points of view in technique and theory. *Int. J. Psychoanal.*, 6:5-12.
Strachey, J. (1934). The nature of the therapeutic action of psycho-analysis. *Int. J. Psychoanal.*, 15:127-159.

1

FIGURES AND
THEIR
FUNCTIONS:
ON THE OEDIPAL
STRUCTURE OF A
PSYCHOANALYSIS

FIGURES AND THEIR FUNCTIONS: ON THE OEDIPAL STRUCTURE OF A PSYCHOANALYSIS

BY CHRISTOPHER BOLLAS

In the very heart of psychoanalytic practice resides a stunning opposition of aims. The patient presumably comes for treatment because of psychic ailments—which invite concentrated attention and interpretative hard work on the part of each participant—and yet both are meant to abandon intentions that logically arise from the assumed task and instead give themselves over to the free association of ideas. Will is immediately defeated. Both participants must not allow their wish for knowledge to interfere with a method that defers heightened consciousness in favor of a dreamier frame of mind in order to encourage the free movement of images, ideas, pregnant words, slips of the tongue, emotional states, and developing relational positions.

Freud never had an easy time with this. For although he clearly advocated the patient's right of free association—knowing full well that it was only through such unpremeditated speaking that a certain truth asserted itself—he simultaneously believed he was in possession of universal truths, such as the oedipus complex and other ubiquitous organizing structures, that bound the network of associations. So he wanted to find his truths in the material. Yet he never won the day against his own method. It is still possible to see where the analysand's introduction of unexpected ideas and unconscious complexes took him by surprise and dislodged one of his theories about to take hold.

The record of his treatment of the Rat Man (1909), for example, illustrates how he collaborated with patients. Telling the patient that his omnipotence dated to the first death in his fam-

3

ily, "that of Katherine—about which he had three memories" (p. 299), he found that the Rat Man "corrected and enlarged the first of these" (*ibid.*). Or again: "While I was discussing the possible reasons for his feeling guilty of her death, he took up another point which was also important because here again he had not previously recalled his omnipotence idea" (p. 300).

He enjoys announcing truth—"He was astonished when I explained that his masturbation was responsible for . . ." (p. 269)—but he also relishes the unexpected: "He told me the whole dream, but understands nothing about it; on the other hand he gave me a few associations to WŁK. My idea that this meant a W.C. not confirmed; but with W ['vay'] he associated a song sung by his sister '*In meinem Herzen sitzt ein grosses Weh*' [also pronounced 'vay']" (p. 294). He does not know what will happen next—the patient will lead the way—and when the Rat Man discloses fantasies about Freud's daughter, the analyst can barely suppress his delight at being led into new terrain by the patient's unconscious.

Throughout this text—as with all his writings—Freud is forever full of summary discoveries and truths just waiting for their right to universal placement; yet, he still takes pleasure in the capacity of the unconscious to upset certainty. Session after session establishes the ambiguities of any psychic life, not the least occasioned by the analyst's own unconscious responses to the material. Listening to the Rat Man's account of early losses, Freud tells us that he had not mentioned three memories from a previous session, in part because he is not certain if the third memory—of the patient's father bending over a weeping mother—was the Rat Man's memory or "Ph's," another patient. "My uncertainty and forgetfulness on these last two points seem to be intimately connected," he writes, "(They were forgotten owing to complexes of my own.)" (p. 264), thus entering in his account those movements of his own unconscious life that always arise in work with any patient. We see here something of the self-analyzing Freud of the dream book: the provider of material in a dense articulation of packed unconscious interests (the dream), the self who unravels this gift through free association, and the self who searches for points of convergence in the "material."

Did he realize that he had discovered the nondialectical relation between several ways of knowing? The dream condenses into imagery a thousand differing strands of thought which have arisen in light of events of the dream day. Author of a script which bears considerable knowledge, the patient does not comprehend his own creation, and, although psychoanalysis offers a way to know something of this dream, in turn it introduces a different means of knowing. Free association informs through destruction: destruction not only of a conscious wish to give the dream immediate meaning, but destruction of the dream itself, as its text is cracked open and dispersed by free speech. A third type of knowing is gained through interpretation, when the analyst searches amongst the debris for a "tissue of thought" that reveals the trail of a wish or an unconscious interest.

Importantly, however, none of these forms of knowing is displaced in a hieratic order by any of the other forms of knowing. If the knowing that is the dream is destroyed by the logic of free association, the truth to be found through the forming of any dream is never eradicated by free speaking. If an interpretation brings together several themes latent in the network of associations, it does not displace the truth evoked by dissemination.

Each of these authors—the dreamer, the associater, the interpreter—renders lived experience in differing ways and makes his own truth. Each of these ways of knowing is vital to the function of the human personality. We need to make dreams, just as we need to disseminate them, just as we need to form interpretations. Even though Freud privileged the analyst's interpretation of meaning, his fascination with dream contents and the matrix of unconscious material and his fidelity to the process of free association meant that at no point in his writings did his belief in his interpretive truths ever displace a method that would always undermine him.

These ways of knowing reflect the three different psychic

positions in the oedipal triangle. And just as the oedipus complex involves three distinctive persons who yet overlap—the mother, the child, the father—so do these processes derive from the members of this triangle. To make the dream—as Freud indicated—is to think like an infant again: in intense hallucinatory imagery that conjures a reality. To recline next to a quiet yet present other, evokes the half dreamy state of a free associative being—the infant and mother engaged in differing states of solitude and relatedness. When the analysand reflects on his communications and the analyst provides an interpretation, he always bears the name of the father: the outsider who breaks the unhindered movement of desire and defense.

The psychoanalytic way of knowing gives functional place to the analysand's prior ways of knowing: the infant's pure hallucination of his reality, the participation in the mother's way of knowing, the encounters with the father. Each of these authorings of meaning is essential not to some ultimate truth that will derive, but, as a triad, they are the constituents of finding truth.

As the patient makes her dream, breaks it up through free speech, and searches amongst the remains for fragments of meaning she keeps alive—or discovers for the first time—the interactive yet intermittent exchange of three mentalities: the infant's, the mother's, and the father's. With three types of comprehending and rendering existence fully available—as I argue in the method of a psychoanalysis—each analysand is put through the paces of these constitutive orders.[1] The self that is alone yet in the presence of the other (the dreamer),[2] the self that is unknowingly involved in uttering contents to a reverential other (the infant and the mother together), the self that

---

[1] Being an infant, becoming a child, taking in the mother, introjecting the father are the constituting tasks of a childhood. Rather than emphasize the person of the mother or the father as objects to be internalized, I prefer to speak of them as bearing "orders": sets of functions which engage and process the infant.

[2] The object relation here is purely intrapsychic: of consciousness to unconsciousness, or the awakened thinker considering the events that occurred to the sleeping self.

comes to account for and accept responsibility for knowing the internal world through penetrating insights (the child and the father) are an essential *family* of authors.[3] If one member of this triad becomes too influential, or, if one function is altogether eliminated, then full knowing is not possible.

Any emphasis on one of the three constituents to the subtle exclusion of the others automatically undermines the structure of knowledge derived from psychoanalysis. Yet an exhaustive review of psychoanalytic writings—not offered here—would indicate a surprising number of essays in which authors favored one or another of these three structures of knowing. Winnicott, for example, stressed the dreamy free associative state of the patient in which he offered "uninterpretation," clearly elbowing out the function of interpretation. Kleinian writing consistently stresses the interpretive work of the analyst and admonishes analysts for emphasizing the function of holding and the generative work of silence. Yet the group of analysts that surrounded these writers no doubt did so for internal political reasons—so the Kleinians overemphasized the internal world because the Winnicottians overemphasized the holding environment—polarizing each other and in turn distorting a more complete view of psychoanalysis.

---

[3] I trust it will be clear that attributes placed under the name of the father, such as interpretation, or reverie placed under the name of the mother, are not equivalent to stating that the father is incapable of reverie or the mother without her own form of interpretation. A full articulation of all the qualifications needed to explore the concepts of the maternal order and the paternal order would lead us into interesting observations on the kind of interpretation that proceeds from the maternal process and the kind of reverie that derives from the paternal process. A disadvantage of such enumeration, however, is that it suggests a clear distinction in how any person should perceive these two orders, while it is closer to the truth, I think, for differing psychoanalysts to determine for themselves functions under the name of one parent or another. Finally, it is important to bear in mind that these orders are not descriptions of how all mothers or fathers behave, but of processes associated with and usually conducted by the mother or the father, who assume differing forms of significance for the developing infant and child. Behaviorally, the mother will perform paternal functions and the father will operate the maternal order.

These debates are not without irony. The Kleinians focus much of their theory on the first year of life, and privilege the mother's body, yet advocate a highly active interpretative stance surely conducted in the name of the father. ("As my account shows," wrote Melanie Klein in the preface to her account of the analysis of ten-year-old Richard, "I could *penetrate* into very deep layers of the mind . . ." (1961, p. 13, italics added). The Lacanians, many of whom barely conceal contempt for the British emphasis on holding, are curiously maternal: the patient is free to speak with only rare interruption and even then the analyst's speech is allusive, elliptical, and porous.

It is more than a matter of curiosity that psychoanalytic schools of thought—many of which are built around single persons—break the oedipal triangle of unconscious structures operating in a psychoanalysis and either kick out the mother or kick out the father. Thus we have embarrassing oedipal debates in psychoanalysis—interpretation versus holding, or nature versus nurture, or internal world versus external world—which inevitably pressure the reader to favor one oedipal object over another. For example, read "mother" versus "father" in the title "holding" versus "interpretation." Psychoanalytic conferences or essays often operate around oedipal divisions of this kind. Indeed, entire regions or cities of the world—depending on which order they have followed—would appear to have marginalized one of the parents and appropriated the other. Thus the breasts—good and bad—seem to have become the intellectual property of the British to be found in London, while the phallus resides in Paris as the intellectual property of the Lacanians. Psychoanalytic groups continue to appropriate treasured parts of one or another parent's bodies—breast, penis, womb—or to appropriate attributes in an oedipal manner; to caricature this a bit: "we can tell you about envy and destruction," "we know about empathy," "we have potential space in our house," "we have language and the name of the father!"

Those who favor the maternal order suggest all too often, when listening to clinical material, that one must look to the preoedipal elements, where here preoedipal amongst other things means "deeper" and therefore closer to the truth. Those who favor the paternal order stress the oedipal, suggesting in clinical debates that focusing on the preoedipal evades the more troubling problematics of sexuality. To look at the oedipal, not its preoedipal elements, is to face the true challenge of the enigmatic. Depending on their oedipal positions, many analysts assert a more intimate knowledge of the truth, which can be understood as a special claim to be the more favored child of psychoanalysis: the one closest to the mother or closest to the father of true knowledge.

As we witness important parts of human life being singled out to become flag bearers of entire psychoanalytic movements— i.e., *self* psychology, *intersubjective* theory, *relational* theory—it is little wonder that a stampede to grab other essential parts of the total picture is not taking place. One could envision movements springing up in the name of desire, or meaning, or . . . how about authenticity? Authentic psychoanalysis. Each of these appropriations tends to put off those who are outside the more narrow political group surrounding them, perhaps because it is unintentionally offensive to feel that one group assumes it knows about the relational, another the instincts, another the body, another the self. Psychoanalysts from other territories invited to give a talk before a group that has formed its identity around a single word or a set of privately coveted parts of the body of psychoanalysis may be unaware that their wording has either used an unconsciously "patented" word—thus leading to profound irritation on the part of the hosts about the failure to cite the new parents who have made it a born again word—or worse, have failed to employ words or concepts in such a way as to pay homage to the clan hosting the event.[4] This is less intel-

---

[4] Not infrequently, a visiting psychoanalyst is asked what might appear to be a rather simple question, but members of the host institution know that it is a "coded" message. It contains key words around which a subclan has formed and in this moment becomes an iconic gesture. It may contain a word used by one of the society

lectual development than it is intellectual totemism.

Psychoanalysts who are outsiders to these causes[5] often either take up rather irrational dislikes of the signifying terms of the above groups—how many times have we heard analysts wince at the utterance of "empathy" or "relational" or "self"—and thus find themselves opposing an exceptionally important idea intrinsic to the development of psychoanalytic theory, or they are left to plead a kind of forlorn plurality, appearing to favor an "anything and everything is fine" attitude. It is not a matter of restoring a "one happy family" inclusion of ideas but of deterring the politically driven dismantling of the body of psychoanalytic theory. This could only be eclectic if the body was in pieces to begin with, not if there were a set of models held by Freud and the early group of analysts that has since been cannibalized by his analytic children. The primal horde—brothers who devour the body of the father—is an inadequate account of the origins of humankind, but at times it is all too apt a myth for the nature of the psychoanalytic movement.

Is one simply jesting in pointing out the partition of the body, the psyche, and the other, or, as I believe, is there some important truth to be found in a battle that takes place between groups across the globe, as first years battle with fifth years, as mothers and infants battle with fathers and children, as the phallus battles with the breast, as the fetus tries to take the cake?

The breaking up of the oedipal structure essential to a full analytic freedom is no laughing matter, however, and it is of psychoanalytic interest to consider why we may be in this unfortunate situation. I shall take the view that psychoanalysis needs to objectify and resolve its own oedipus complex—defined here as the killing off by one group of the other group's

---

analysts in a book or a paper and is something of a local offering to a well-respected individual. Needless to say, however, these cryptic communications are often not appreciated by the visitor, and unwitting offense is given.

[5] Arguably no one in the psychoanalytic movement is truly outside tribal thought, and this author is certainly aware of the part he has played in intellectual territorialism.

affiliation with one parent—in order for that knowing to take place that Freud invented but was himself instrumental in compromising. Jung, for example, embodied qualities that Freud both admired and feared. He enacted the maternal and feminine—as did Winnicott later—which Freud found faintingly fetching but also wished to keep outside his affiliation to the father. Ridding himself of Jung also expelled from his field of consideration other matters which he found irksome—aesthetics, philosophy, music—which may have felt like the wish(y) wash(y) world of maternal knowledge. To this day, too many Freudian analysts marginalize Jung, whom they find flaky, impressionistic, otherworldly, or lacking in rigor, apparently unaware of the contempt expressed toward the maternal order that saturates much of Jung's work.

Psychoanalysis continues to struggle with and against its oedipal dilemma. However important the great thinkers of psychoanalysis have been to the development of our knowledge—Klein, Lacan, Kohut, Winnicott, Bion—each of them has favored one of the parental members of the triangle over another. Each of these thinkers—like Freud himself—unconsciously opposed full and cognizant inclusion of all three members of the oedipal family and, intriguingly, the discipline that founded the concept of the oedipus complex and that prides itself on insight into its unconscious appearances has yet to objectify the anti-oedipal dimensions of its own formations.

The psychoanalytic ways of knowing have become politicized and have inevitably affected the different forms of authority in the consulting room. On closer inspection, there would seem to be a longstanding split of the oedipal couple. Although there is widespread disagreement in the analytic world among many groups, it is possible to see how this world is divided between those analysts who apparently remain fundamentally quiet and say relatively little and those analysts who are interactive and regard the relationship as dialogical. Thus, classical analysts in the United States and France—who imagine their patient's inner worlds differently—nonetheless see the analyst's silence and parcity of comment as an essential factor in clinical work. While interpersonal psychoanalysts and Kleinians would make very different comments to their patients, they both regard the analytic relation as interactive and believe their task is to interpret what the patient is doing to the analyst moment to moment. Naturally, there are shades of difference, the inevitable grey areas in which analysts operate in domains where hard and fast rules of technique seem to be of little value.

We may wonder quite why this fundamental difference has occurred. What does it mean if analysts of different schools of thought nonetheless divide over such a fundamental approach to their task?

It may come as no surprise that these differing attitudes toward the fundamental object relation of a psychoanalysis pivot around whether the analyst chooses to affiliate with the mother's way of being or the father's way of being. There is the other who is quiet, waits, privileges the movement of the barely articulate, appreciates the nuance of developing meaning, and comments in an allusive or elliptical manner, contributing to the flow of life existing between the two: "in" the maternal order. Or there is the interpretative other who brings the patient to thoughtful account for what the patient is doing "right now": i.e., "in" the paternal order.

When we think of the figure of authority in these analyses, we may turn around Paula Heimann's (1956) question about the patient's transference—who is speaking to whom and why now—and ask of the analyst, "Who is this speaker, and to whom is he speaking, and why?" This is not an easy question to answer, and one must avoid the temptation to oversimplify. The Kleinian enacts the interpretive presence of the father while fundamentally orienting the patient to the mother's body. European classical analysts would object to the idea that they speak with the voice of the mother, for in making an interpretation they often see such a comment as the introduction of a third element, brought into the analytic couple by the insight of the father. But placed between the maternal voice of the analyst—the "umm-ming" being who listens and receives—and the infant's or child's playing out of his desire in the transference and through free association, the analyst operates in the maternal order. Thus, there are subtle and important differences when we ask who the analyst is when speaking, and justice cannot be done to them here.

Important theoretical differences between analysts may partly derive from "the order" of their speech. Kohut and Kernberg, for example, have different views of the narcissistic personality. In a certain sense, Kohut works more from the maternal order—and is occasionally simplistically seen as cosseting—and Kernberg writes from the paternal order, and is sometimes unfairly seen as too confronting. Surely the solution to this difference is neither to pick sides in a debate of its kind nor to attempt a false synthesis of their differences. Each position is valid so far as it goes and represents an important perspective. Most psychoanalysts would find, I think, that they work differently with narcissistic analysands, sometimes more in the manner of Kohut and other times more in the manner of Kernberg: and often in the same session.[6]

One way or another, then, fundamentally different analytic positions either speak in the name of the mother or in the name of the father but simultaneously enact the attitude of the opposite parent. In this respect it could be said that both members of the parental couple are present in the conducting of an analysis, although one of the partners is forced into a silent role. To my way of thinking, this is an unfortunate outcome in the evolution of a psychoanalysis. We may wonder, for example, why a typical analytic session or, perhaps better yet, a series of sessions could not naturally be a mixture of these two positions, with the analyst sometimes quiet for long spells of time, implicitly supporting the generative development of internal associations (in the

[6] Although I suppose we shall never know, I would not be surprised if detailed sessional reports of the way of working of these two remarkable psychoanalytic thinkers and clinicians would reveal each of them "crossing over" and working in the manner of the presumed opposite.

patient and in himself) and other times talkative, bringing both himself and the patient into a more "objective" place. The associative place would be operating within the maternal order, the interpretive within the paternal order, and the patient's participation in both worlds—indeed the patient's need for both positions—would constitute a structural use of the parental couple.

Functioning within both positions is essential to *full* analysis. The analysand needs to use the elements of the maternal order that support dreamy and sentient production of unconscious material. Provision of the maternal process facilitates that unconscious freedom that analysts conceptualize as part of the primary process. At the same time, however, the patient's psychic life requires the creative interventions of the paternal order.

Winnicott might well have disagreed with this. He wrote that a psychoanalyst's interpretation was like the shining object presented to an infant: much like a spatula (1941, p. 67). Certainly, the experience of receiving something "from the outside"— beyond the bounds of immediate self experience—has precedent in an unseen part of the mother bringing something from the outside world into the intimate relation to the child. Winnicott and many other analysts have argued at the same time, however, that this outside object links the mother's function with the father's presence, as he is the ultimate arbiter of the outside and associated in the unconscious with he who is outside the dreamy world, waiting with a different frame of mind and different expectations. Thus, the shining object that comes from otherwhere—introduced through the hands of the mother— already points in another direction, toward the father. In turn, the father bears in his processional identity[7] elements of the maternal order, and when the child encounters him, the child

[7] The identity that resides in the particular way of being and relating: in the self as a process.

can feel elements of the maternal order within the father's personality.

Many of the analyst's comments are more associative than interpretive. Interpretation brings many elements together and is an implicit act of confrontation. The analysand is expected to recognize this and to make use of this object. Failure to do so, or dismissal of the interpretation, will often be regarded as a resistance and will bring the analyst back to why the comment was deflected. More associative remarks, however, bear less expectation and demand and sustain the stream of consciousness essential to unconscious collaboration between patient and analyst.

Viewed this way, a typical series of sessions would be authored by three different orders—the infantile or childish, the maternal, and the paternal—as the patient oscillates between periods of silence which facilitate dense internal experiencing,[8] periods of talking that open up such inner experience through free speech that disseminates the self in an infinite series of directions,[9] and moments of reflective concentration when the analyst and the patient collect meaning from the prior time.

All three ways of knowing are experienced in differing ways

[8] Masud Khan (1974) would term this "the experiencing of one's being" (see "Vicissitudes of Being, Knowing, and Experiencing in the Therapeutic Situation" in *The Privacy of the Self*, pps. 203-218). Such inner evolutions, in which the patient feels the unconscious logic of his own existence—even if he cannot grasp it in consciousness—is an important part of the deep work of an analysis, and such silences are not to be confused with resistance when the patient is remaining silent in order to stop the flow of association or to conceal a particular mental content.

[9] Of course, this is what Lacan meant by the Symbolic order, which, as a self experience, opens any person out into an infinite chain of signifiers that immediately link the subject to networks of meaning well beyond the nuclear moment that sponsored the utterance in the first place. Psychoanalysis has quite rightly looked back to find the link between the networks of signifiers and the originating moment—as this is the more immediately meaningful search for a patient—but at the same time, birth of the subject through his utterance means that speech also delivers the subject into other worlds to which he ultimately may travel. This is less a sublimation—of the original contents—than it is a directional force: each utterance points to future utterances and interests that emerge out of it.

by the two participants of a psychoanalysis. The analyst also has infant-like experiences in her daydreams and those mental contents that emerge while one is lost in thought. The patient emerges from free association and suddenly sees something unseen before: the patient may interrupt the analyst's reverie to make an objectifying comment.[10]

The image (dream or dense inner experience) arriving in the still center of being (at night or in a day reverie), its break-up through free utterance, its facilitation by a sentiently welcoming other who desires and shares this swing from quiet to intense experience, its interruption by an other who comes from the outside (and yet is part of our own way of thinking all along), these movements are the ways of knowing that are true to all life but brought together in no other way than in a psychoanalysis. This *is* the oedipal structure of a psychoanalysis. These participants—ghosts of at least three human others—live on as functions. Different ways of knowing, they are equally different types of authority. Who is to say that the dream or the image or the psychic intensity or the affect is to be privileged over all else? To do so would be to cosset the infant and worship it yet again. Who is to say that the reverentially sentient receptive order, the world pregnant with meanings yet to come, is the sacred author of knowledge? To do so would be to worship the Madonna of silence and being. Who is to say that until the duty-bound part of the mind brings the self to account through interpretive grasp of the truth that all the above may be nice but is meaningless?

These three forms of authorizing knowledge and these three quite different ways of entertaining the truth are as essential to a full analysis as the presence of the mother, the father, and the child are essential to the true realization of the oedipal family. It

---

[10] Readers will at some point rightly ask how any of this applies to the borderline patient, or to the schizophrenic, or to the . . . , and one could add many another patient. An essay of this kind cannot address the many different variations on the above, although the family of authors described above all have a place in the analysis of any patient regardless of diagnostic type.

bears restating a well-known fact, that Sophocles' *Oedipus* is not the tale of an oedipus complex, but the story of a family that did not happen. The oedipal family—the one the loving Oedipus desired—constitutes a creatively destructive child, a receptive other taking in the child and playing with him, and the outsider who is to become part of the inside: the father who is always there and ultimately to be included as the bearer of laws and prohibitions that are essential to thinking and establishing one's being in a social world.

If we set aside one of the most important tasks of a psychoanalysis—the deconstructive working through of symptoms, pathological structures, and character ailments—we may ask what else is it that a psychoanalysis accomplishes?

Psychoanalysts would describe the development of a psychoanalytic attitude[11] as an important outcome of a psychoanalysis; like Lacan, they might say that it is time to stop an analysis when the patient can tell the analyst about himself, or like Kohut, they might point to the momentum of the patient's "health potential" (1984, p. 44). These views are, to my way of thinking, very important. Indeed, it is arguable that the psychic changes illustrated above are ultimately only accomplished if the patient can discover the analytic attitude. This would have to be a particular capacity to operate according to the three elements of authoring and knowing: a celebration of the dreamer, the infant, the child, the producer of vivid ideas; a capacity to receive life and to bear a not knowing about what is taking place even though a profound mulling and playing is the medium of such reception; and finally, a search for the truth that necessitates a toughminded organization of the dream world. The analysand at the end of an analysis, therefore, is a dreamer who values his dreams, receptive to the essentials of a lost-in-thought elaboration of dreams and vivid ideas,[12] and intermittently given to

---

[11] See Schafer (1983), "The Analytic Attitude: An Introduction" in *The Analytic Attitude*, pps. 3-13.

[12] By vivid thoughts I mean those inner associations—which might very well be

insights that bear the unmistakable feel of a truth about the self.

It follows therefore that for a psychoanalysis to live up to itself, the analyst must be sensitive to the need in each patient of these different forms of knowing. The patient must be a true author of the sessions, as she produces and recollects dreams, narrates vivid moments from the day before, and bears the contents of her own unconscious life. The analyst must sustain the maternal order by comprehending and utilizing the essentials of analytic quiet and reverie, a vital presence that receptively introjects the analysand's contents and is essential to the constant flow of unconscious communicating that is always beyond words alone. Finally, the analyst must use the function of the father. The analyst is not there simply to celebrate the analysand's capacity, nor there only as a holding environment. It is vital to the provision of the third way of knowing that the analyst interrupt the flow of associations with well thought out interpretations that bear psychic change within them.[13]

A psychoanalytic session is an inevitable regression to the early orders of existence, not because the analyst acts like a mother or a father, nor even because the patient acts infant or childlike, but because those psychic structures that typify these orders and constitute the very core of mental functioning are amplified in a psychoanalysis. Dreaming and recalling the dream, freely speaking with little sense of the direction of thought, articulating one's inner life through fragments of speech that are incomprehensible metonyms of the denser and thicker world of self experience: these features of analysis call

---

evoked by actual objects in ordinary everyday life—that arise saturated with feeling, memory potential, and porous to instinctual derivatives.

[13] When an analyst makes an inspired interpretation—collecting together disparate elements for the first time—she actually bears psychic change in her comment. If the patient tolerates the interpretation and proceeds to work on it, such a working through constitutes the patient's introjection of a truth that will in itself be the catalyst of change. Inspired interpretations are usually the outcome of unconscious collaboration between patient and analyst and announce the arrival of the nascent psychic structure that is addressed in the content (see Bollas [1992], "Psychic Genera" in *Being a Character*, pps. 66-100).

up the maternal order. One self still inside this order, a different frame of mind ensues: more focal, more intense, more accountable, penetrating into the network of material to find a core truth. The patient is inside the paternal order. In a session the patient may oscillate between these two orders, but no position annihilates its opposite. The free associating analysand is still in part affiliated with the law of the father, and when the stream of consciousness naturally converges toward a sentient point, the patient turns to the paternal functioning to discern what he knows.[14]

Is there an opposition between these two differing ways of thinking and being? A battle of the sexes? In the best sense, one is inclined to agree. The maternal and paternal orders are engaged opposites, each essential to the child's evolution. The analysand who seeks his own truths in a psychoanalysis will succeed only to the extent that the maternal and paternal orders combine in him. It is never a matter of one form of knowing being superior to another. The dreamy, associating, free-speaking process is meaningless without the discerning, judicial, truth-seeking paternal order. Patients, of course, have difficulty in tolerating the one or the other, and psychoanalysts will make clinical adjustments. A narcissistic patient may find the paternal order too persecuting, and the analyst may wisely opt for a long time to be more maternal, slowly introducing the father. An obsessive-compulsive personality may feel a deep contempt for the loose world of maternal processes and seek only the lucid hard objects of the father's world. The analyst will take her time introducing the patient to the deconstructive invitation of silence and self-abandonment.

Consideration of the types of authority and knowledge in a psychoanalysis could certainly have been cast in different terms than those I have selected. Writings about a maternal order or a

---

[14] These orders do not in fact reflect the patient's mother or father so much as they express a part of the subject who has come to use these orders to constitute important forms of experiencing and knowing.

paternal order can feel somewhat archaic and clumsy. They may seem too arbitrary and typecasting. Surely *the* mother and *the* father are not to be so clearly defined. We know that both share qualities of the opposite sex. Am I not allegorizing where abstract terms would do us better? This may be so. But I prefer the strength of these terms. The maternal and the paternal in us—a self as inevitably a combination of differing persons and their functions—appeals to me because I believe our constitutions derive from our inherited form and its transformation not only by two unique but distinct persons with particular attributes but by two persons who have come to embody quite different ways of being and thinking. We can talk about who the mother is and who the father is and talk and talk: it is an endless conversation. Do the terms "primary process" and "secondary process" have that life to them? I do not think so. Nor do the functions these terms designate bear their own histories, while if we think of the mother and the father we simultaneously evoke our own precise histories with these persons and their structures: shared in common among all people. So we are immediately part of our personal history and a universal order, as all of us have *our* mother and *our* father, and yet each of us participates in psychic orders that are properly listed under the name of the mother and the name of the father.

Under the regressive move of a psychoanalysis the three participants of the oedipal triangle are revived, not only in the specular sense, but more importantly in their structural relation to one another. Perhaps Freud's construction of the psychoanalytic process was simply an oedipal enactment, but if so, it is surely a deployment in the clinical theater of the most essential parts of us. An adult self is an outcome of these functions. Capable of generating inspired ideas that derive from the insulated regions of any self, yet able to fully use the complex range of processes introduced by the mother and finally able to use those functions held in the name of the father. A mix. The adult in analysis knows instinctively how to regress and what parts of the roles on offer to make use of in this profoundly deep revision of one's self.

The political movement that is psychoanalysis—distinguished here from the clinical practice that also bears this name—too often cannibalizes parts of the body, elements of the self, dimensions of the other, and constructs a group around the part object. It is disconcerting that an important motivation in the psychoanalytic movement is murder of one parent or the other—at the core easily seen in the bifurcation of practice around silence or speech. The failure to combine the parental processes in psychoanalytic practice means that patients are all too often having to live either within a space that is overly maternal or a space that is overly paternal. Efforts to resolve this division are regarded as pluralistically watering down a more pure approach, which may well be a purity based on expulsion of an undesirable object. The oedipal violence that generates too much of the psychoanalytic movement has inspired a "part object theory": taking a part of the overall theory of meaning available in psychoanalytic theory and founding either a school or body of thought around that particular part object and then treating it as a sufficient ground of knowledge. This is more a form of intellectual cloning than it is a true development of theory, with "supporters" standing in for critical examination, sheer numbers ultimately determining the validity of the theory and its perpetrators.

For the maternal order and the paternal order to be reproductive processes generating a full analysis, psychoanalysis will need to critically examine the "movement's" violence against this pair. To give birth to truly creative formulations of theory as it relates to practice, the movement will have to appreciate the combined virtues of what derives from the mother and father as a couple. Otherwise our intellections will continue in their matricidal and patricidal ways, and psychoanalytic theory—and consequently the practice—will continue as a single-parent family.

REFERENCES

BOLLAS, C. (1992). *Being a Character*. New York: Hill & Wang.

FREUD, S. (1909). Notes upon a case of obsessional neurosis. *S.E.*, 10.

HEIMANN, P. (1956). Dynamics of transference interpretations. In *About Children and Children-No-Longer. Collected Papers 1942-80*. London: Routledge, 1989, pp. 108-121.

KHAN, M. M. R. (1974). *The Privacy of the Self. Papers on Psychoanalytic Theory and Technique*. New York: Int. Univ. Press.

KLEIN, M. (1961). *Narrative of a Child Analysis. The Conduct of the Psycho-Analysis of Children as Seen in the Treatment of a Ten Year Old Boy*. London: Hogarth, 1975.

KOHUT, H. (1984). *How Does Analysis Cure?* Chicago/London: Univ. of Chicago Press.

SCHAFER, R. (1983). *The Analytic Attitude*. New York: Basic Books.

WINNICOTT, D. W. (1941). The observation of infants in a set situation. In *Collected Papers. Through Paediatrics to Psycho-Analysis*. London: Tavistock, 1958, pp. 52-69.

2

THE NATURE OF
KNOWLEDGE AND
THE LIMITS OF
AUTHORITY IN
PSYCHOANALYSIS

THE NATURE OF KNOWLEDGE AND THE LIMITS OF AUTHORITY IN PSYCHOANALYSIS

BY CHARLES BRENNER, M.D.

The topic to be discussed in the group of papers of which this is one comes under the heading of technique. It concerns the question of the relation between analyst and patient: is an analyst in a position of superior knowledge and authority to a patient or not?

Current psychoanalytic thinking on this and related aspects of the analytic situation contains so many diverse and conflicting ideas that it is worthwhile to go back to basics at least briefly. Any technique is a way of doing something. What is it that a psychoanalyst wishes to do? Is the principal task of an analyst to create an environment in which the patient will feel secure? Or is it to assist the patient to become able to analyze him or herself? Or to repair defects in the patient's ego functioning? Does an analyst wish mainly to improve the patient's sense of self? Or to help the patient discover how the patient reacts to the analyst's words, tone of voice, and general behavior? Or is an analyst's chief wish to discover the nature and development of the patient's pathogenic conflicts and to convey that information to the patient?

The answers to these questions greatly influence an analyst's technique. So much so that it has been said that an analyst's technique is determined by the analyst's theory of pathogenesis (Arlow, 1986). One's decision about how to help a patient get well is bound to be at the least substantially influenced by one's ideas about what is making the patient ill enough to seek treatment in the first place.

For example, Kohut's belief that his patients' symptoms were due primarily to disturbances in their sense of self and that any

25

sexual conflicts must be secondary to fragmentation of the self is consistent with the fact that he paid no attention to Mr. Z's homosexual conflicts despite their apparent significance in the case material that he presented (Kohut, 1979). Similarly, Hoffman's conviction that the aim of analysis is that the patient learn how he or she reacts to another's behavior makes understandable Hoffman's emphasis on the necessity of consistently interpreting to every patient how he or she is reacting to the analyst in the analytic situation (Hoffman, 1994).

My own conclusion from the data available to me is that patients' symptoms are pathological compromise formations due to conflicts over sexual and aggressive wishes of childhood origin. It is a conclusion that was reached early in the history of psychoanalysis (Freud, 1894, 1896) and that has been, I believe, repeatedly confirmed by the observations of the majority of analysts, including myself (Brenner, 1982, 1994). It is consistent with this belief that I see the task of analysis to be the understanding of and the interpretation of pathogenic conflict. In what follows I shall limit myself to a discussion of how questions of knowledge and authority are involved in an analysis aimed at the discovery of the nature and origin of pathogenic conflicts and their interpretation to patients. To go beyond this self-imposed limit would necessarily involve a discussion of the relative validity of other theories of pathogenesis and psychodynamics. Such a discussion would go far beyond the limits of this paper.

To stay with basics for just a little longer, it is obvious that a prospective analysand expects, correctly, that an analyst is more knowledgeable than is the analysand about analysis in particular and about psychopathology in general. When an analyst suggests to a patient that the patient lie on a couch and speak freely, it is equally obvious that in doing so, the analyst is exerting authority based on the analyst's superior knowledge of analysis. An appeal to knowledge and the exertion of authority are essential parts of every therapeutic relationship, including that between analyst and analysand. An analyst stakes his or her professional reputation with every patient on the authoritative statement that the thing for the patient to do, in order to obtain relief, is to talk as freely as possible and to listen to what the analyst has to say when the analyst speaks. Not many analysts, I think, would take the position that each patient knows best what sort of treatment is appropriate for her or him and that an analyst should defer to the patient's ideas about how his or her therapy should be conducted.

Granted that authoritative knowledge plays a role at least to the extent just indicated at the beginning of treatment, there is real question about the exercise of authority by an analyst during the course of analysis. Analysts often (always?) think they know what is going on in a patient's mind better than the patient does. Should an analyst ever say this to a patient? Should the patient ever even glean from the analyst's manner and mode of speech that the analyst thinks this to be the case? Should an analyst ever, on the basis of presumed better knowledge, set her or himself up as an authority or, still worse, be seen as authoritarian?

In this connection critical reference is often made to Freud's statement that patients are persuaded of the correctness of an analyst's interpretations by the power of the benign, positive transference, that is, by the fact that patients as adults trust and believe their analysts as, when they were children, they trusted and believed their parents (Freud, 1917). To this extent, and to this extent only, according to Freud, suggestion plays a role in psychoanalysis.

It does not seem difficult to guess at the reasoning that underlay Freud's conviction. In 1917 therapeutic analyses rarely lasted longer than a few months. The idea that defenses are something to be analyzed, rather than something to be overcome or circumvented, was not even in the offing. The analysis of the patient commonly referred to as the Wolf Man, an analysis that lasted for four years, was Freud's first experience with a fairly long analysis (Kris, 1955). Even as late as 1918, in reporting that case, Freud referred to the first three and a half years of work as consisting largely in clearing away the obstacles to analysis, rather than as analyzing his patient's defenses. As Freud conceived of analysis at that time, real, consistent analysis of the Wolf Man began only after a time limit had been set, some four months before termination. In 1917 and for many years to come the task of analysis was thought to be to ferret out the fixation points of a patient's libido and to help the patient to free up the fixated libido so that it could be properly discharged through direct, sexual gratification and/or healthy sublimation.

It was only after several decades that it became generally recognized that the analysis of defenses is an indispensable, centrally important part of analytic work. As the recognition that this is so gradually dawned during the thirties through the work of such analysts as Fenichel (1941) and A. Freud (1936), there was a corresponding diminution of emphasis on the role of suggestion in analysis. Thus, for example, it was no longer considered to be of crucial importance whether a patient agreed with an analyst's interpretation (Fenichel, 1941; Freud, 1937). A patient might disagree and still give evidence by subsequent behavior and/or associations of the correctness of the interpretation, or a patient might agree with an incorrect or inept interpretation for reasons to be discovered and analyzed. The analyst's influence, its suggestive effect, was to be minimized, not relied upon to help accomplish the task of analysis. It was to be recognized and analyzed when necessary to do so.

Many years ago, in the course of a spirited discussion of a reported case, Waelder made a remark that sounded so trite and self-evident that it was taken by the audience as a joke and provoked considerable laughter. What he said was that it is always good to understand one's patient. Trite and obvious though it seems, it is profoundly wise in my opinion. The better one understands what is going on in the mind of a patient at any given time, the better able one is to decide what, if anything, to say to the patient and how and when to say it. In addition, Waelder's remark warns one against facile generalizations. When one is asked, "What do I say to a patient who . . . ?," the only sensible answer is, "That depends." Specifically, it depends on what one understands about "the patient who. . . ." Two patients may behave in a very similar way for quite different reasons or in quite different ways for very similar reasons. What one does or says in any clinical situation depends on one's understanding of that patient's motives and conflicts.

Since it is an understanding of the nature and origins of a patient's conflicts that one is after, one structures the therapeutic situation in such a way as best to further one's efforts in this direction (Brenner, 1995). Of the many elements of the analytic situation, in addition to the analysand's participation, the one that is indispensable is the analyst's attitude. Whatever a patient may say or do, an *analyst's* attitude toward it should be a questioning one, i.e., an attitude in keeping with the analyst's attempt to understand better what these particular words and behavior, these particular compromise formations, can contribute to the analyst's understanding of the patient's conflicts over the patient's sexual and aggressive wishes of childhood origin. Fenichel's (1941) prescription that an analyst should behave naturally with patients has been echoed many times since, but it must be borne in mind that what is natural behavior for an analyst in an analytic situation is different in important respects from natural behavior in any other social context. If one conceives the task of an analyst as the attempt to understand a patient's conflicts, one realizes that it may be quite natural and "human" for an analyst to refrain from what in other situations would be the natural and tactful thing to do, like giving voice to an expression of sympathy or answering a direct question. It is natural and humane for an analyst qua analyst to do what the analyst is convinced is the best thing that can be done to help a patient. It need only be added that patients should not be left in the dark about the reasons for their analysts' behavior in these regards. They should be told, if they do not already know it, that, for example, one may at times refrain from answering questions because one thinks that not answering is likely to be more helpful than answering or, for our other example, that a prompt expression of sympathy may be, under certain circumstances, more a hindrance to analysis than a help.

How is one ever sure that one understands a patient's conflicts correctly? How can one be certain that one is not led astray by one's own wishes, by the memories of one's own childhood calamities, and by the need to control, deny, and otherwise ward off both? After all, analysts are just as human as are patients. Does not the fact that every analyst is a participant observer make the task of understanding any patient impossible, in the sense that the words "understanding a patient" have in the present discussion? Are not the answers to these questions dispositive of any assumption of superior knowledge and consequent authority in the psychoanalytic relationship? Here are two persons, analyst and patient, each with conflicts of childhood origin that determinatively influence their current thought and behavior. How can one justifiably claim to be more objective or realistic than the other? Doesn't such a claim fly in the face of both fact and logic? Should not an analyst's attitude be one in which "the clinical enterprise is conceived of as a true collaboration between peers" (Renik, 1995, pp. 491-492)?

In attempting to answer these questions to the best of our ability at the present time, one may start by discarding as irrelevant the first question: "How can one be sure that one understands a patient's conflicts correctly?" As I have argued elsewhere (Brenner, 1995), one can never be sure in the sense implicit in the question. In science one can never be "sure." One can only draw the best conclusion possible from the available data. Further than this one cannot go. What one can say is that in the opinion of many analysts the best conclusion that can be drawn from the available data is that an experienced analyst, with the help of a personal analysis, is in a much better position to understand the nature and origin of a patient's conflicts than is the patient. One may always make mistakes. One may always overlook something. When either of these happens, the patient is not likely to be a reliable court of last resort. One should always listen with attention to what a patient has to say, but not as to an arbiter.

I recall one of my first analytic patients who, after several years of analysis, persisted for months in a tearful complaint that analysis was not for her, that I was of no help to her, and that she should leave a treatment that yielded nothing but daily misery and a sense of helplessness. Both her history and such current analytic material as dreams seemed to me to point clearly to the fact that her suffering and lack of progress expressed both her wish to render me impotent and her consequent, unconscious guilt and need to punish herself, but my interpretations to that effect seemed useless, however well supported they were by dreams and other analytic material. After months of what seemed to be a complete stalemate I decided that perhaps I was wrong and she was right and that it would be best for her to stop analysis. When I told her so, she sat up on the couch, faced me, and burst into a broad smile as she wiped away her tears. Her immediate thought was that she had won at last! She had finally made me give up!

A beginner, as I was at that time, may perhaps be pardoned for being hesitant and uncertain in dealing with such difficulties in the analysis of the transference of a very sadomasochistic patient. In fact the patient continued in analysis with me for some months after the incident just reported, though she eventually terminated and resumed treatment some time later with a more experienced colleague, with whom she finally achieved a satisfactory analytic result. The point I wish to make is simply that when analyst and patient differ, the patient is not necessarily right. Patient and analyst are not on an equal footing in the analytic situation. Here was a patient who, though she was successful in hiding the fact from herself, had an intense desire both to defeat me and to punish herself for that desire. Despite her conscious protestations to the contrary, there was ample evidence in the analytic material that this was the case. When such evidence is present, the analyst is usually best advised to

depend upon it and to remain convinced by it rather than to
defer to the patient's arguments to the contrary. Should the
analyst have reason for serious doubt about the correctness of
her/his conviction, a consultation with a colleague is much more
likely to be helpful than a misguided deference to the patient as
a presumed peer.

To return to the line of objection raised above, the fact that,
as a participant observer, one necessarily affects (alters) the data
of observation does not justify the conclusion that one's observations are never reliable or objective. The problem of the influence of observation on data is a general problem. It arises in
every field of scientific inquiry, not just in psychoanalysis. The
fact that Heisenberg demonstrated that it is logically inconceivable that one can simultaneously determine both the position
and the velocity of an electron, because of the influence of the
observer on the observed, does not mean that one cannot, for
example, accurately weigh a chemical sample or determine the
temperature of a liquid. In both the latter examples the presence and activity of the observer does, in fact, influence the
result, but one can safely disregard that influence. It is not great
enough to matter, whereas in the case of an electron, the influence is too great to disregard. What is at issue in any scientific
observation is what are called significant figures. If one were
faced with the task of weighing a chemical sample to the last
electron, quark, or string, one simply could not do it. But one
can, without too much difficulty, weigh such a sample to a tenth
or a hundredth of a milligram. Similarly in psychoanalysis. The
question is not whether the observer influences the data. Of
course the observer does. Always. The question is whether the
observer's influence is a significant one for the purpose of the
observations made and the generalizations one hopes to be able
to draw from them. I believe that in a properly conducted analysis or, if one prefers, in a proper analytic situation the effect of
the observer on the data is not so great as to render the data
unreliable for the purpose to which one hopes to put them, i.e.,
as a basis for understanding the nature and origin of a patient's

conflicts and, by extension, as a basis for conveying that understanding to a patient.

The way in which one does convey one's understanding to a
patient deserves some consideration here, since questions of authority and authoritarianism are involved. There are no prescriptions about phrasing, about tone of voice, about the use of
metaphor or humor, that fit every situation. It is the analyst's
attitude that is of fundamental importance, in my opinion. As I
see it, an analyst in making an interpretation is in the position of
trying to explain to another person, the patient, what the analyst
thinks might be motivating the patient even though the patient
is not fully aware of the fact. When one is trying to explain
something to another person one may talk more softly at one
time, more loudly at another, more hesitantly now, with more
certainty then, and so on. One may be persuasive at times, factual at times, humorous at times, as the situation warrants and as
one happens to feel. What one should not be in an analytic
situation is either angry, arrogant, and disapproving on the one
hand or seductive or disingenuous on the other. An analyst's
attitude should be that of an explainer who hopes that the explanations offered are both correct and helpful, but one whose
chief interest beyond those considerations is not in convincing
the patient but in observing the patient's reaction to whatever
interpretation has been made.

As I have pointed out previously (Brenner, 1976), every interpretation is a conjecture that the analyst communicates to the
patient. An analyst's conviction about the correctness of a conjecture varies greatly from instance to instance, but whatever the
degree of conviction the analyst may have about a particular
conjecture, the patient's reaction is always a matter of prime
importance. One naturally hopes for a confirmatory reaction,
perhaps one of the various sorts outlined by Freud (1937) and
Fenichel (1941), although the list given by those authors is by no
means an exhaustive one (Panel, 1955). Under certain circumstances one may support one's interpretation by referring to the
analytic data from previous days, months, or years that support

it. What one should not do is to attempt to intimidate or to argue with a patient, but neither should one treat a patient's objections as necessarily correct. They may be correct, but the fact is that neither analyst nor patient can claim unimpeachable accuracy for any given conjecture. In the majority of cases the analyst is in a better position to decide for two obvious reasons. The first is that the analyst usually knows more than does the patient about the workings of the mind. The second is implicit in the analytic situation. Every patient is engaged in deceiving her/himself about her/his most powerful motives. Defense is an essential part of conflict, and self-deception is the essence of defense. In most instances, therefore, a conjecture of the analyst, who has less need to deceive her/himself than does the patient, is more likely to be accurate. Nonetheless, the best test of the correctness of any conjecture comes from the analytic material that follows the presentation of the conjecture as an interpretation (see Brenner, 1976, Chapter 2).

An analytic situation cannot be created simply by applying rules of thumb or simply by making certain physical arrangements. The essence of any analytic situation is the attitudes of the two persons involved. One comes for help, the other offers it. On the basis of what she/he has learned and of her/his own analysis, the analyst tries to understand the nature and origins of the patient's pathogenic conflicts and compromise formations. Whatever authority the analyst exercises in the form of instructing the patient how to proceed is to be understood by the patient as the analyst's expert opinion about how the analyst can best help the patient. Those should be the limits of the analyst's authoritative attitude and behavior. Beyond those limits the question of authority is beside the point. In the course of analytic work an analyst is engaged in forming conjectures, in communicating those conjectures as interpretations, and in observing the patient's response to whatever interpretations are offered. The exercise of authority does not enter in. Even in such extreme cases, by no means uncommon, as when a patient refuses to speak, or refuses to speak about certain topics, or refuses to listen to what the analyst says, an analyst does best, not by attempting to exert authority, however benevolently, but by attempting to understand and to interpret. In brief, an analyst's job in analysis is to analyze.

REFERENCES

ARLOW, J. A. (1986). The relation of theories of pathogenesis to psychoanalytic therapy. In *Psychoanalysis, the Science of Mental Conflict*, ed. A. D. Richards & M. S. Willick. Hillsdale, NJ: Analytic Press, pp. 49-63.
BRENNER, C. (1976). *Psychoanalytic Technique and Psychic Conflict*. New York: Int. Univ. Press.
———— (1982). *The Mind in Conflict*. New York: Int. Univ. Press.
———— (1994). The mind as conflict and compromise formation. *J. Clin. Psychoanal.*, 3:473-488.
———— (1995). Some remarks on psychoanalytic technique. *J. Clin. Psychoanal.*, 4: 413-428.
FENICHEL, O. (1941). *Problems of Psychoanalytic Technique*. New York: Psychoanalytic Quarterly, 1969.
FREUD, A. (1936). *The Ego and the Mechanisms of Defence*. New York: Int. Univ. Press, 1946.
FREUD, S. (1894). The neuro-psychoses of defence. *S.E.*, 3.
———— (1896). Further remarks on the neuro-psychoses of defence. *S.E.*, 3.
———— (1917). Introductory lectures on psycho-analysis. *S.E.*, 16.
———— (1918). From the history of an infantile neurosis. *S.E.*, 17.
———— (1937). Constructions in analysis. *S.E.*, 23.
HOFFMAN, I. Z. (1994). Remarks in discussion. Meeting of the American Psychoanalytic Association, December.
KOHUT, H. (1979). The two analyses of Mr Z. *Int. J. Psychoanal.*, 60:3-27.
KRIS, E. (1955). Personal communication.
PANEL (1955). Validation of psychoanalytic techniques. J. Marmor, Reporter. *J. Amer. Psychoanal. Assn.*, 3:496-505.
RENIK, O. (1995). The ideal of the anonymous analyst and the problem of self-disclosure. *Psychoanal. Q.*, 64:466-495.

3

Reflections on the Authority of the Past in Psychoanalytic Thinking

---

REFLECTIONS ON THE AUTHORITY OF THE PAST IN PSYCHOANALYTIC THINKING

BY NANCY J. CHODOROW, PH.D.

Structural thinking, it seems, is on the wane. The analytic encounter is seen as mutually constructed and contingent rather than intrapsychically caused by one person; we pay increasing attention to the analyst's personally idiosyncratic countertransference, experience, and activity. Analysts have become more aware that intersubjective and intrapsychic meanings are ambiguous and paradoxical, and we emphasize partial interpretations and the multiplicities of narrative consonance.

Such a view of meaning focuses us on ongoing psychological agency and activity—fantasies and self-other constructions that are fluid, ever-changing processes rather than libidinal fixations or ego or self structures that are being enacted. The depth psychology expressed in transference—of unconscious conflicts, fantasies, emotions, projective and introjective exchanges—is continually created and transformed, and we as analysts are more likely to pay careful attention to the unconscious fantasies and affects—the subjectivity, rather than the developmentally created objective structures—that transferences express. What is expressed in the analytic encounter is fed by infantile sources, but it is also fed by many sources in daily life—by the moment-to-moment animating of and investing the world with subjective meaning and by the new meanings that emerge in interchanges between two (or more) people, each involved in creating mean-

I am indebted to Maureen Katz, Maurice G. Marcus, Owen Renik, and Victor Wolfenstein for careful reading and helpful comments on this article. I was supported during the writing by the National Endowment for the Humanities and the Guggenheim Foundation.

ing both from within and through their encounter. Some writers question the ease with which analytic theory once distinguished the transference relationship from the real relationship, as if transference is created through distortions carried over from the past, whereas reality reflects an accurate perception of objective actuality and the analyst's actual behavior (Hoffman, 1983; Loewald, 1960).

In the broader view of transference-countertransference, all experience is subjectively imbued and created, even as it also works with and reacts to that with which it is presented. Even if we know or become aware of someone's general patterns of reaction and construction, or if we have hypotheses about the objective structural sequelae of their development, we cannot predict the specificities of how or when these will be expressed. Psychobiological structures and capacities enable such processes, but the processes themselves are constructed at the moment, calling the fixities of development into question: meanings may build on infantile memories, fantasies, and stances, but they also seem to build on yesterday's experiences and fantasies, both with the analyst and in the world. Psychological activity is a process as much as an outcome.

A clinical emphasis on contingency and ambiguity of emergent personal meaning makes things more messy and indeterminate than accounts that tie clinical observation or interpretation to putative developmental determinants. Traditionally, we could rely, among ever-shifting clinical communications, on one or another theory of the childhood past and its determinative effects on the psyche throughout life, but our contemporary focus on the here-and-now has moved us away from such rooting. Indeed, just as much developmental theory moved in more fixed, causal, and objectivist directions—with elaborated accounts of developmental lines, interrelated systems or structures, and theories about stages in object relations or self development, deficits and flaws—we increasingly came to understand the analytic process in subjectivist and intersubjectivist ways as contingent, not predictable, ambiguous, and emergent. This creates discomfort: indeterminacy provides a less immediately comfortable account than determination, explanation, and cause, and psychoanalysis in particular has claimed throughout its history to have a causal, explanatory theory.

Moreover, we continue to be faced with transferential meanings—emotionally toned projections and introjections and conscious and unconscious fantasies—that seem to be at the same time situated, evoked, and emergent, and stable, repeated, and determined. As we focus our interpretive attention on the here-and-now of the psychoanalytic encounter, we also find ourselves trying to explain repeated and predictable patterns of interaction and expression. Especially if these patterns seem tenacious, repeated, stable, and resistant to transformation, we seem unable to give up the view that what the patient expresses comes from childhood, from the past, from without.

There is a further contribution to the tenacity of psychoanalytic attention to the past. I have argued elsewhere (Chodorow, 1994) that psychoanalytic concepts often unwittingly reflect culturally normative assumptions. One of these, I believe, is a pretheoretical, taken-for-granted belief that having a coherent sense of one's life as a whole is a necessary psychological universal. Moreover, our Western cultural narrative and our professional narrative both tend to create this coherence (or to assume that it is created) by giving temporal continuity to the self. We fuse wholeness and continuity with biographical terms like case history and personal narrative. In spite of our richly elaborated theoretical and clinical sense of unconscious mental processes (often considered "timeless"), we do not, finally, seem to have a way to imagine human life outside of a life cycle tying past and present, childhood and adulthood. It makes intuitive sense to us to interpret a "life cycle" as biologically driven, regularly progressing, having a beginning, unfolding, and end. But it is not self-evident that temporality is the only way to conceptualize a coherent life, nor that the Western life cycle story is the only possible way to provide such temporal coherence (for instance, Hindus and Buddhists explain and conceptualize a life story in terms that include previous and future lives).

Several forces, then, lead to an extraclinical appeal to childhood. Partly, our taken-for-granted cultural and professional narratives assume a coherent, unfolding life cycle from past to present and into the future. Partly, the subjective past seems imbued in current transferences. Partly, the complexity, contingency, ambiguity, and indeterminacy of continually changing transferences and countertransferences make us too uneasy, both psychologically and epistemologically. The relations between subjective and objective past and between past and present, and the unpacking of the present in its own terms, all pose a challenge.

All these forces lead contemporary writers across the theoretical spectrum to strive toward a both-and position. These writers claim that when they refer to the role of the past in the transference, they are referring to an inner psychic past rather than to an actual environmental, historical, or even fantasied past. They are not concerned with reconstructing what actually happened, including the fantasies constructed in the past about the past. Or, if they are concerned with what actually happened, it is for particular reasons only—for instance, because *patients themselves* feel a sense of continuity if they can create a life story that links past and present; or because it shows the analyst's interest in the patient; or because it is a route back to transference interpretations that the patient resists. Joseph, for example, claims that the transference is "a living relationship in which there is constant movement and change, . . . in which something is going on all the time but we know that this something is essentially based on the patient's past and the relationship with his internal objects or his beliefs about them and what they were like" (1985, pp. 167, 164). For Malcolm, the transference expresses "the past in the present," so that the analyst's "understanding of the present is the understanding of the patient's past as alive and actual" (1986, p. 75). Similarly, for Schafer, "reconstructions of the infantile past and the transferential present are interdependent" (1983, p. 196). For purposes of assessing the "relevance of the here-and-now transference interpretation to the reconstruction of early development," the analysand's past and present become virtually identical: "what was is, and what is, was; the narrated present originates in the narrated past and vice versa" (Schafer, 1982, p. 78). Sandler and Sandler (1984) create a topography of depth and surface that distinguishes the "past unconscious" from the "present unconscious," thus tying topography to past and present. The "present unconscious" is close to Freud's preconscious, while the "past unconscious" is a structuring agency that shapes the intrapsychic content of deeper, more infantile unconscious wishes and fantasies. Ogden speaks of the "two forms of history . . . the consciously symbolized past and the unconscious living past" (1989, p. 193).

Loewald, reminding us that transference is most centrally from unconscious to conscious rather than from past to present, notes that the "patient's behavior, while importantly determined by transference displacements from his past, often is triggered by the analyst's behavior or words," and that "[c]ountertransferences are influenced, but not wholly determined, by past experiences" (1986, p. 279). Transference comes equally from present and past: it "is a new rendition, shaped by these [past] origins, by later experiences and growth, and increasingly modified by the libidinally based transactions in the analytic encounter" (p. 286). Subjective past and present are, finally, mutually determinative and constitutive: "reliving the past is apt to be influenced by novel present experience. . . . Inasmuch as reenactment is a form of remembering, memories may change under the impact of present experience. . . . It is thus not only true that the present is influenced by the past, but also that the past—as a living force within the patient—is influenced by the present" (1975, p. 360).

All these formulations—"past unconscious and present unconscious," "unconscious living past," "alive past," "the past in the present," "the present in the past"—represent an attempt to resolve two apparently contradictory views: on the one hand, that current psychical reality is created subjectively and intersubjectively in the here-and-now; on the other, that current psychical reality (especially as it interests the analyst) was created in the there-and-then past. There is in these accounts (with the possible exception of Sandler and Sandler) an explicit attempt to tie past to present subjectively—to move away from the causal determinisms of developmental theory. What is important for the analytic conversation, these writers insist, is the patient's creating a subjective past, rather than discovering, as in previous psychoanalytic times, an objective past. The work of interpretation goes to elicit and bring emotional conviction to the "past in the present" or "alive past," without regard to the actual past or the "inferred historical past" that "the past in the present" represents.

However, although they are striving toward a nondeterministic integration of past and present, these accounts in my view tend to retain a metaphoric vagueness that substitutes for convincing argument. I believe this is at least partly because they still retain implicit objectivist and determinist assumptions about the past. No one holds that transferences are direct impositions of previous object-imagoes onto current relations, but these new accounts, finally, do not have an alternative view of development to accompany their alternative clinical account. Even the privileging of alive over inferred past retains a universalized objectivist quality: there are particular clinical situations in which attending to the actual past is vital and relevant.

Developmental as well as transference theories may also reach toward a both-and view. Klein and her followers conceptualize the paranoid-schizoid and depressive positions developmentally but also claim that a person may move between these positions in any particular analytic hour, over the course of an analysis, and throughout life. Loewald (1978, 1979) points to a lifelong oscillation between differentiated, oedipal, secondary process, ego autonomous forms of existence and thought and merged, preoedipal, nonlinguistic, primary process forms, an oscillation, seemingly, between nontemporally distinct modes of being and between earlier and later developmental modes. Mahler and her co-workers (1975) describe the rapprochement negotiation of self and other as the central crisis of childhood and the main dilemma of human life. Erikson's (1950) epigenetic cycle began as a developmental stage account modeled on time-dependent biological unfolding, but he transformed it into a weaving in which every stage of the life cycle was interwoven with every other stage (perhaps it was at this point of eight-by-eight nuance and multiple mutual determinations that analysts gave up trying to think in Eriksonian terms). All these conceptions embed developmental notions—preoedipal precedes oedipal, the paranoid-schizoid precedes the depressive position, and merging precedes separation—but they also portray what we have thought of as developmental stages as modes of operation going from infancy throughout life, the one never permanently transcended by the other.

Even the strongest narrativists and intersubjectivists seem to hold objectivized as well as subjectivist views of the past in relation to the present. Schafer has elaborated extensively the methodological program to follow a narrative, yet his hermeneutics, finally, require a (however potentially polysemic) signified as well as a signifier. He notes that the analyst uses "specifically psychoanalytic abstracting and organizing concepts" (1982, p. 78) and that "interpretations are redescriptions or retellings of action along the lines peculiar to psychoanalytic interest" (1983, pp. 255, 219). These "specifically psychoanalytic organizing concepts" and "lines of psychoanalytic interest" include a developmental theory of childhood and its effects. The multiplicity of analytic theories all lead to "life-historical narratives" (1982, p. 77), so that a "narrative strategy" organizes one narrative (that which the patient is telling you) into another, which "expresses the desired point of view on the past . . . along lines laid down by pre-existing theoretical commitments or life-historical strategies" (pp. 77, 81). The transferential present and the infantile past may be constructed or reconstructed narratively, but Schafer does not question the necessity of centering the analytic narrative on past and present in the first place.

In a related vein, Hoffman (1983) argues that what occurs in the analytic encounter is generated by that encounter itself, but he nonetheless suggests that one of the best ways out of tenacious transference-countertransference enactments is the analyst and patient's "evolving understanding of the patient's history." In a familiar way, he likens the patient's interpretation of the analyst's experience to her childhood interpretation of her parents' experience and claims that the patient will come to understand her reactions on the basis of "what has happened in the past" (p. 419).

Thus, even as we argue for transference as an expression of an "alive" or "unconscious" past—to all intents and purposes, a present—it seems hard for us not to assume or make explicit the actual past roots of present-day psychical reality. Case descriptions and theoretical discussion frequently describe a past whose contours are shaped by childhood experience read in terms of the specific developmental theory that the analyst holds. Despite alternate claims, these accounts also imply that this actual past causes or is expressed in the transference. Such tendencies cross the analytic spectrum. Kleinians describe how fluctuations in early internal object relations and oscillations between internal and external experience mirror and give rise to fluctuations and oscillations in the transference. Object relations psychoanalysts claim to talk about "internal" rather than real mother-infant relationships but make assumptions about the psychodynamic and behavioral reality and consequences of a patient's past (see, e.g., Bollas, 1987; Ogden, 1986, 1989). Self psychologists draw upon countertransference experiences and experiences of being used as a selfobject to make definitive conclusions about failures in early maternal mirroring and early parentally instigated barriers to positive narcissistic development. Ego psychologists and structural theorists observe the operation and failure to operate of different developmental lines or structures (e.g., self structures or superego structures) in their patients and make conclusions about whether these patients developed a true infantile neurosis or achieved a true oedipal crisis and resolution.

Our views, then, are caught between two perspectives. Most contemporary analysts hold that psychoanalytic theory and practice are principally about what goes on in the clinical consulting room. This *sui generis* experience is related to that which goes on outside and before, but it is not simply an epiphenomenon—a result, reproduction, or expression—of these. In the clinical encounter, we see how people process and create their psyches in ways that take more or less account of early psychic realities and are more or less influenced by them. Childhood determination cannot explain these contingent, intrapsychically and interpersonally emergent clinical processes.

Yet it seems that one cannot do psychoanalytic work (at least it is an empirical observation that analysts for the most part do not do psychoanalytic work) without conceptions of a patient's early experiences and theories about early development and its challenges. Many of us seem not ready to give up assumptions about the determinative importance of childhood in adult psychic life. Further to complicate matters, most conceptions of the psychoanalytic process are themselves intertwined with theories about childhood: the clinical encounter is conceptualized in terms of the mother-child encounter, of childhood fantasies like an oedipal fear of castration or a search for paternal protection, of primitive (first year of life) projective and introjective processes, and so forth; the psychoanalytic process is conceptualized as a developmental process (e.g., Loewald, 1960; Settlage, 1980, 1993). We focus on the "here-and-now" both because it is the here-and-now and inherently interesting as such (we are more interested than we were formerly in the emergent present) and because it is the best route to understand the "there-and-then" (we still want to know the past and reshape its effects).

This apparently unresolvable dual reality suggests that another solution to our epistemological and empirical dilemma is to assess accounts of childhood and development in terms of their compatibility with clinical understanding. It seems to me that developmental theories compatible with clinical understanding require two elements. First, a perspective on psychic life in the clinical here-and-now of transference-countertransference puts us immediately in a mutually constructed relational world in which the emotional meanings of situations and interactions are negotiated. Transference-countertransference expresses intrapsychic fantasy and feeling, but it is created in an interpersonal matrix (even one-person conceptions of the psychoanalytic encounter imply an other to the self who transfers). Clinically, feelings are always located in a relational field, even if this field is internally fantasied or created, and even if its main relational experience is of absence of an other.

Second, analyst and analysand create transference-countertransference as a contingent, continually emergent process. Both draw upon conventional cultural and linguistic usages in their interaction and have overlapping repertoires of metaphor, cultural images, stories, and sayings that help construct their conversation. Each has also a lifetime of creating self and other through emotion- and anxiety-laden, fantasy-driven unconscious projective and introjective constructions. All of these go into the analytic interaction, but each moment of the analytic encounter itself creates new meanings. The interaction itself is emergent in the here-and-now of intrapsychic process and intersubjective interaction and is not fixed once and for all in infancy or childhood. Transference-countertransference focuses us away from universals of psychic structure, system, or content and toward the particularity of the individual and the unique encounter between two people.

Developmental theories in accord with our clinical understanding, then, need to situate development in an internal and external relational matrix, and unlike the classical psychosexual stage-developmental model, the structural-ego psychological model, or the Kleinian model, they need not tell us what is set down and enacted or determinative of psychic contents and modes of functioning. Rather, they must describe for us how people function throughout life, documenting the development and operation of processes of creating unconscious fantasy and emotional meaning. Of empirical importance only is the extent of fixity—the possibility that for many people, special conditions of childhood, childhood in general, or their own particular childhood make these early experiences especially shaping or resonant. By definition such models must accord with a view that the expressions and processes we find in the clinical encounter are also found throughout life.

In what follows, I point to useful directions for such a theory and suggest what is wrong with other developmental approaches, for conceptualizations of clinical processes. Developmental theories useful for clinical thinking seem to be couched in the same phenomenological register as clinical interaction and transference rather than in terms of the observer's nonexperiential causal or structural models. They do not so much tell us about particular sequential childhood stages that determine later psychic contents, modes of functioning, personality, or pathology. Rather, they document extensively and in great detail human psychological life as a whole.

Loewald begins from the premise that for the subject there is initially no inner and outer, no ego versus reality, no drives versus ego. All these are created or differentiated out of a global structure at the same time (see 1980, *passim*). He thus describes those primary processes that create the existence and meaning, one in relation to the other, of self and object. In this view, inner and outer are not qualities given in any direct empirical for-all-time sense. From the outset, they have both emotional and physical-perceptual meanings, and this initial creation sets off a life-long process in which not only the meaning but also the constitution of inner and outer are negotiated. Drives also are created. Loewald does not start from the givenness of drives but from the premise that the developing person shapes what come to be her drives, her characteristic experiences and invocations of aggression and libido. The child's emotionally laden interpersonal experiences influence this shaping: "instincts . . . are to be seen as relational phenomena from the beginning and not as autochthonous forces seeking discharge" (Loewald, 1972, pp. 321-322).

The Kleinian (1940, 1952, and elsewhere) and Fairbairnian (1952) contributions extend that of Loewald. These developmental clinicians focus on the character of the relations between inner and outer—the way an inner object world is created through processes which also create and form the basis for later self-orientations and transferences. Throughout development, as throughout life, inner and outer reality are continually reconstituted through anxiety, fear, and other affect-driven projective and introjective fantasies, so that the experience of people is shaped or filtered through an internal world and in turn reshapes this world: "an inner world is being built up in the child's unconscious mind, corresponding to his actual experiences and the impressions he gains from people and the external world, and yet altered by his own phantasies and impulses" (Klein, 1940, p. 345). Transferential reshaping is ubiquitous: "altogether, in the young infant's mind every external experience is interwoven with his phantasies and on the other hand every phantasy contains elements of actual experience" (Klein, 1952, p. 54).

Kleinian and Fairbairnian language is sometimes overly concrete and simple, but its very concreteness mirrors the underlying assumption founding our notion of transference. In her account of the doubling of experience (1940, pp. 345-346), for example, Klein attempts to characterize and answer the difficult clinical question concerning how fantasies shaping and reshaping the inner world and their results exist both in the inner realm of fantasy (in the transferential reality) and yet have actual effects on our perceptions, experiences, and feelings of external reality. It is, of course, especially in the analytic situation that one can see most extensively these "real" effects, as the analysand unconsciously represents a conception of the analytic relationship and engages in splitting, projective fantasies about what the analyst is doing to the patient, projective identification of feelings into the analyst, and so forth. Klein and Fairbairn also describe the almost dizzying continual activity of doing and undoing, reversing bad and good and self and other that characterizes transferential shifts.

Winnicott's (1971) developmental account of transitional phenomena and transitional process contributes further to a here-and-now-consonant developmental theory of the there-and-then past. Here, we have a *sui generis* relational space in which internally created personal meaning also takes account of the actual presence of the other. Winnicott thus adds a conception of how the object or other itself plays a role to accounts of how fantasy and affective meanings are created from within and accord personal animation to self, other, and objects. This concept helps us see how meanings in transference-countertransference are both emergent (created from within) and have regular features (given from without or from before). This developmental account has been elaborated clinically in conceptions, for examples, of the potential space of the analytic situation (e.g., Ogden, 1986), the evocative analytic object (e.g., Bollas, 1987), and the inherently ambiguous but generative behavior of the analyst for the patient (Hoffman, 1983).

Because they are attuned to emergent psychological activity and to subjective meanings—fantasy, affect, and drive processes that continually create and re-create relations to others and an internal world—these developmental approaches all resonate with descriptions of transference-countertransference. For these theorists, the focus is on *meanings* of ego and object. These meanings must be created: the infant invests ego and objects with fantasies, drives, and affect and in the process creates an inner object world and sets in motion anxiety- and defense-driven processes of splitting, projection, and introjection that continue throughout life. Even the structural outcomes they describe have this phenomenological cast—having to do with patterns of fantasy, drive, and affective construction of self and other that have become relatively stable.

Such theories can also be read exclusively as accounts of developmental stages, yet whether or not infants engage in the processes that these accounts describe, any clinician experiences and observes such processes daily. These developmental theories document the emergence in childhood of that very psychic activity that enables and creates transferential processes throughout life, rather than the emergence of a structured unconscious, psyche, or cognitions that determine later transferences. Rather than portraying a fixed developmental schema concerning psychosexual stages, developmental lines, or interrelated systems, these accounts are consonant with the emergent complexity and indeterminacy of transference, multiplicities of potential meaning, and ambiguities in interpretive possibility. Transitional phenomena and transitional space portray a world of paradoxical, situated meaning—the object, experience, or person objectively perceived and subjectively conceived and negotiated between two people. Contingent fluidity characterizes primary and secondary internalizations and externalizations. These accounts reformulate, but they do not undermine, the psychoanalytic insistence on the importance of early development. They lead to a notion of continual emergence rather than a correlational replaying in the transference relationship.

Infant researchers also contribute developmental accounts consonant with contemporary views of the clinical encounter. Stern (1985), for example, describes the fluidity and transformational possibilities of affect and perception. Infants translate information from one perceptual mode to another and experience qualities of intensity in different affects or perceptions as equivalent: intense anger has something in common with intense joy; intense light is more like forceful than soothing music; the dynamic components of fading, exploding, and rushing give some equivalency to different affects. Directly expressing the both-and position, Stern speaks of "clinical-developmental" issues and claims that in contrast to psychosexually linked developmental stages, different aspects of the sense of self both develop sequentially over the first two years of life and are "issues for the life span" (p. 12).

Attachment theory (Bowlby, 1969, 1973, 1980) and intersubjective theory (Stern, 1985; Trevarthen, 1979, 1980) may also indirectly influence our current refocusing on the analytic relationship and changes in analytic stance, authority, and technique. Contemporary infant researchers document emotional signaling between infant and caregiver and the way the feeling tone of this relation goes to form an "affective core of the self" (Stern's term). They show how the child imbues objects with emotional meaning through sharing her perceptions with the mother or caregiver: emotional interchanges are not just about me and you but about "our" experience and communication concerning the world of physical and cultural objects (Emde, 1991; Emde and Sorce, 1983). Similarly, the meanings of words used by the mother, though drawn from a common language, have the particularized resonance for the child of the relational and affective context in which they are used. Self development is also an interpersonal project on the level of unconscious fantasy: infants develop from birth onward within the sphere of "interfantasy"—within the matrix of the mother's fantasies of the meaning of their exchanges, which in turn are ingredient in (but do not determine) the infant's fantasies (Stern, p. 134). There are thus from the beginning connections among language, word, interpersonal, emotional, and fantasy context and primary process density that become gradually interwined with secondary process articulation. These are also the intertwinings found in the analytic encounter and in other interchanges that are meaningful subjectively to the individual. The carefully theorized research in these fields makes us all more aware of how human experience and selfhood are interpersonally constituted. Just as analysts once thought that drive gratification was the primary human goal, we now know that people seek attachment, response, recognition, and meaning.

All these accounts describe a childhood mental life that emerges from a relational matrix and creates an unconscious, emotion- and fantasy-imbued inner object world of personal meaning and a coloring and animation of the external world through transference, interfantasy, and mutual projective processes. They show that transference and countertransference happen not only in daily life but also in the initial processes of perception and meaning creation. Such developmental accounts enable us to reread childhood, as we read psychoanalytic process, in a less determinist fashion. In them, psychological meaning and subjectivity are not laid down in early childhood, though children from infancy create psychological meaning and subjectivity. Because psychological meaning is constitutive of internal and external perceptions and experiences from childhood, the past is always drawn into the present. But this drawing in is always complex and indeterminate, perhaps not invented anew but nonetheless created at each moment. These developmental accounts do not eliminate the importance of childhood, but they regard subjective experience as a continual process to be engaged intersubjectively and interpretively rather than assuming that childhood causes, determines, or correlates with present functioning.

Such accounts contrast with those that make the empirical fantasy contents of the psyche primary (psychosexual drive stages, oedipal conflicts, destructiveness, rage, and envy of the breast, separation-individuation fears or conflicts) and with developmental accounts cast in nonexperiential terms of psychic structures, systems, or developmental lines. Our ostensibly universal developmental theories, I would suggest, often describe nonuniversal yet empirically widespread patterns of fantasy, ego, and object-relational psychic contents and turn nonnecessary developmental possibilities into tasks (the oedipus complex is a major case in point). They have been misconstrued as universal theories of mental operation with universal fantasy as well as structural consequences. Patterns and tendencies are useful clinical reminders of possible empirical repertoires and orient us in a generalized preconscious way in our listening. They are useful in the individual case, or at different times in the analytic process, but they cannot, for a particular patient at a particular moment, be more. (I am not in a position to assess the relevance of such developmental theories for child treatment, and, as should be apparent, I do not question the intrinsic interest of developmental investigations and theories in themselves.)

We recognize patterns and possibilities partly by having in mind the varieties of developmental knowledge (many of which, incidentally, are incompatible one with the other: it is only by using them in a case- and moment-specific way that they can coexist for us). Similarly, particular childhood traumas seem to affect development (statistically, perhaps, tend to "arrest" development), but not always negatively, not for all people, and not in the same predictable way. Speaking of a young patient with organic brain problems (at the extreme end of what we might take for granted as developmentally or constitutionally determinative), Erikson (1950) says: "the damage . . . would, of course, constitute only a potential, albeit necessary, condition to convulsion. It could not be considered the cause of the convulsion, for we must assume that quite a number of individuals live with similar cerebral pathology without ever having a convulsion" (p. 34). He goes on: "we know of no 'cause.' Instead we find a convergence . . . which make[s] the catastrophe retrospectively intelligible, retrospectively probable. The plausibility thus gained does not permit us to go back and undo causes. It only permits us to understand a continuum, on which the catastrophe marked a decisive event, an event which now throws its shadow back over the very items which seem to have caused it" (pp. 37-38).

This paper argues that we should be wary of clinical explanations in terms of objectivized universal childhood stages or psychobiological drives that determine or predict later psychological experience, and of universalist claims about the panhuman content of unconscious fantasies. And we should be wary of developmental theories that promote such interpretation and explanation. If psychological meaning in the clinical encounter is emergent and created through fantasy, interfantasy, collaborative and tentative transitional negotiations, transferences and countertransferences created in the here-and-now, then it cannot also be the case that an oedipus complex, castration fears, fantasies about "the" primal scene, or envy of "the" breast or "the" mother's insides, are universally given or universally determined by the conditions of early infancy or by a panhuman psychobiology. We must sustain an inductive openness to the content of psychic fantasy and look for evidence not from a universal childhood or psyche but from a particular subjective childhood and the unique evidence of individual transferences. Analytic focus on transference-countertransference in the here-and-now entails a rethinking of childhood and of the relations of past and present in psychoanalytic explanation. It decouples analytic knowledge and interpretation from developmental understandings and reconstructions, except insofar as these reconstructions or conceptions of the past play a role in a particular analysand's fantasy and affective life or in the analytic interchange. I suggest that processual conceptions of childhood that focus on human capacities to create personal and intersubjective meanings virtually from birth, rather than theories centered on developmental stages, lines, structure formation, or tasks, point us to a more promising understanding of psychic functioning throughout life. These conceptions may generate less clinical certainty, but they promise more consistency in our understanding of the analytic encounter.

REFERENCES

BOLLAS, C. (1987). *The Shadow of the Object: Psychoanalysis of the Unthought Known*. New York: Columbia Univ. Press.
BOWLBY, J. (1969). *Attachment and Loss, Vol. 1. Attachment*. New York: Basic Books.
———— (1973). *Attachment and Loss, Vol. 2. Separation: Anxiety and Anger*. New York: Basic Books.
———— (1980). *Attachment and Loss, Vol. 3. Loss: Sadness and Depression*. New York: Basic Books.
CHODOROW, N. J. (1994). *Femininities, Masculinities, Sexualities. Freud and Beyond*. Lexington: Univ. of Kentucky Press; London: Free Association Books.
EMDE, R. N. (1991). Positive emotions for psychoanalytic theory: surprises from infancy research and new directions. *J. Amer. Psychoanal. Assn.*, Suppl., 39:5-44.

————& SORCE, J. F. (1983). The rewards of infancy: emotional availability and maternal referencing. In *Frontiers of Infant Psychiatry, Vol. 2*, ed. J. D. Call, E. Galenson. & R. Tyson. New York: Basic Books, pp. 17-30.

ERIKSON, E. H. (1950). *Childhood and Society*. Second edition. New York: Norton, 1963.

FAIRBAIRN, W. R. D. (1952). *An Object-Relations Theory of the Personality*. New York: Basic Books.

HOFFMAN, I. Z. (1983). The patient as interpreter of the analyst's experience. *Contemp. Psychoanal.*, 19:389-422.

JOSEPH, B. (1985). Transference: the total situation. In *Psychic Equilibrium and Psychic Change*. London/New York: Routledge, 1989, pp. 156-167.

KLEIN, M. (1940). Mourning and its relation to manic-depressive states. In *Love, Guilt, and Reparation and Other Works, 1921-1945*. New York: Delacorte, 1975, pp. 344-369.

———— (1952). The origins of transference. In *Envy and Gratitude and Other Works, 1946-1963*. New York: Delacorte, 1975, pp. 48-56.

LOEWALD, H. W. (1960). On the therapeutic action of psychoanalysis. In *Papers on Psychoanalysis*. New Haven: Yale Univ. Press, 1980, pp. 221-256.

———— (1972). Freud's conception of the negative therapeutic reaction, with comments on instinct theory. In *Op. cit.*, pp. 315-325.

———— (1975). Psychoanalysis as an art and the fantasy character of the psychoanalytic situation. In *Op. cit.*, pp. 352-371.

———— (1978). Primary process, secondary process, and language. In *Op. cit.*, pp. 178-206.

———— (1979). The waning of the Oedipus complex. In *Op. cit.*, pp. 384-404.

———— (1980). *Papers on Psychoanalysis*. New Haven: Yale Univ. Press.

———— (1986). Transference-countertransference. *J. Amer. Psychoanal. Assn.*, 34:275-287.

MAHLER, M. S., PINE, F., & BERGMAN, A. (1975). *The Psychological Birth of the Human Infant. Symbiosis and Individuation*. New York: Basic Books.

MALCOLM, R. R. (1986). Interpretation: the past in the present. In *Melanie Klein Today, Vol. 2*, ed. E. B. Spillius. London: Routledge, 1988, pp. 73-89.

OGDEN, T. (1986). *The Matrix of the Mind. Object Relations and the Psychoanalytic Dialogue*. Northvale, NJ: Aronson.

———— (1989). *The Primitive Edge of Experience*. Northvale, NJ/London: Aronson.

SANDLER, J. & SANDLER, A.-M. (1984). The past unconscious, the present unconscious and the interpretation of the transference. *Psychoanal. Inquiry*, 4:367-400.

SCHAFER, R. (1982). The relevance of the 'here and now' transference interpretation to the reconstruction of early development. *Int. J. Psychoanal.*, 63:77-82.

———— (1983). *The Analytic Attitude*. New York: Basic Books.

SETTLAGE, C. F. (1980). Psychoanalytic developmental thinking in current and historical perspective. *Psychoanal. Contemp. Thought*, 3:139-170.

———— (1993). Therapeutic process and developmental process in the restructuring of object and self constancy. *J. Amer. Psychoanal. Assn.*, 41:473-492.

STERN, D. N. (1985). *The Interpersonal World of the Infant. A View from Psychoanalysis and Developmental Psychology*. New York: Basic Books.

TREVARTHAN, C. (1979). Communication and cooperation in early infancy: a description of primary intersubjectivity. In *Before Speech: The Beginning of Interpersonal Communication*, ed. M. M. Bullowa. New York: Cambridge Univ. Press, pp. 321-347.

————— (1980). The foundations of intersubjectivity: development of interpersonal and cooperative understanding in infants. In *The Social Foundation of Language and Thought: Essays in Honor of Jerome Bruner*, ed., D. R. Olsen. New York: Norton, pp. 316-342.

WINNICOTT, D. W. (1971). *Playing and Reality*. New York: Basic Books.

4

PSYCHOANALYSIS AT ITS LIMITS: NAVIGATING THE POSTMODERN TURN

PSYCHOANALYSIS AT ITS LIMITS: NAVIGATING THE POSTMODERN TURN

BY ANTHONY ELLIOTT, PH.D. AND CHARLES SPEZZANO, PH.D.

In a 1929 essay, T. S. Eliot wrote about Dante that "he not only thought in a way in which every man of his culture in the whole of Europe then thought, but he employed a method which was common and commonly understood throughout Europe" (cited in Trachtenberg, 1979, p. 1). Dante may have been the last writer to enjoy this guaranteed rapport with his audience. Certainly no psychoanalytic author can expect anything like it. Quite the contrary, it is guaranteed that all psychoanalysts writing for their "colleagues" today will encounter, among at least some readers, disbelief at their failure to grasp basic principles, headshaking over their hubris in imagining that what they have written contains new ideas, or disinterest from readers not of their "school" because they talk "another language" that is too "old fashioned" or "not really psychoanalysis."

Further, in the theorizing and clinical reports contained in contemporary analytic journals one does not only find authors whose work is intended to advance (or fits neatly into) a project called ego analysis, self psychology, object relational theory, or Kleinian analysis. One also finds authors whose work seems harder to pigeonhole; but, as philosopher Iris Murdoch (1993) has suggested: "We fear plurality, diffusion, senseless accident, chaos, we want to transform what we cannot dominate or understand into something reassuring and familiar, into ordinary being, into history, art, religion, science" (pp. 1-2). We want to say: "That is classical analysis, self psychology, relational psychoanalysis. The author is an element of one of our reassuring unities."

As the individual voices in psychoanalysis proliferate, we need more unifying labels to maintain order and ward off chaos. "Postmodernism" is the most recent. As with other labels, it relies for its appearance of usefulness and validity on the availability of a contrary perspective: "modernism." In this case, for the first time in the history of psychoanalysis, the dueling labels have been imported from other disciplines. This has tended to increase the confusion about their usage beyond the level that has beset the use of other psychoanalytic dichotomies. The aim of our article is not so ambitious as to clear up this confusion, but rather simply to describe it. We will argue, in fact, that it might be a good idea to allow it to remain confusing.

Modernism and Postmodernism: The Alleged Dichotomy

The "thing" against which postmodernism is most often described as setting itself—the thing called modernism—was midwifed into existence by Kant's angry reaction to the blindness of metaphysics and the emptiness of empiricism. Although he championed it with some qualifications, what Kant offered in place of these pretenders was that most precious child of the Enlightenment: reason. Through reason (and only through reason) "could the universal, eternal, and the immutable qualities of all humanity be revealed" (Harvey, 1990, p. 12). As such knowledge accumulated, "rational modes of thought promised liberation from the irrationalities of myth, religion, superstition," and, especially, "release from the arbitrary use of power as well as from the dark side of our own human natures" (*ibid.*).

As might be expected, once such a monolithic entity as modernism has been constituted, it becomes convenient and compelling to write as if everything that is not it is one other thing, in this case postmodernism. If modernism has been a quest for truth and reality and if its modus operandi has been positivism or objectivism, then everything that is not positivistic and objectivist is assumed to be thoroughly antagonistic to truth and reality. If, however, modernism itself was a cubist painting—with ambiguously related surfaces of reason, truth, certainty, objectivity, and positivism made to look like a unified whole—then a contemporary theorist who takes issue with one of these points might not take issue with all of them. This, it turns out, might well be the messy truth of postmodern thinking in psychoanalysis and other disciplines. Consider the following epistemologies.

British philosopher Roger Scruton (1994) argues that Kant's take on human beings knowing the world is not the final word, but it is the best one. We cannot look at the world from outside our concepts and know the world as it is. We cannot see it from no particular point of view, as God might. In fact, we could not even begin to think about the world if we did not believe that we were viewing it through concepts of objectivity and that our judgments of it would represent reality.

German critical theorist Jürgen Habermas argues that all human beings possess the same faculty of reason. We experience the results of reason's successful application when we find ourselves with dialogical consensus or in coordinated action with others. "The intersubjectivity of the validity of communication rules is confirmed in the reciprocity of actions and expectations. Whether this reciprocity occurs or fails to occur can be discovered only by the parties involved; but they make this discovery intersubjectively" (1970, p. 141).

In his highly readable introduction to postmodernism, John McGowan (1991) uses the term "to designate a specific form of cultural critique that has become increasingly conspicuous in the academy since about 1975" (p. ix). He understands postmodernism as referring to an antifoundationalist critique, but adds to this a positive dimension: a search for freedom and pluralism that accepts the necessity, if not the virtue, of norms to which people, institutions and practices are responsive.

American philosopher Simon Blackburn (1993) takes what he calls a "quasi-realist" position: "that truth is the aim of judgment; that our disciplines make us better able to appreciate it, that it is, however, independent of us, and that we are fallible in our grasp of it" (p. 4).

Jacques Derrida suggests that we read all texts deconstructively. We must "work through the structured genealogy of its concepts in the most scrupulous and immanent fashion, but at the same time to determine from a certain external perspective that it cannot name or describe what this history may have concealed or excluded" (1981, p. 6). We might paraphrase Norris (1987), in his excellent account of Derrida's philosophical project, and say that the effect of Derrida's philosophy is to render "intensely problematic" much of what passes for "rigorous" thought in psychoanalysis (as well as in philosophy and literary theory). "But this effect is not achieved by dispensing with the protocols of detailed, meticulous argument, or by simply abandoning the conceptual ground on which such arguments have hitherto been conducted" (p. 20).

Barnaby Barratt (1993), in his book *Psychoanalysis and the Postmodern Impulse*, offers a vision of psychoanalysis as a process of free-associative deconstruction—"deconstructive and negatively dialectical in a subversively postmodern sense" rather than "insight establishing and reflective in the modern philosophical sense" (p. xiv).

Italian philosopher Gianni Vattimo (1980), during a discussion of Nietzsche's reduction of truth to morality, takes the following position: "Whenever a proposition seems evident, there operates a series of historical premises and predispositions towards acceptance or rejection on the part of the subject, and these predispositions are guided by an overriding interest in the preservation and development not simply of 'life' as such, but of a particular form of life" (p. 43).

Neopragmatist philosopher Richard Rorty (1982) argues that there "are two ways of thinking about various things." We can think of truth "as a vertical relationship between representations and what is represented" (p. 92). We can also think of truth "horizontally—as the culminating reinterpretation of our predecessors' reinterpretation." He adds: "It is the difference between regarding truth, goodness, and beauty as eternal objects which we try to locate and reveal, and regarding them as artifacts whose fundamental design we often have to alter" (*ibid.*).

In *The Postmodern Condition: A Report on Knowledge* Jean-François Lyotard (1984) writes: "I define postmodern as incredulity toward metanarratives" (p. xxv). For Lyotard, the postmodern world is made up of Wittgensteinian language games and "the social subject itself seems to dissolve in this dissemination of language games" (*ibid.*). Even science needs to have rules that prescribe what moves are admissible into its language game. These prescriptions are the same sorts of presuppositions that form the foundation of any language game.

Where would one draw a line, on this roughly arranged continuum of perspectives, to separate modern from postmodern, given the blend of continuities and breaks that simultaneously link and separate each one from its neighbors? "Modernism" and "postmodernism" are not homogeneous or unambiguous facts, but only partially successful attempts to locate and define intellectual centers of gravity. Psychoanalysts looking to this epistemological debate, in their effort to assess their attitudes toward their own interpretations, must tolerate greater heterogeneity than they might have hoped to find.

Three Faces of Postmodernism

The modernity/postmodernity debate can be seen to fall into three realms, each of which must be fully considered when tracing the impact of postmodernity upon psychoanalytic theory and practice. First, there is the aesthetic debate over modernism and postmodernism, which concerns above all the nature of representation in the contemporary epoch. Postmodernism, in this particular sense, concerns a particular set of aesthetic or cultural values which were first given expression in the domains of architecture, the plastic and visual arts, poetry and literature. In contrast to the high modernist ambitions of uncovering an inner truth behind surface appearances, postmodernism exhibits a new playfulness, a mixing of previous aesthetic distinctions of content and form, high and low culture, the personal and public realms. The modernist attempt to discover a "deeper" reality is abandoned in the postmodern in favor of the celebration of style and surface. The preoccupation of modernism with principles of meaning and rationality is replaced with a tolerance for diversity and difference, the characteristics of which are reflected in a postmodern criticism which values irony, cynicism, pastiche, commercialism, and, in some cases, relativism (see Jameson, 1991). To portray the complexity of aesthetic surfaces and signs in the postmodern, Deleuze and Guattari (1977) invoke the metaphor of "rhizome": a peculiar rootstock that is multidirectional, chaotic, and random in its expansion. In this new aesthetic experience, postmodernism is a self-constituting world, determined by its own internal movement and process.

The second area of debate has focused on the philosophical and cultural concepts of modernity and postmodernity. Here it has been argued that a postmodern approach is necessary to avoid the realist assumptions of the Cartesian-Kantian-Hegelian tradition. Perhaps no other text has marked the intellectual terms of reference here as much as Lyotard's (1984) short treatise, *The Postmodern Condition: A Report on Knowledge*. Postmodernism, writes Lyotard, "designates the state of our culture following the transformations which, since the end of the nineteenth century, have altered the game rules for science, literature and the arts" (p. xxv). The "game rules" to which Lyotard refers involve a letting go of the grand narratives of traditional philosophy and science and an acceptance of the "heteromorphous nature of language games." Reason comes in many varieties. Two groups applying it effectively and adaptively to the same situation might well end up inventing, and living in, different Wittgensteinian language games without common ground rules. Here, the emphasis is away from forms of thought that promote uniformity and universality, and toward an appreciation of particularity, especially as regards the holding in mind of ambiguity and difference. Lyotard's position on postmodernism has been described as extreme insofar as it presents a radical separation of the nature of language games from their sociocultural context, and, as such, is said to threaten a complete fragmentation of subjectivity (see Norris [1993] and Eagleton [1990] for critical appraisals of Lyotard's more recent work).

Under postmodern theories of knowledge, there has been a profound questioning of foundationalism. Derrida (1978) argues that Western metaphysics is haunted by impossible dreams of certitude and transparency. Derrida, and the deconstructionism that his work has promoted, draws attention to the binary oppositions of textual practices and rhetorical strategies, using a poststructuralist conception of language as a differential play of signifiers to uncouple language from the world it seeks to colonize through acts of description. There will be in everything a writer writes or a patient says a contradiction that the author of the statement cannot acknowledge. As Stanley Fish (1989) sums up the goals of a Derridean deconstructive reading, it will "surface those contradictions and expose those suppressions" (p. 215). As a result, such a reading will expose those ideas or feelings which have been suppressed (repressed or dissociated, we might add). These exposures "trouble" the apparent unity of the text. We say that this unity has been defensively constructed. Deconstructivists say that such a unity was achieved in the first place "only by covering over all the excluded emphases and interests that might threaten it." According to Fish, Derridean deconstruction does not uncover these contradictions and dialectic hiding operations of rhetoric in order to reach "the Truth; rather it continually uncovers the truth of rhetorical operations, the truth that all operations, including the operation of deconstruction itself, are rhetorical" (p. 215). From this standpoint, there is no philosophical or ideological position that is able to claim *ultimate* authority or justification. On the contrary, the justification of knowledge, as the postmodern pragmatist Richard Rorty has argued, is always a matter of argumentation from different positions and perspectives, such that our beliefs about the world are necessarily local, provisional, and contingent.

The third area of debate is concerned more explicitly with the personal, social, and cultural aspects of postmodern society. Here the issue concerns the way in which postmodernity affects the world of human selves and of interpersonal relationships. And it is at the level of our personal and cultural worlds, we suggest, that postmodernism most forcefully breaks its links with the ontological premises of modernity. By this we mean to focus attention on contemporary culture and its technologies, and in particular the ways in which globalization and instantaneous communication is transforming self-identity and interpersonal relationships. Globalization, transnational communication systems, new information technologies, the industrialization of war, universal consumerism: these are the core institutional dimensions of contemporary societies, and most students of contemporary culture agree that such transformations carry immense implications as regards selfhood, self-identity, and subjectivity (Frosh, 1991; Giddens, 1991; Thompson, 1990). The transformation of personal experience that postmodernity ushers into existence concerns, among other things, a compression of space and mutation of time, rapid and at times cataclysmic forms of change, an exponential increase in the dynamism of social and economic life, as well as a growing sense of fragmentation and dislocation. Such transformations, to repeat, are not only social in character; on the contrary, they penetrate to the core of psychic experience and restructure unconscious transactions between human subjects in new, and often dramatic, ways (see Elliott, 1996).

It is from this flux and turmoil of contemporary social life that many commentators have branded postmodernity as antihistorical, relativist, and disordered. Postmodernism, in this reading, represents the dislocation of meaning and logic, whether of society or of the mind. It is possible to hold a more optimistic view of this apparent cultural disorientation, however, once the irreducibility of the plurality of human worlds is accepted. The social theorist Zygmunt Bauman (1990, 1991, 1992, 1993), for example, argues that postmodernity represents a new dawning, rather than a twilight, for the generation of meaning. "Postmodernity," Bauman (1991) writes, "is marked by a view of the human world as irreducibly and irrevocably pluralistic, split into a multitude of sovereign units and sites of authority, with no horizontal or vertical order, either in actuality or in potency" (p. 35). This emphasis on plurality and multiplicity highlights that postmodernity involves a rejection of the typically modernist search for foundations, absolutes, and universals. Postmodernity is a self-constituting and self-propelling culture, a culture which is increasingly self-referential in direction. From cable TV to the information superhighway: postmodern culture is a culture turned back upon itself, generated in and through reflexive systems of technological knowledge.

The strength of Bauman's interpretation is that it demonstrates that modernity and postmodernity are not dichotomous. Culturally, we have not transcended modernity, nor have we entered a postmodern society writ large. Instead, it can be said that contemporary Western societies deploy modern and postmodern cultural forms simultaneously. Postmodernity is better understood as "modernity without illusions." It is a form of life, or perhaps state of mind, in which the messiness of life is directly embraced and dealt with as challenge. Pluralism, contingency, ambiguity, ambivalence, uncertainty: these features of social life were assigned a negative value—they were seen as pathologies to be eradicated—in the modern era. For Bauman, however, these are not distortions to be overcome, but are the distinctive features of a mode of social experience which has broken with the disabling hold of objectivity, necessity, law.

Thus, the picture that we are presenting is that modernity and postmodernity are not homogeneous or unambiguous facts; nor are they dichotomous entities. Rather, as modes of contemporary experience, modernity and postmodernity locate and define cognitive-affective centers of gravity for individuals seeking to come to terms with the difficulties of day-to-day life. As a result, psychoanalysts looking to this epistemological debate, in their effort to assess their attitudes toward their own interpretations, must tolerate greater heterogeneity than they might have hoped to find.

In the following section of this essay, we will consider two typically reductive critiques of the postmodern turn in psychoanalysis—reductive in that postmodernism is reduced to a single meaning, and thus the complexity of postmodernity is screened from view. We will argue, in contrast to much recent thinking on the subject, that there are indeed alliances between certain thinkers known in their own fields as postmodern and some contemporary psychoanalysts. We will also argue that, contrary to dominant assumptions concerning the inescapability of fragmentation, all but the most extreme forms of postmodernity permit an "opening out" to reflective psychical activity, a space for the thinking or processing of uncertainty, ambivalence, otherness, and difference. Similarly, although some postmodern thinking is relativistic, it is perspectivism and not relativism that is essential to postmodernism. Acknowledging the viability and plausibility of multiple perspectives does not consign one to accepting that any interpretation is as good as any other.

James Glass's Critique of Postmodern Theorizing

In *Shattered Selves: Multiple Personality in a Postmodern World*, James Glass (1993) accepts that many of the objectivist ambitions of modernity should be renounced. He supports the postmodern critique of all-inclusive and dominating metanarratives, and he underscores the importance of recent French psychoanalytic feminist critiques of the phallocentric values and assumptions of modernity in promoting personal and political change in the contemporary epoch.

Glass, however, also sees a costly price tag on this postmodern agenda. If the identity of the self, as some post modernists assert, following the French psychoanalyst Jacques Lacan, is imaginary—a kind of papering over of the indeterminacy of desire itself—then the human subject is fully desubjectivized. That brand of postmodernism isolates the self and argues that there is nothing hidden or split off in psychological experience, nothing inaccessible to ideological explanation. We share that concern about Lacanian and similar brands of postmodernism, but since Glass assumes that postmodernism is homogeneous, he believes that all postmodernists carry this subject-destroying virus.

> In their insistence on freeing the self from any historical or structural conception of what the self is, the postmodernists reject, in coming to an understanding of what identity "is," the influence of infancy, the psychoanalytic notion of the preoedipal, the Freudian conception of the unconscious (drive theory), and the idea that actions of the self may be represented in severe forms of internal psychological conflict whose origins lie in primitive emotional symbolization (p. 5).

Postmodernist theories, in this reading, are not only attempting to destabilize modernist conceptions of subjectivity, meaning, and truth, they are out to do away with the basic tensions or contradictions of self and world altogether. As a result they must all end up criticizing and rejecting everything modern in Freudian psychoanalysis: "multiplicity of self" will lead to the psychological repudiation of difference and of language; the fragmentation idealized in the postmodernity discourse is really multiple personality disorder and schizophrenia; flux threatens the self, subjectivity and identity.

Finally, we are presented with a list of postmodern theorists, a list which includes Derrida, Lyotard, Baudrillard, Cixous, Irigaray, and others (all quite different) who are all said to be indifferent to the harm or injury of psychological fragmentation as well as ignorant of the post-Freudian stress on relationality and intersubjectivity. (That some of these theorists have produced some of the most important critiques of psychoanalysis in France since the Second World War is something that seems to have escaped Glass's attention; as well as the point that some of them are practicing analysts.)

Kimberlyn Leary's Critique of Postmodern Theorizing

For most clinicians questions about selves, subjects, and truth become important insofar as they suggest options to be considered and decisions to be made in the analytic situation. Kimberlyn Leary in "Psychoanalytic 'Problems' and Postmodern 'Solutions' " (1994), an article that appeared in this journal, argued that "postmodern solutions" suggest illusory answers to real clinical problems. She used the writings of Hoffman and Schafer as examples of postmodernism.

The "implication that follows" from postmodern writings, Leary argues, "is that we can, at will, assume a self that suits us if the proper audience can be assembled" (p. 454). This is a hyperbolic rendering of the postmodern argument that, given a different social context, we might imagine people coming to have other senses of what it means to be a self than the sense they now have in our culture. This is especially the case, in that the postmodern deconstruction of subjectivity is precisely an attempt to criticize and rethink modernist notions of the will, intention, agency, and the like. Leary, however, argues that there is no difference between imagining that one might be whomever one wants to be if only the right audience could be assembled (or that one is only stuck being who one is because one has always had the wrong audience) and being diagnosable as borderline or narcissistic.

Before considering whether Schafer or Hoffman might be construed, from anything either has written, to have ever embraced a "choose your own self" position, we want to note that, as many readers might have noticed, Leary's marriage of Hoffman and Schafer is itself problematic. She recognizes that there are significant differences between the various positions they take in their writings, and she details some of these. Yet, she cannot resist the temptation to conclude, after all, that, despite these differences, their theoretical projects are variations on the postmodern theme of relativism about truth and fragmentation of the self.

This lumping together of Hoffman and Schafer under the

postmodern label glosses over the unique features of their quite different theories that are crucial if one wants to use them as examples of postmodern theorizing in psychoanalysis (and it also buries the modernist features of both men's work). Hoffman sees analysts' participation as a function of their subjectivity (countertransference, in the broadest sense). They will neither be aware nor want to be aware of every aspect of this unconscious subjectivity. Thus, they ought to remain (or realize that they are) more uncertain of what they mean and what they are doing than many analysts—of all the major schools—have been. If a patient claims to know or suspect something about the analyst's personality or experience, then the analyst does not necessarily affirm or deny, but shows interest in the patient's observations and wonders what conclusions the patient might draw from them.

Schafer, by contrast, emphasizes that the way in which the analyst understands and interprets is always partly a manifestation of the analyst's theory. He says little or nothing about the analyst's unconscious psychology. For example, Schafer (1992) writes of a teacher, S.M., who "derives pleasure from regularly treating his students cruelly" (p. 52). In Freud's psychosexual language, the patient is sadistic. "He, however, thinks that he treats his students fairly, dispassionately, professionally." As Schafer points out, we, as analysts, along with many other observers, might conclude that he is deceiving himself. "The attribution of self-deception is, however," Schafer argues—and here is where he becomes postmodern—"based on a number of unstated assumptions, interpretations, and evidential claims."

> Far from this deception being an unmediated perception by an "objective" observer of what S.M. is "really" doing, it is a rather elaborate construction (p. 52).

> . . . it is the storylines that establish the facts of the case, which of these facts are to be taken as significant (for example, as evidence of sadism), and how these facts are to be situated. . . .
> The case of S.M. could be told differently; it often is (p. 55).

Yet, as if in anticipation of critiques like Leary's, Schafer adds: "I am not proposing that any account is as acceptable as any other." What he does propose, in a hermeneutically postmodern argument, is that "when we speak of true and false accounts of actions, we are positioning ourselves in a matrix of narratives that are always open to examination as to their precritical assumptions and values and as to their usefulness in one or another project" (p. 56).

Where Schafer is interested in how the analyst's theory reshapes the patient's account of her or his history (which account is itself already one of many possible narratives), Hoffman talks about how the analyst chooses to shape the evolving relationship with the patient by doing or not doing, saying or not saying certain things at specific junctures. The analyst can no longer be certain that unwavering adherence to a specific technical stance (whether empathy or resistance analysis) simply serves to bring forth a clear picture of what has been inside the patient's psyche or guarantees the most effective route to what has been called structural change. Further, such unwavering adherence does not mean that the analyst is not deciding over and over to shape the analytic relationship in a specific way.

As an example of a specific decision he made in his own work, Hoffman (1994) reports that when he called an angry patient's internist during a session in response to the patient's demand that he do something immediately to help her get Valium, the "enactment helped me and the patient to begin to see how much she wanted me to be frantic about her in a way similar to how she thought her mother was frantic about [a sister], the difference being that my 'getting hysterical' was also an object of curiosity and critical reflection. Thus there was reason to believe that the quality of my attention, taken as a whole, was better than what either the patient or [the sister] got from their mother" (pp. 212-213). What Hoffman emphasizes here is his awareness that his choices are rooted in his subjectivity, which includes countertransference even when it is theoretically informed. The choice therefore invites critical reflection as to its meaning in the relationship. The countertransference is not condemned since the entire transference-countertransference enactment is an object of critical reflection.

Neither Schafer nor Hoffman has been implying that analysands have no enduring unconscious psychology, nor that people are an endless flow of abruptly appearing selves unrelated to each other in time and space. What each, in quite different ways, has argued at times is that his clinical observations have led him to think that one enduring feature of human unconscious psychology is a greater sense of discontinuity and contingency than was recognized by previous theories.

By the time Leary was ready to move from Hoffman and Schafer to the realms of body and gender, she was in high positivist and objectivist gears. Postmodernists, she says, forget that people have bodies and that these bodies come in male and female versions—an especially intriguing criticism, given that the contemporary focus on the body and its pleasures by the social sciences and the humanities is generally understood to derive from postmodernism (see Butler, 1993). Having forgotten this, they probably talk to their female patients as if these patients are free to forget those realities as well. Further, she suggests, postmodernists probably tell patients that death is just another version of life, just as they must believe that Terry Anderson could have made anything he wanted out of his captivity once he got past putting too much stock in treating as real such facts as his captors' controlling when he could use the toilet (Leary, 1994, p. 458).

Hoffman, after briefly considering it, Leary tells us, gives up on the idea of an external reality. He does not. He simply argues that the variations of what we claim is out there are not constructed privately by each mind but by minds in interaction. Similarly, Hoffman's emphasis does not argue that every account of the analysand must be treated by the analyst as credible and tenable. He suggests a shift in technique in which the analyst is much more likely, than was once (in the history of psychoanalysis) the case, to treat as plausible that the patient did in fact evoke and then find some element of the analyst's experience (including unconscious experience) or behavior on which to hang the enduring representation of a ragefully attacking other. Further, Hoffman nowhere says that he automatically agrees with his patients that everything they say about him is true. He portrays himself as doing exactly what Leary suggests analysts should do: he appreciates the patient's view of the analyst by more often treating it as plausible than theories of transference-as-distortion had encouraged us to do. He argues, however, that such appreciation has been crude when embedded by analysts in clear statements that while they appreciate the patient's infantile view of them, there is simply not a shred of current truth in it.

If an analyst was persuaded by Hoffman's writings and if that analyst gradually internalized a constructivist attitude, we might expect a shift to more often and more automatically considering the possibility that a patient's statement about the analyst's experience (including the analyst's unconscious experience) has captured something true not only about the analyst but also about the patient's ability to evoke experience in others and the patient's selective attention to certain aspects of the experience of others. Similarly, such an analyst might also feel more free to judge (out loud) the patient's assessments of the analyst's experience with the proviso that the analyst understands such judgments as arising out of subjective experience and as having the potential to contribute in part to the enactment of transference-countertransference patterns. What makes the difference in Hoffman's view is that the analyst appreciates that his or her judgment is born out of his or her full subjective participation in the process.

What is unfortunate about articles such as those by skeptics of "postmodern psychoanalysis" like Glass and Leary is that they raise important issues about the psychical and social implications of postmodernism in such a divisive and dismissive way. Their respective critiques of the "inescapable fragmentation" which postmodernity promotes does specify quite well a dilemma which psychoanalysts face today: the contemporary world is marked by constant turmoil and dislocation, yet to embrace the insights of postmodernism risks a further escalation of fragmentation itself—of knowledge, expertise, and meaning.

In our view, such an understanding of postmodernism is misplaced (even if the anxiety registered is expressive of a fear of "not-knowing"). In fact, the critiques made by Glass and Leary are critiques that many postmodernists would also make against the extreme forms of postmodernism that Glass and Leary set up for criticism. Leary, especially, having set things up this way, then simply claims that any nonpositivist, nonobjectivist theorist of the analytic process must, prima facie, be one of those extreme postmodernists; since she can see only those two places for a theorist to stand. Because, as we have said from the start, those points of view labeled as postmodern are heterogeneous; postmodernity permits other conceptual options than those imagined by Glass and Leary.

In the next two sections of this essay we want to go beyond the specific arguments of Glass or Leary and take up two general categories of critique written against attempts to use postmodern discourse to reshape psychoanalytic theory: that it forces on us an untenable notion of the self as inescapably fragmented, and that it leaves us with no hope or even ambition of finding the truth about anything. In each case we hope to show that these criticisms should not frighten away or deter interested analysts from pursuing the possibility that a study of postmodern ideas will enhance their clinical effectiveness. In considering each of these criticisms, we offer distinctions between what is and what is not being said about selfhood and subjectivity in the postmodernity discourse. In brief, postmodern thought does not force upon us the notion that the self is incoherently fragmented (rather, it is decentered); and, postmodern thought does not leave us lost in the belief that any interpretation is as good as any other (rather, all views are interpretive and perspectival).

The Critique of "Inescapable Fragmentation"

Postmodern conceptions of plural selves and worlds are informed, in broad terms, by the poststructuralist notion of the decentering of the subject. This is a decentering initiated by Freud himself, who suggested in the strongest theoretical terms that the ego is not master in its own house, and this is an insight that has been fruitfully extended by Lacan to include a focus on the creative and coercive effects of language.

The central point to note at this stage is that this decentering should not be equated with a disintegration of the human subject. The criticism that the postmodernist decentering of selves amounts to a wiping out of subjectivity is perhaps better seen as a defensive reaction to the dislocation of modernist fantasies of self-control and mastery. The postmodernist stress on ambiguity, ambivalence, difference, plurality, and fragmentation, on the contrary, underlines the psychical capacities and resources that are needed to register such forms of subjectivity, or, psychoanalytically speaking, to attach meaning to experience in open-ended ways.

Seen in this light, postmodern conceptions of multiple selves actually situate the subject in a context of heightened self-reflexivity, a reflectiveness that is used for exploring personal experience and fantasy. This intertwining of experience, fantasy, and reflexivity is conceptualized in terms of the capacity to think about—that is, to symbolize and to process—unconscious communications in the interpersonal world, of projective and introjective identifications, splitting, denial, and the like. Broadly speaking, what is being stressed here is the prising open of a space between fantasy and words (the chain of significations) in which meaning is constituted, such that the subject can reflect upon this self-constitution and creatively alter it.

In some circumstances, of course, self-reflexivity is debilitating rather than emancipatory. An openness to multiple worlds of fantasy can produce extreme pain and anxiety, as well as a dislocation of the capacity of the mind to register thinking itself

(Bion, 1962; Ogden, 1989). In general terms though, and in a diversity of contexts, it produces the contrary: an "opening out" to the multiplicity of fantasy and imagination at the intersection of self and world. This is conceptualized, as we will examine later in this essay, in differing ways by postmodern analysts. Cornelius Castoriadis speaks of a self-understanding of "radical imagination," Julia Kristeva of "semiotic subversion," and Christopher Bollas of our "personal idiom." This focus highlights a reflexive awareness of imagination, and of the key role of ambivalence, difference, and otherness in human relations.

Criticisms of the Postmodern Collapse of Signification

What about "reality" and "truth"? Some critics of postmodernism have reached the erroneous conclusion that so-called hermeneutic, relational, deconstructionist, intersubjective, or constructivist perspectives imply that the conditions of interpretation are such that no true or correct interpretations are possible—a position that some philosophers (Bohman, 1991) label "interpretive skepticism" (p. 136) or "strong holism" (p. 130). These terms refer to the arguments by certain postmodern thinkers that all cognitive activity is interpretive and so warrants deep skepticism and that it is holistic in the sense of always taking place against the background of all our beliefs and practices. "Together these two theses imply that no interpretation can be singled out as uniquely correct, since the assertion that it is so would itself be an interpretation within a particular context" (p. 130)—the so-called hermeneutic circle.

A number of philosophers and literary critics have strongly identified with this epistemological claim while others have partially or moderately embraced it at times in their writings. We do not, however, believe that postmodern analysts have to embrace this strongly skeptical and strongly holistic position on interpretation. To varying degrees Schafer and Hoffman (who are as much modern as postmodern), along with other analysts who work within the modern/postmodern dialectic, seem to agree that interpretation is indeterminate and perspectival, while also maintaining that interpretations can produce revisable, shared knowledge based on identifiable evidence. Thus, in the clinical situation a postmodern attitude does nothing so radical as to force the abandonment of the quest for truth about the patient's unconscious psychology. It does, however, question and make problematic any rigidly modernist pursuit of this truth. Consider, for example, this clinical event:

> A 25 year old woman fell silent after I made an interpretation. After a few minutes, she said she felt my voice was too "insistent," and she became silent again (Busch, 1995, p. 47).

One could easily imagine any analyst influenced by postmodern trends asking the patient to tell him or her about his or her insistence. Busch almost does that, but the contrast is vital. He reports: "I immediately recognized what she was responding to" (p. 47). Postmodernism would urge a little less certainty about what the patient was responding to until the patient had a chance to elaborate (or associate to) her representation of the analyst as too insistent.

What happens next is, at first, a bit confusing. We might expect that Busch would tell us, the readers, what it was that he immediately recognized; but he only tells us that the "interpretation was one that I had speculated about for some time, and the analysand's associations confirmed it in a way that she seemed ready to understand" (p. 47). We read this in two ways. First, Busch wants us to know that he has waited until the patient was already saying whatever it was he told her in the interpretation she claimed he made too insistently. Second, he wants us to know that he was not speculating about the unconscious wishes that make her anxious. This matters because in most of his writings Busch identifies himself as working along the lines suggested by Paul Gray, and Gray has made it clear throughout his writings that he does not think analysts should do that sort of speculating about what *absent content* catalyzes defenses—just interpret resistance, especially in the form of superego projections onto the analyst, and the patient will get to the anxiety that triggers the resistance and the sexual excitement or rage that triggers the anxiety. Busch has to make this apologetic because sooner or later he will say something about that *absent content*, and he does not want to emphasize the subjective nature of the judgment call involved in deciding when one is simply pointing to it in the patient's associations and when one is getting it from one's own thought. Like Leary, he wants there to be a ground in the data of the patient's associations upon which we stand free of constructions or narratives.

Having made these points, Busch then tells us that what he immediately recognized was that he, too, thought there had been a shift from his more questioning voice to another kind of voice. It is crucial here, however, that he does not label that new voice. It is hard to imagine that he does not have a label for it in his mind, just as the patient has the label "too insistent" attached to it in hers. He does, after all, have a label for the voice he shifted from: it was "questioning." What a postmodern analyst might say at this point is that Busch has his shift in voice constructed one way in his mind and the patient has it constructed another. How can Busch be so positive (as in positivistic) that her construction ("too insistent") is wrong? This does not mean that Hoffman or Schafer thinks every construction is as plausible here as any other, simply that if Busch shifted from questioning to telling or from questioning to asserting, there is a range of constructions that might make sense of what he had done.

What Busch does next is return to his questioning voice. A bit later in his article he complains that object relational analysts, whom he believes he is critiquing in his essay, might simply "turn down the volume" of their voice to make the patient feel safe, so we assume he wants us to understand that, while he too did that, he also did more. It is the subject matter of another essay that no object relational analyst whose work we have read has suggested that if the patient complains about something we are doing, we simply stop doing it and do not try to work with the patient to understand the complaint.

What matters here is that Busch, too, changed his voice but attributes little or no significance to this as influencing what happens next. Further complicating things, his lack of attention to how he is participating in constructing this complex relational event with his patient allows him to say simply in passing that the first thing he did after returning to his *questioning* voice was to *tell* her something: that he could see how she heard his voice as "different." Finally, he has been forced to do what we have been suggesting, from a postmodern perspective, cannot be avoided: he tells us how he has constructed his changing of his voice. He has applied the word "different" to it. He will implicitly claim that anything more descriptive than that is entirely the patient's resistance. We believe that this is precisely the sort of clinical work, in counterpoint to which theories such as Hoffman's stand. Leary's use of the extreme example of a patient's claiming the analyst is always ragefully attacking her, when he has never overtly done so, masked this problem of the clinical position her stance implies.

What Critics of Postmodernism Such as Glass and Leary Fail To Do

Some of the most important changes taking place in postmodern culture concern the restructuring of emotional relationships, sexuality, intimacy, gender, and love (Beck and Beck-Gernsheim, 1995; Giddens, 1992). In the light of the postmodernist critique of the grand narratives of Western rationality, how can psychoanalysts rethink the relationship between subjectivity, unconscious desire, and interpersonal processes? (For an extended treatment of these issues, see Elliott [1992].)

Critiques such as those of Glass and Leary, in our opinion, occlude the epistemological interest of postmodernism in psychoanalysis. That is, they fail to deal with what is most important and significant in the postmodernity debate as regards psycho-analysis.

Glass focuses on the work of Michel Foucault and his thesis that "subject positions" are determined by networks of power/ knowledge relations. He then makes the criticism—quite rightly against Foucault—that the unconscious and libidinal desires are rendered mere products of wider social forces, of power and knowledge. But the critical point here is that this is not a criticism of postmodernism: Foucault was not a postmodernist, and in fact rejected the notion of a transition from modernity to postmodernity (see Macey, 1993).

Leary makes use of the term "postmodern" to marginalize the potential usefulness to analysts of the theorizing of Hoffman and Schafer (rather than, say, showing how their clinical work links them to specific modern or postmodern thinkers). She then implies that because they are postmodern, they would be inclined to do various absurd things during analytic hours. Her suggestion—that if we consider Schafer and Hoffman as gad-flies for positivistically inclined analysts (rather than purveyors of clinical theories of their own), then maybe they are useful after all—hardly mitigates her previous severe criticizing of them, which is based on having first linked them, via labeling them "postmodern," with total fragmentation of the self and total relativism in the assignment of meaning to experience.

Postmodernity and Psychoanalytic Heterogeneity

Whereas Glass and Leary proceed by bundling very divergent postmodern social theories together and then developing a neg-ative assessment of this shift in thinking as regards psychoanal-ysis as a discipline, we propose a different tack. In our opinion, it is too simple, and indeed erroneous, to imagine that divergent postmodern theories can either be imported into, or excluded from, psychoanalysis at the level of theory as well as the level of clinical practice. Such an approach treats the very nature of psychoanalytic thought as something that develops outside of our general culture. That thing known as "postmodernism" appears as something that does not really affect the structure of mind; and if its conceptual and practical implications seem a little too threatening, then it is something that psychoanalysis would also do well to avoid. Postmodernity and psychoanalysis, in this reading, have absolutely nothing to do with each other, unless it is decided otherwise by the psychoanalytic community at some point when the profession might more actively consider a radical change in its system of beliefs.

In our view, the development of psychoanalysis is not so self-contained. On the contrary, recent trends in psychoanalysis indicate a transformation in theorizing as regards subjectivity, the status of the unconscious, the nature of intersubjectivity, and of thinking in terms of what analyst and patient know about themselves and each other (Elliott and Frosh, 1995; Mitchell, 1993; Spezzano, 1993). Such changes in theorizing take many forms throughout contemporary psychoanalytic literature, and it is a central aspect of our argument that this direction in psychoanalytic theorizing is part of our postmodern world-view.

Consider, for example, the question of epistemology. In traditional psychoanalysis, practitioners tended to pride themselves on their knowledge of the unconscious as a distinct psychical system. The unconscious, having been fully explored and colonized by Freud, was seen as a realm of mind that can be known and subsequently placed under rational control, once patient and analyst are brave enough to face sexual repression and its difficulty. In post-Freudian psychoanalysis, however, there is a range of approaches to thinking of the unconscious and the anxiety-provoking nature of desire, which generally displace this emphasis on certitude toward more open-ended forms of knowledge and of experience. Indeed, the capacity to tolerate periods of "not-knowing," at both subjective and theoretical levels, is positively valued in some contemporary versions of psychoanalysis (see Hoffman, 1987; Ogden, 1989).

Here the focus is on a suspension of preconceived thoughts

and beliefs, coupled with the intersubjective exploration of fantasy and desire. Human knowledge is no longer understood as being subject to singular, rationalistic control (once the secrets of the unconscious are unlocked); on the contrary, knowledge is regarded as perspectival and decentered. Knowledge, of the self and of others, is discovered, according to Winnicott, in that "transitional space" of intermediate experience; the connections between subjectivity and truth unfold at the margins of thinking and in intersubjective reverie, according to Bion; and fantasy is embedded in human relationships through a dialectical interplay of paranoid-schizoid and depressive positions of generating experience, according to Klein. We mention Winnicott, Bion, and Klein in this context to highlight the beginnings of that psychoanalytic shift away from understanding knowledge as rationality and control. The point is not that any of these psychoanalysts may, at the current historical juncture, be reread as "postmodern." Rather, the point is that the development of psychoanalytic theory, to which their contributions are seminal, at once contributes to and reflects our postmodern world-view and culture.

Many psychoanalysts have been contributing to a shift away from realist aspirations or impersonal objectivity. They have rejected the traditional view that the clearest form of understanding occurs when secondary-process thinking is separated out from the unconscious fantasy. Instead, they pay explicit attention to the creative power of human imagination as regards issues of subjectivity, intersubjectivity, truth, desire, fantasy and personal meaning, and authenticity. As Stephen Mitchell (1993) summarizes this rescaffolding of the discipline:

> What is inspiring about psychoanalysis today is not the renunciation of illusion in the hope of joining a common, progressively realistic knowledge and control, but rather the hope of fashioning a personal reality that feels authentic and enriching. . . . The hope inspired by psychoanalysis in our time is grounded in personal meaning, not rational consensus. The bridge supporting connections with others is not built out of a

rationality superseding fantasy and the imagination, but out of feelings experienced as real, authentic, generated from the inside, rather than imposed externally, in close relationship with fantasy and the imagination (p. 21).

It is this explicit attention given to fantasy and the imagination that, in our opinion, helps to define the stakes of contemporary psychoanalysis. The stakes are necessarily high if only because no one knows with any degree of certainty how, and with what success, contemporary selves and societies will frame meaning and truth based on an appreciation of the ambivalence, ambiguity, and plurality of human experience.

All of this raises the thorny question: has psychoanalysis, whether it likes it or not, become postmodern? Is there such a thing as "postmodern psychoanalysis"? To this, we would respond with a qualified "yes"; save that the issue cannot really be understood adequately if put in such terms. To grasp the trajectories of psychoanalysis today, we suggest, it is necessary to understand that the self-reflexivity which psychoanalysis uncovers and promotes (and which, according to Jürgen Habermas [1968], is Freud's central discovery) is radicalized and transformed in postmodern culture. With the eclipse of custom and tradition as embedded in modernity, the relationship between self and society becomes self-referential in postmodern times. Without the binding cultural, symbolic norms of modernity in arenas such as sexuality, love, relationships, gender, and work, people become increasingly aware of the contingency of the self, of relationships, and of society itself. They also become profoundly aware of the contingency of meaning and of the sign; they see that meaning is not fixed once and for all, but rather that signification is creatively made and remade by desire-and-anxiety-driven human relationships. In this sense, postmodern culture can be said to directly incorporate certain core insights of psychoanalysis into its framing assumptions, especially as concerns the role of fantasy as being at the root of our traffic with social meaning. (For a detailed discussion of the intricate

connections between postmodernity and psychoanalysis see Elliott [1996].)

There are strong indications that this cultural self-awareness
of contingency, ambivalence, and plurality—key features of the
postmodern world-view—are theorized in contemporary psychoanalytic dialogues. In contemporary psychoanalysis, in the
work of its most radical clinicians and theoreticians, the subjectivity of the self is approached as comprising multivalent psychical forms, embedded in a field of interpersonal relationships,
and in close connection with unconscious fantasy. In recent
years, such writers as Castoriadis, Kristeva, Anzieu, Ogden, and
Bollas have radically reconceptualized the nature of psychic processing, and in particular of the constitution of psychic meanings. It is beyond the scope of this article to discuss in any detail
the specific contributions of these authors, or of the significant
conceptual differences between their approaches to psychoanalysis. However, some of the common threads in their visions of
psychoanalysis, and of their understandings of psychic constitution and meaning, will be briefly touched on here, in order to
draw out the wider cultural links to postmodernism.

Cornelius Castoriadis (1987, 1995), an analyst living in Paris,
theorizes subjectivity in terms of a "radical imaginary," by which
he means an unconscious architecture of representations,
drives, and affects in and through which psychic space is constituted and perpetuated. The precondition for the self-
reflection upon subjectivity, says Castoriadis, is fantasy: the capacity of the psyche to posit figuration *ex nihilo*. "The original
narcissistic cathexis or investment," he writes, "is necessarily
representation . . . (otherwise it would not be psychical) and it
can then be nothing other than a 'representation' (unimaginable
and unrepresentable for us) of the Self" (1987, p. 287).

In Castoriadis's reading of Freud, the unconscious is not so
much the psychic depository of that which cannot be held in
consciousness, but rather the essential psychical flux which un-
derpins all representations of the self, of others, and of the social

and cultural world. Such psychical flux, necessarily plural, multiple, and discontinuous, is that which renders identity nonidentical with itself, as Adorno would have it, or, in more psychoanalytic terms, it is that which means that every self-representation is intrinsically incomplete and lacking since the subject arises from a primary loss which remains traumatic at the level of the unconscious. Here Castoriadis's emphasis on the radically imaginary dimensions of self and society parallels the postmodernist stress on the demise of external foundations as an anchoring mechanism for thought, and his stress on psychical flux mirrors certain postmodernist themes which highlight the ambiguity, ambivalence, and radical otherness of contemporary social life.

So too Kristeva (1984, 1989) underscores the profoundly imaginary dimensions of unconscious experience in terms of her notion of the "semiotic," a realm of prelinguistic experience (including drives, affects, and primal rhythms) which is necessarily prior to symbolic representation and entry into cultural processes. Seeking to account for an internally disruptive presence as regards the space of the Other in Lacanian psychoanalysis, Kristeva argues that contemporary psychoanalysis is increasingly concerned with the complexities of semiotic displacement, or unconscious rupture, as that point of otherness which derails symbolism and intersubjectivity. One way of understanding Kristeva's reconceptualization of the unconscious in post-Lacanian theory is as an explicit attempt to account for the multiplication of fantasy (and of multiple selves) in its trading with received social meanings, or external reality.

Extending Kristeva, Elliott (1995) argues that this multiplication of fantasy is underlined by a "representational wrapping of self and other," a preliminary ordering of pre-self experience, otherness, and difference. Such wrapping lies at the core of intersubjectivity space—indeed it is the unconscious investment in the shapes, textures, surfaces, and pre-objects that comprise psychic space itself—and it functions as a kind of perpetual self-constitution, or what is termed "rolling identification" (pp. 45-47). In a Kleinian vein, Thomas Ogden (1989) also speaks of such a preliminary ordering of pre-object relations as the "autistic-contiguous mode of generating experience" (p. 30), the sensory floor of psychic space which underlies paranoid-schizoid and depressive processes.

Along similar lines, Anzieu (1985) links fantasy and interpersonal experience with the notion of a "skin ego," an imaginary registration of maternal holding. Influenced by Klein and Winnicott, Anzieu argues that the skin ego is constituted in relation to maternal bodily experiences, a contact from which the beginning separation of inner and outer worlds takes place through introjective and projective identification. The skin ego is thus a kind of "containing envelope" for the holding of emotional states in fantasy, from which human experience can become known, symbolized, and developed. So too Bollas (1992) argues that selfhood is generated in and through our "personal idiom," a psychical grid (or unconscious space) between experience and fantasy.

In the preceding accounts, psychical life is portrayed as a nonlinear movement of fantasies, containers, introjects, representational wrappings, semiotic sensations, envelopes, and memories. Such a focus has much in common with postmodernist theory insofar as the radical imagination of the psyche is treated as central to the constitution and reproduction of subjectivity; a self-reflexive subjectivity. This is not to say, however, that the subject of contemporary psychoanalysis is without grounding, set adrift within the logics of disintegration. On the contrary, the multivalent psychical forms of contemporary selves are said to be patterned in and through an interpersonal field of interactions with significant others, theorized variously as the Lacanian Symbolic Order, the Kleinian depressive position, or social imaginary significations.

Beyond Hermeneutics and Constructivism

The hermeneutic and constructivist perspectives of Hoffman and Schafer are not the whole story of a "postmodern turn" in psychoanalysis. We emphasized their work because a previous article in this journal (Leary, 1994) had risked leaving an impression that might easily limit interest not only in the important work of these two analysts but also in anything else associated with postmodernism. As we argued above, psychoanalysts cannot remain impervious to the postmodern ideas swirling around them—any more than any domain of twentieth century Western thought was able to decide not to be bothered by psychoanalysis.

Psychoanalysts believed, for most of this century, that we could choose not to study outside our discipline. We needed only to master our techniques and theories. Then came a period of time during which some analysts looked to philosophy, neuropsychology, infant research, or literary criticism to adjudicate our theoretical and clinical debates. Leary's essay, although we disputed it, might be treated as a harbinger of a third phase in the relationship between psychoanalysis and other disciplines. In this emerging third phase, we would neither ignore nor annex ideas from, say, contemporary philosophy. Instead, we would recognize that as broad cultural shifts occur in our way of viewing the human condition (and in our way of understanding our ways of viewing the human condition), then psychoanalysis will both contribute to and be moved by these shifts. As a result we would understand that we are thrown into relationships with activities in other disciplines—from rereadings of Hegel to studies of affect and intersubjectivity by neuropsychologists and infant researchers—through which psychoanalysis (clinical and applied) both reacts to and shapes the human world.

REFERENCES

ANZIEU, D. (1985). *The Skin Ego*. Translated by C. Turner. New Haven/London: Yale Univ. Press, 1989.
BARRATT, B. B. (1993). *Psychoanalysis and the Postmodern Impulse. Knowing and Being since Freud's Psychology*. Baltimore/London: Johns Hopkins Univ. Press.
BAUMAN, Z. (1990). *Modernity and Ambivalence*. Cambridge: Polity Press.

—— (1991). *Intimations of Postmodernity*. London: Routledge.
—— (1992). *Mortality, Immortality, and Other Life Strategies*. Cambridge: Polity Press.
—— (1993). *Postmodern Ethics*. Oxford: Blackwell.
BECK, U. & BECK-GERNSHEIM, E. (1995). *The Normal Chaos of Love*. Cambridge: Polity Press.
BION, W. R. (1962). *Learning from Experience*. New York: Basic Books.
BLACKBURN, S. (1993). *Essays in Quasi-Realism*. Oxford: Oxford Univ. Press.
BOHMAN, J. (1991). Holism without skepticism. In *The Interpretive Turn*, ed. D. Hiley, J. Dorman & R. Shusterman. Ithaca: Cornell Univ. Press, pp. 129-134.
BOLLAS, C. (1992). *Being a Character*. New York: Hill & Wang.
BUSCH, F. (1995). Resistance analysis and object relations theory. *Psychoanal. Psychol.*, 12:43-54.
BUTLER, J. (1993). *Bodies That Matter*. New York: Routledge.
CASTORIADIS, C. (1987). *The Imaginary Institution of Society*. Translated by K. Blamey. Cambridge, MA: MIT Press.
—— (1995). Logic, imagination, reflection. In *Psychoanalysis in Contexts: Paths between Theory and Modern Culture*, ed. A. Elliott & S. Frosh. London: Routledge, pp. 15-35.
DELEUZE, G. & GUATTARI, F. (1977). *Anti-Oedipus: Capitalism and Schizophrenia*. New York: Viking.
DERRIDA, J. (1978). *Writing and Difference*. Translated by A. Bass. Chicago: Univ. of Chicago Press, 1980.
—— (1981). *Positions*. Translated by A. Bass. Chicago: Univ. of Chicago Press.
EAGLETON, T. (1990). *The Ideology of the Aesthetic*. Oxford: Blackwell.
ELLIOTT, A. (1992). *Social Theory and Psychoanalysis in Transition: Self and Society from Freud to Kristeva*. Oxford: Blackwell.
—— (1995). The affirmation of primary repression rethought: reflections on the state of the self in its unconscious relational world. *Amer. Imago*, 52:55-79.
—— (1996). *Subject to Ourselves: Social Theory, Psychoanalysis and Postmodernity*. Cambridge: Polity Press. In press.
—— & FROSH, S. (1995). *Psychoanalysis in Contexts: Paths between Theory and Modern Culture*. London: Routledge.
FISH, S. (1989). Rhetoric. In *Critical Terms for Literary Study*, ed. F. Lentricchia & T. McLaughlin. Chicago: Univ. of Chicago Press, pp. 203-222.
FROSH, S. (1991). *Identity Crisis: Psychoanalysis, Modernity and the Self*. New York: Routledge.
GIDDENS, A. (1991). *Modernity and Self-Identity. Self and Society in the Late Modern Age*. Stanford, CA: Stanford Univ. Press.
—— (1992). *The Transformation of Intimacy. Sexuality, Love, and Eroticism in Modern Societies*. Stanford, CA: Stanford Univ. Press.
GLASS, J. M. (1993). *Shattered Selves. Multiple Personality in a Postmodern World*. Ithaca, NY/London: Cornell Univ. Press.
HABERMAS, J. (1968). *Knowledge and Human Interests*. Translated by J. J. Shapiro. Boston: Beacon, 1971.
—— (1970). *On the Logic of the Social Sciences*. Translated by S. W. Nicholson & J. A. Stark. Cambridge, MA: MIT Press, 1988.
HARVEY, D. (1990). *The Condition of Postmodernity*. Cambridge, MA: Blackwell.

HOFFMAN, I. Z. (1987). The value of uncertainty in psychoanalytic practice. *Contemp. Psychoanal.*, 23:205-215.

—— (1994). Dialectical thinking and therapeutic action in the psychoanalytic process. *Psychoanal. Q.*, 63:187-218.

JAMESON, F. (1991). *Postmodernism, or, The Cultural Logic of Late Capitalism.* Durham, NC: Duke Univ. Press.

KRISTEVA, J. (1984). *Revolution in Poetic Language.* Translated by M. Waller. Ithaca, NY: Cornell Univ. Press.

—— (1989). *Black Sun: Depression and Melancholia.* New York: Columbia Univ. Press.

LEARY, K. (1994). Psychoanalytic "problems" and postmodern "solutions." *Psychoanal. Q.*, 63:433-465.

LYOTARD, J.-F. (1984). *The Postmodern Condition: A Report on Knowledge.* Translated by G. Bennington & B. Massumi. Minneapolis: Univ of Minnesota Press.

MACEY, D. (1993). *The Lives of Michel Foucault.* London: Hutchinson.

McGOWAN, J. (1991). *Postmodernism and Its Critics.* Ithaca, NY: Cornell Univ. Press.

MITCHELL, S. A. (1993). *Hope and Dread in Psychoanalysis.* New York: Basic Books.

MURDOCH, I. (1993). *Metaphysics as a Guide to Morals: Philosophical Reflections.* New York: Viking Penguin, 1994.

NORRIS, C. (1987). *Derrida.* Cambridge, MA: Harvard Univ. Press, 1988.

—— (1993). *The Truth about Postmodernism.* Oxford: Blackwell.

OGDEN, T. H. (1989). *The Primitive Edge of Experience.* Northvale, NJ/London: Aronson.

RORTY, R. (1982). *The Consequences of Pragmatism: Essays 1972-1980.* Minneapolis: Univ. of Minnesota Press.

SCHAFER, R. (1992). *Retelling a Life. Narration and Dialogue in Psychoanalysis.* New York: Basic Books.

SCRUTON, R. (1994). *Modern Philosophy.* London: Sinclair-Stevenson.

SPEZZANO, C. (1993). *Affect in Psychoanalysis. A Clinical Synthesis.* Hillsdale, NJ: Analytic Press.

THOMPSON, J. B. (1990). *Ideology and Modern Culture. Critical Social Theory in the Era of Mass Communication.* Stanford, CA: Stanford Univ. Press.

TRACHTENBERG, A. (1979). Intellectual background. In *Harvard Guide to Contemporary American Writing*, ed. D. Hoffman. Cambridge, MA: Harvard Univ. Press.

VATTIMO, G. (1980). *The Adventure of Difference: Philosophy after Nietzsche and Heidegger.* Translated by C. Blamires & T. Harrison. Baltimore: Johns Hopkins Univ. Press.

5

REFLECTIONS ON FEMININE AND MASCULINE AUTHORITY: A DEVELOPMENTAL PERSPECTIVE

REFLECTIONS ON FEMININE AND MASCULINE AUTHORITY: A DEVELOPMENTAL PERSPECTIVE

BY CHARLES M. T. HANLY, PH.D.

Is there a difference between feminine and masculine authority? If so, does affiliation to authority figures in psychoanalysis make a difference according to the gender of the authority? Is there a difference in the thinking of Kleinian analysts as compared with Freudian analysts that in some way underlies the theoretical and technical differences and arises out of the relation each has to the authoritative figure who founded the school of thought? Could a male analyst have established Kleinian thought? Could a female analyst have established Freudian thought? Is a choice of authority based on gender involved in the choice by an analyst to be a Kleinian or a Freudian?

Immediately, other questions crowd in. Are not these foolish questions? Is it not obvious that we analysts adopt theoretical ideas according to the evidence for them that emerges from our personal analysis, our studies, and our clinical observations in our analyses of others? What does the fact that Klein was a woman and Freud a man have to do with finding the theories of one more plausible than the theories of the other? I shall argue later that these are foolish question in certain respects. But fools and their foolish questions may be worth thinking about. Shakespeare made the fool the bearer of truths denied by others, as, for example, in *King Lear*. So I shall dare to play the fool, although without any claim to the wisdom of Shakespeare's fools.

If the authority of the father is based upon law, the authority of the mother is based upon desire. This formulation suggests a gender difference in the way in which we experience the authoritative object. It might be thought that in this differentiation

95

there is a debasement of the mother and of women. The mother (the woman) is able to command because she is the object of the desire of her child or her lover. The father (the man) is able to command because he is the source of the law—of prohibitions and permissions. But we now must ask how the father becomes the source of law. Part of the answer must be that he is the object of fear. Thus, just as the mother is the object of desire, the father is the object of fear and, hence, of idealization. The one is not more or less an object than the other. It is the affects they arouse that differentiates them.

The mother's capacity to satisfy need gives her authority over those whose needs she satisfies. She bears in her own person the power to give life, to sustain life during its most helpless state, and to give the first and, because all of instinctual life is simultaneously involved, the most unitary and intense of life's pleasures. To the extent that infants are able to experience the mother only as a part object scarcely differentiated from themselves, their experience of the mother as a breast is symbiotically invested with omnipotence. This symbiotic investment is the precursor of the projection of omnipotence that the mother receives as infants slowly begin to come to terms with their own precarious and helpless finitude (Hanly, 1992). The symbiosis and projection are the source of an aura that unifies and envelopes the infant's experience of the good mother.

Grunberger (1971) has traced narcissism to a prenatal elational state generated by the illusion of uterine self-sufficiency. The belief in immortality, the feeling of infinity, ideas of a disembodied, blissful state, beliefs in nirvana, utopian ideals, pantheism, nature mysticism, etc., are on Grunberger's hypothesis, adult elaborations of the memory of this primordial, biological tie to the mother and derive from a longing to return to it. If there is such a retained memory, its first elaborations are the infant's symbiosis with the mother, followed by the projection of his or her narcissism onto the mother. If the infant does not retain intrauterine sensations, it is my view that the phenomena Grunberger explains by means of them can be as well explained by the elational aura with which symbiosis and narcissistic projection envelop first the mother's breast and then the mother.

In either case, in these beliefs, psychic states, intimations, and experiences of adult life there is an implicit evocation of the benign presence of the mother of the beginning of life. These beliefs, states, intimations, and experiences are the soil from which law and morality of various kinds with various contents spring up. An unconscious longing for reunion with a perfect being or for the attainment of an ideal state are powerful motivating forces for a morality and a way of life that promises their fulfillment. The melodies, tonalities, and rhythms of great religious music express these motivational sources of moral striving. It turns out that there was a false dichotomy in our first formulation that based the authority of the mother on desire and the authority of the father on fear. Desire, and specifically desire for the mother, is no less important than fear as a source of law. Hence, there is an elemental feminine contribution to the authority that gives rise to law, or put differently, we unconsciously experience the mother's authority as that of a lawgiver.

But there is yet another falsification in our initial formulation. The mother, like the father, is an object of fear. Klein (1946) saw that if the ego life of the infant were more organized at birth than Freud had thought it to be, the infant would be assailed by nameless fears of disintegration and annihilation by the death instinct and would be forced to project its aggression upon its first, only, and most loved object—the scarcely differentiated mother's breast. As a result, the infant begins to feel endangered by the breast. This intolerable state of affairs triggers a splitting of the object, giving rise to the paranoid-schizoid organization of infantile experience. The nameless anxieties would now have become a nameless dread and would be attached to the steadily differentiating breast of the mother. Thus, an alien, dangerous presence, identified with the mother, would be introduced into the child's world.

Even if one is skeptical about Freud's death instinct (which I am) or finds Klein's hypothesis of infantile ego functioning implausible (which I do not), it is necessary to acknowledge the infant's fear of the mother. Klein describes what happens phenomenologically and developmentally under conditions that are not good enough—for example, conditions of oral deprivation. The differences are two: the cause of the phenomena of projection and splitting is a trauma from without rather than a drive; with good enough care the paranoid-schizoid position does not occur until later. In good enough circumstances, the growing infants are progressively thrust forward into self-object differentiation and into awareness of their own helplessness in a strange, alien, massive world that escapes their perception and defies their control. Their anxiety causes them to project their narcissism onto their mothers, who thus become their omnipotent caretakers—their sun by day, their moon by night. This projection of narcissism does not exactly correspond with, but it is at least to some extent functionally equivalent to, the same processes Klein (1946) described as the idealization of the object by the projection of the loving ego, which Segal (1979) identifies as the source of narcissistic object relations.

From this situation a new anxiety arises as the child becomes aware of the mother's moods and learns that her care depends on her love. The loss of the mother's love is dangerous. The child must struggle to preserve it. The struggle is sanctioned from within by signal anxiety in the form of shame. The child's retained narcissism makes him or her believe that if the mother is angry, it is because the child has made her so. At the least, the child feels her withdrawal and feels life to be out of joint, helpless, and worthless. The child's vulnerability to the loss of love gives to the mother an extraordinary power over the child. By withholding her love, she can cause him or her to experience a fall in her eyes and hence in the child's own eyes. The first internal sanction for obedience, the first experience of authority, and therefore the first experience of the law arises out of the relation with the mother. The incipient rebellions, the hitting and biting, the various robust defiances of the small child toward the mother, do not contradict this view; they are made possible by the child's confidence in the mother's love, a confidence that he or she does not always enjoy.

But what of the father? Is his contribution to the developing child's sense of authority also caricatured by his identification as lawgiver? Because he cannot exercise the authority of the breast, the father's contribution during the oral phase is only accidentally connected with the drives, the events that they cause, and the structures that begin to develop as the ego acquires and strengthens its defensive capacities. The father's presence and his care for the infant are less fateful, less inexorable in their influence, under the ordinary circumstances of good enough mothering.

Probably, the father is at first an acceptable, only partially differentiated substitute for the mother, insofar as he is significantly involved in the care of the infant. Through his caring activities he may find his way into the mother-infant monad. Grunberger (1989) introduced the idea of the monad as a virtual space that includes the mother and protects the infant from the world and from the infant's own instinctuality. It is the developmental precursor of what I have called narcissistic projection (Hanly, 1992). But unless the infant is being bottle-fed, the father is barred from entering into the central nursing ceremony of the monad or from becoming the object of the intense attachment that it forms. If nature takes its course during the first months of life, the father is an ambiguous presence who is both included in and left out of the infant's maternal world. It is this ambiguity, which is based on biological differentiation, that allows the father to function for the infant as a referent to, representative of, and intruder from the world beyond the monad. The physical, biological differences come specifically into their own with particular clarity if the father is called upon to comfort and help a child who is experiencing difficulty in giving up the breast—an instinctual resignation which forms the portal through which the child can enter into a world that is shared with mother and father.

Chasseguet-Smirgel (1984) has illuminated the importance of the boy's idealizing identification with the father by showing that the consequences of the failure to do so rests upon a denial of the father's "prerogatives and capacities" in order to maintain the illusion that his own "little pregenital penis is as valid as his father's" (p. 70). The boy's primary identification with the father (Freud, 1923) comes to have the part Freud attributed to it in the formation and resolution of the oedipus complex, because it gradually leads the child out of the mother's world, where the oral and anal stages are for the most part lived out, and into the parental world where the oedipus has to take place. This idea assumes that triangulation and a rudimentary superego development take place before the onset and resolution of the oedipus complex, as Klein (1945, 1957) affirmed. However, I am inclined to think that while aggressive rivalry and jealousy, along with sporadic phallic/clitoral interests, are involved, the triangulations of the oral and anal phases are not strictly oedipal for two reasons: the phallic/clitoral interests are secondary to and derive from the oral and anal drive organizations and their leading erotogenic zones; and for the most part, the rivalry for both boys and girls is primarily with the father for the mother. For this reason, the mother's pride of place as the source of self-authorization only gradually diminishes until it gives way to the reorganizations of the oedipal stage.

Despite the importance of the drive determinants, however, one must not lose sight of the role of the relation to the father and of the father himself in this transition. Various authors from various points of view, including Lacan's "name-of-the-father" and "law of the father" and Grunberger's (1989) "father principle," have focused upon the role of the father in leading the child out of the maternal world. This office is performed by the father for the boy through the child's identification with him and for the girl through her object love. The identification and love have very important oedipal precursors, but they are brought to fruition developmentally by the oedipus complex, the resolution of which further completes and lays down crucial templates for maturation.

If the father is enlisted in this way by the burgeoning developmental needs of children, what are we to infer concerning the paternal contribution to the definition of authority? Where is the maternal contribution left? Is it simply left behind? Is it assigned a permanently secondary place?

One thing is clear. The dichotomy, maternal authority/desire and paternal authority/law, is as inadequate to the role of the father as it is to the role of the mother. No doubt the child may fill his or her maternal world with polymorphously perverse delights. No doubt adult men and women may have a potent unconscious fantasy of the enjoyment of the blissful, unconstrained, sensual, gratifying plenitude of the mother's body, a fantasy that is threatening because of its regressive pull.

Evidence of the generality of such fantasies can be found in the trials of heroes and knights, as in Homer's *Odyssey* and in Spenser's *The Faerie Queene*, in which "The Bower of Bliss" is a powerful evocation of dangerous beauty and pleasure. The maternal authority that desire assigns is nowhere more powerfully evoked than in Hesiod's cosmological and genealogical poem, *Theogony*. During the work of creation, Ouranos, the sky god, became jealous of his progeny and would not let them be born to Gaea, who became overburdened, "and she contrived a crafty evil device . . . she sent [Kronos] into a hidden place of ambush, placed in his hands a jagged-toothed sickle, and enjoined on him the whole deceit" (Kirk and Raven, 1957, p. 35). A variation on a grand sociopolitical yet human scale is the power of women to corrupt their sons, and thus the state, accorded them by Plato (*Republic*, Book VIII, 549-550). In the ruling families of the timocracy (the rule of the military elite) there are mothers who complain to their sons that their soldier fathers are unmanly, neglectful of them, and indifferent to the good things of life that wealth could provide, leading the sons to be ruled by the pursuit of material goods and causing them to bring about a degeneration of the state into an oligarchy (the rule of the wealthy few). This descent, according to Plato, passes via democratic anarchy into the sensual, appetite-driven tyranny symbolized by Spenser's "The Bower of Bliss." One is reminded of the mother who, in Chasseguet-Smirgel's example, encourages her son to believe that, indeed, his little penis is better than his father's. These are mothers from whom children need to be rescued by fathers strong enough in their masculinity to sustain some of the maternal functions needed by the child.

However important these fantasies are, they are not a reliable basis for understanding the role of the mother in the creation and definition of authority. It can hardly escape our attention that the fantasy of the all-satisfying mother is more likely to be a fantasy that denies memories of painful disappointments rather than the derivatives of memories of abandonment to her enjoyment and that there is surely a measure of denying projection in Hesiod's and Plato's mythic portrayals of the malignant power of women over their sons.

May we not hypothesize that these fantasies evade and deny the maternal authority created by the child's fear of the loss of her love, by which mothers discipline rather than gratify their sons and daughters? They also deny the biological and psychological forces within women that move them—because of fatigue and the wish to repossess their own bodies, their adult sexuality, and their own identities—to encourage the disruption of the monad and to lead their offspring roughly or gently out of the maternal world. These are the motives in healthy mothers that facilitate the process of gradual education to reality that Ferenczi (1913) brilliantly described. But these motives, when supported by a sadistic-narcissistic need for the reflecting glory of perfect children, can cause mothers to risk traumatizing their children by pushing them beyond their tolerance for instinctual and ego maturation. When the sadism is unmitigated by narcissism, the use of authority by the mother turns into psychopathogenic violence. The images of this violently punishing mother, as seen in works on object relations and in the subjectively originated persecutory figures explored by Klein (1957), are also found in legend, myth, and literature: the awesome beauty of Helen of Troy, the destroyer of ships, of men, and of cities; the ruinous Erinyes of ancient Greek mythology; the envious murderous Lady Macbeth in whose domiciles kings are unsafe.

If the virtues of women are not always soft, neither are the virtues of men always hard. The boy's identification with his father is from the beginning a form of love. Anaclitic love for the mother on account of her nourishing would be no more than for the father as protector, except for the orality and the anality of the libidinal drive and the consequent attributed, as well as real, protectiveness of the mother herself. Freud's (1914) account is too simplified, correct as it may be in its fundamentals. Also, a good enough father, who has no reason to be afraid of his identification with his own mother, knows how to soften with mercy the violence of his wife's exercise of maternal authority when it is unnecessarily severe and possessive. Even the mother who, in anger, warns her wayward child of the punishment he or she can expect when father arrives, while restraining her wish to punish the child physically, has already punished him or her with the withdrawal of her love, intensified all the more by the treachery of her alliance with the father. However, a father can serve well as a substitute mother in this way only if he is secure enough in his own male identity to be able to act maternally toward his children without compromising their sense of his masculinity. Successful parents are able to share parental authority in this fashion without contributing to gender confusion in their children.

This issue brings us to the question of the oedipus complex and its contribution to the formation of a viable and valid recognition of paternal and maternal authority implanted in the parent-child relation. Such a relation is essential to the formation of a conscience that is sufficient for the degree of internal instinct mastery required by decent, civilized life and for the internal sustenance of a legitimate self-esteem. It is for this reason that I attach as much importance as did Freud (1923) to the place of the resolution of the oedipus complex in psychic development generally and to the development of a valid internal and external relation to authority in particular, while acknowledging the importance of oedipal precursors of the kind recently described by Britton, Feldman, and O'Shaughnessy (1989).

The essential point is that the resolution of the oedipus complex requires an intensification of the identification with both the mother and the father as a consequence of the urgency of the child's need to modify her or his relationship to them. The girl must moderate her hatred for her mother and her too dangerous rebellious rivalry with her by an intensification of her identification with the mother, as must the boy in his identification with his father. The aggression that had been invested in the relationship is now directed against the self and becomes a major factor in self-restraint and aim inhibition. The girl is also driven to modify her love for her father, without which the necessary alteration in the relation to the mother could not take place, since it is the love of the father that converts tolerable jealousy of the mother into dangerously envious hatred. In this, there is a loss that is repaired by an intensification of the identification with the father. The same transformation is required of the boy in relation to his mother. The authority of conscience is based on these dual identifications.

This description of oedipal identifications differs from Freud's (1923) account in two respects. It avoids the paradox involved in attributing an intensifying identification with the same-sex parent directly to the loss of the incestuous love relation with the opposite-sex parent and that concept's inconsistency with Freud's (1917) formula for the genesis of melancholia. And, it does not imply that the male superego is more effective than its female equivalent, even though they are qualitatively different. This avoids both the invidiousness of Freud's (1923) comparison and its inconsistency with his death instinct hypothesis, which is, presumably, as mortifying in women as in men; death, after all, is as frequent among women as among men.

The problem for this rather different account is to explain gender difference insofar as it depends upon the greater strength of the identification with the same-sex parent. Let us try. The positive oedipus complex is itself a heterosexual organization. The transformation of these relationships brought about through their internalization by means of strengthened identifications with parents need be informed only by their original libidinal and aggressive investments. The boy substitutes the wish to become like his father for the wish to replace him now. He substitutes the wish to have someone in the future like his mother for the wish to have her now. Gratification is deferred and can be realized later when the boy becomes a man like his father. The idealizations that motivate the preparations for deferred pleasures are themselves grounded in anxiety. The prohibitive efficacy of these idealizations will be proportional to the anxiety which will in turn be proportional to the strength of the incestuous and aggressive envious wishes.

Since I see no reason why such wishes should be less demanding in girls than they are in boys, I do not see, either, why the boy's castration anxiety should be a more effective source of moral guilt than the girl's fear of being poisoned, of being imprisoned for life, of becoming the victim of a witch's spell, or of having deformed, ill, or dead babies. What is lost in specificity, immediacy, and the dreaded irreversibility of the physical injury of castration in the girl's fantasies of punishment is at least made up for by the fact that, for her, it is the mother who has loved and cared for her from birth who is now her most dangerous enemy. The mother, whose cunning is powerful enough to cast a spell upon the father which the small oedipal girl can see with her own eyes, is certainly able to cast a mortifying evil spell upon her. It is perhaps for this reason that it is primarily the fear of the loss of love that gives the girl's conscience the authority to exact obedience from her, leaving guilt in a secondary place—whereas guilt is primary in the boy, with fear of the loss of love secondary.

Thus, if moral authority is more impersonal and severe in

men, as Freud (1925) claimed, but more object related and compassionate in women, it is equally effective in both. Moral authority in women is not an Adam's rib. If, on the whole, it is true that women place a higher value on love, relationships, seducing, and manipulating, while men place a higher value on justice, obligation, cheating, and law-breaking in their respective relations to authority, it is also true that women suffer guilty prohibitions of pleasure on account of duty, and men can learn to temper justice with compassion. The ideal appears to be an integration of the maternal and the paternal identifications with primacy going to the parent of the same sex, which is made possible by the resolution of the oedipus complex. Britton, Feldman, and O'Shaughnessy (1989) have described the pathological consequences of failures to carry out this integration.

But the conclusion of this argument poses a question: if authority is more or less equivalently masculine and feminine, are there psychological as well as cultural and physical reasons why Judeo-Christian women and men have worshiped a male deity for so many centuries? I have argued elsewhere (Hanly, 1988) that the difference has to do with the differences in the oedipus complex in boys and girls. The fundamental attitude toward deity on the part of men is one of supplication on account of awe (sublimated castration anxiety) and sublimated homosexual submission; on the part of women it is because of sublimated love for the father and the longing to be loved by him.

I have thus far failed to attempt an answer to the fool's question that introduced this paper. Does the gender of analysts influence their theorizing? This is a question for which this paper provides at best a background for the search for an answer. Here are some preliminary reflections.

Is it accidental that a group of brilliant women analysts pioneered in exploring the dynamics of the mother-child dyad? Melanie Klein worked out the implications of the death instinct for the earliest phases of the infant's relation to the mother. Annie Reich traced the sources of flaws in women's self-evaluation to the preoedipal relation to the mother. Elizabeth

Zetzel, in the area of technique, attributed the importance of her concept of the working alliance to the influence of early maternal attachment. Women have contributed much else to psychoanalytic theory and practice, and one wonders whether gender has played a part in these contributions. It is easy enough to suppose that gender is a factor in the motivation to explore the psychology of infant and mother. But, however interesting and important the question of motivation may be, it pales before the question of whether gender is an important factor in the creation of ideas for understanding and of perceptions for testing them.

Before attempting even a tentative suggestion about gender and insight, we must remind ourselves that men have also made important contributions to the most womanly of terrains. Abraham first systematically elaborated the preoedipal stages. Grunberger's understanding of narcissism begins in reflections upon the psychological derivatives of intrauterine existence and the mother-baby monad. Winnicott's concepts of transitional object, false self, and facilitating environment are deeply rooted in the mother-infant dyad. Is there, then, no basis for a psychological epistemology that would recognize a cognitive differentiation based on gender?

Psychoanalytic perception and understanding depends in an important way on memory. Is there anything in the girl baby's experience of her very early childhood that is gender specific, the memory of which would give her as an adult woman analyst a distinct advantage in understanding the psychology of the mother-child dyad? Does a baby girl experience her mother differently than a baby boy does? It seems reasonable to suppose that the infant's experience will be different according to the mother's unconscious feelings about the infant's gender. These feelings will influence the care the mother gives and, hence, the infant's experience of her. But may we not assume that the contributions of the infant to the shaping and content of the earliest experience of the mother will be essentially the same for boys and girls? The mother as object of infantile experience will be the same for boys and girls, except insofar as the mother is affected unconsciously by the gender of the infant. If this is so, there seems to be no gender advantage in the search for knowledge of early infancy. However, women analysts may have one cognitive advantage that is gender dependent. The experience of being anaclitically tied to a mother may be no different for girls and boys, but only women can experience being the object of this tie as mothers. The tie to the father in early infancy is a derivative one as a partial substitute. The subject needs further study and reflection.

Thus far, I have pursued an understanding of masculine and feminine authority by means of a somewhat dialectical method. It is not, to be sure, a dialectical method after the fashion of Plato's pursuit of knowledge of the divine, nor does it suppress the principle of noncontradiction as did Hegel's and Marx's use of dialectic. It seeks only to gain a view of the complexities of the authority inevitably exercised by men and by women in relation to their children. It does this by means of a series of affirmations and negations, assertions and qualifications, in the perhaps fond hope of doing some kind of rough justice to the contending contributions of drive development and object relations, as well as being at least open to social and cultural determinants. It is, in a certain sense, a dialectic born of the limitations of our observations, of our categories of thought, and of propositional language.

In this spirit, I wish to conclude with a brief exploration of two qualifications of what I have thus far said, as I promised at the beginning. There is a recognition of authority by men and women that transcends male and female differences. This authority lies within the sphere of knowledge, rather than of morality, which has largely been my focus above. Access to authoritative knowledge is a great and convenient asset. Small children are obliged to rely on their parents for authoritative knowledge about what is safe and beneficial and what is dangerous and hurtful. Children have to trust their parents to carry out the work of reality testing on their behalf which they cannot yet perform themselves. As adults, we are not infrequently thrust again into the situation of being unable to verify some idea of importance to us, so that we are obliged to consult experts and take their word for it: we have to rely for much of our knowledge on the authority of the expert.

To argue from authority is to commit a material fallacy. Children who claim that something is true because father told them so are committing a material fallacy called *argumentum ad verecundiam*, or argument with respect to authority. The truth of a statement depends upon the evidence for it and not upon its source, no matter how worthy of respect the source may be. The strength of the wish to submit to authority in order to be relieved of the burden of responsibility for even remarkably creative discoveries that challenge established ideas is illustrated by Harvey's assertion that he had come upon the idea of the circulation of the blood in the works of the venerable Galen (where it is not to be found) when in reality he had discovered it himself. He dressed up a beautiful truth in the tatters of a fallacy, although given the reverential attitude toward authority among his contemporaries, it would not have appeared so at the time. Freud and Klein seem to have been little troubled by this need; both seem to have taken pride in and courage from the originality of their ideas.

However, even if we cannot avoid reliance on authorities for many of our beliefs because we do not have the means to test them for ourselves, we analysts have no such excuse where psychoanalytic knowledge is concerned. Analysts are the experts and the authorities in the field of depth psychology. We have confidence in the authorities in other fields because we think that they have reliable facts from which to infer the knowledge claims they make. We must demand no less of the knowledge claims that make up psychoanalysis.

Here we come upon a different type of authority—the authority of fact and logic, which gives us access to the impersonal authority of reality, not what we believe there is or what we wish there to be, but what there is. This is an impersonal domain of observation and thought. A fact about male narcissism is not itself male anymore than a fact about female narcissism is female. Men and women have to bow equally before the impersonal authority of the facts of observation, out of which our theories have to be built if the theories are to survive as contributions to scientific knowledge. To be sure, it may well be that men and women have specialized aptitudes for observation based on sexual and gender differences. Differing interests, life experiences, and orientations to life may guide observations differently in the two sexes. However, when the work of observation is carried out successfully, it will issue in an observation that owes its content and meaning to the object observed and not to the subjectivity or the gender of the observer. It is out of such observations that knowledge in any field is constructed. It is our ability to submit our perceptions and thoughts to the authority of fact that enables us to move beyond Tiresias.

The psychological development that makes objectivity possible involves two aspects of the resolution of the oedipus complex: the formation of the superego, which makes self-criticism possible, and the supply of neutralized drive energy to the ego functions through sublimation (Waelder, 1934). Neutralization is currently neglected or repudiated in psychoanalytic theorizing. It is suspect for some on account of its relation to the idea of energy. Neutrality as the desired attitude of the analyst is sometimes repudiated on the grounds that it is an ideal rendered unattainable by the ubiquity of countertransference. I agree that our understanding of neutralization is problematic. Yet surely we can trace, with Freud (1895), the first fragile beginnings of the reality principle in the differentiation of the image of the satisfying object from the object that satisfies; this is followed by the release of interest in things and curiosity about them for their own sake, which, in the aftermath of the resolution of the oedipus complex, eventually finds its highest expression in the observing and thinking of adults that is open to the world. It was to this last stage of neutralized object hunger that Aristotle was pointing in the opening sentences of the *Metaphys-*

ics: "All men by nature desire to know. An indication of this is the delight we take in our senses; for even apart from their usefulness they are loved for themselves . . . ." The recognition of the authority of experience liberates in us the capacity to test the beliefs that we have adopted on the authority of persons.

It is, in my view, essential that analysts develop in themselves and through their training a good measure of this impersonal desire to know the lives of others and that they be able to use it in their analytic work. It is essential if psychoanalysis is to be a body of knowledge as well as a healing art. It is essential because, whether we like it or not, the transferences of our patients inevitably invest us with the struggles they have had with parental authority along with the authority of the experts they expect us to be, for which they pay us a fee to help in ways that they themselves have been unable to do. Whenever we exploit our vicarious, transferential, parental authority as a substitute for the quest for the authority of fact, for observing and understanding the patient, we betray the patient's trust. It has been the purpose of this paper to attempt to clarify some of the developmental commonalities and variations in parental authority that are likely to appear in transferences.

We are left with a dialectic that is different from the dialectic of exposition that I have sought to use in this paper. It is a deeper dialectic that is alive in each of us in our struggle to harmonize the authority of persons to whom we owe much with the authority of the facts onto which we have the good fortune to stumble.

REFERENCES

ARISTOTLE. Metaphysics. In *Introduction to Aristotle*, ed. R. McKeon. New York: Modern Library, 1947, pp. 238-297.

BRITTON, R., FELDMAN, M. & O'SHAUGHNESSY, E. (1989). *The Oedipus Complex Today: Clinical Implications*. London: Karnac.

CHASSEGUET-SMIRGEL, J. (1984). *Creativity and Perversion*. London: Free Association Press.

FERENCZI, S. (1913). Stages in the development of the sense of reality. In *First Contributions to Psycho-Analysis*. New York: Brunner/Mazel, 1980, pp. 213-239.

112   FEMININE AND MASCULINE AUTHORITY

FREUD, S. (1895). Project for a scientific psychology. *S.E.*, 1.

—— (1914). On narcissism: an introduction. *S.E.*, 14.

—— (1917). Mourning and melancholia. *S.E.*, 14.

—— (1923). The ego and the id. *S.E.*, 19.

—— (1925). Some psychical consequences of the anatomical distinction between the sexes. *S.E.*, 19.

GRUNBERGER, B. (1971). *Le Narcissisme. Essais de psychanalyse.* Paris: Payot.

—— (1989). *New Essays on Narcissism.* Translated and edited by D. Macey. London: Free Association Press.

HANLY, C. (1988). Metaphysics and innateness. In *The Problem of Truth in Applied Psychoanalysis.* New York/London: Guilford, 1991, pp. 50-70.

—— (1992). On narcissistic defenses. *Psychoanal. Study Child*, 47:139-157.

KIRK, G. S. & RAVEN, J. E. (1957). *The Presocratic Philosophers.* Cambridge: Cambridge Univ. Press.

KLEIN, M. (1945). The Oedipus complex in the light of early anxieties. In *Love, Guilt and Reparation and Other Works, 1921-1945.* Delacorte, 1975, pp. 370-419.

—— (1946). Notes on some schizoid mechanisms. In *Envy and Gratitude and Other Works, 1946-1963.* Delacorte, 1975, pp. 1-24.

—— (1957). Envy and gratitude. In *Op. cit.*, pp. 176-235.

PLATO. *Republic.* Translated by B. Jowett. New York: Liberal Arts Press, 1948.

SEGAL, H. (1979). *Melanie Klein.* New York: Viking.

WAELDER, R. (1934). The problem of freedom in psychoanalysis and the problem of reality testing. In *Psychoanalysis: Observation, Theory, Applications.* New York: Int. Univ. Press, 1976, pp. 101-120.

6

ABSTRACT:
THE INTIMATE
AND IRONIC
AUTHORITY
OF THE
PSYCHOANALYST'S
PRESENCE

ABSTRACT:
THE INTIMATE AND IRONIC AUTHORITY
OF THE PSYCHOANALYST'S PRESENCE

BY IRWIN Z. HOFFMAN, PH.D.

Irwin Hoffman describes a trajectory from Freud's solitary reflection on his own dreams to a critical contructivist paradigm, in which the idea that analysts can neutralize their influence on their patients by assiduous transference–countertransference analysis is viewed as illusory. Accordingly, he calls for recognition of the moral authority attendant on the analyst's role—freighted as it is with irony in the context of the analysis of the transference coupled with today's climate of cultural relativism and postmodern skepticism.

The analyst's authority derives not only from his or her special expertise but also from the ritualized asymmetry built into the dyad, which very asymmetry is also what gives the mutuality of the partnership its power ("The asymmetry makes our participation in the spirit of mutuality *matter* in an intensified way"). Toward reconciling the polarities of asymmetry and mutuality, ritual and spontaneity, boundaries and intimacy, the actual and representational aspects of the analyst's participation, Hoffman welcomes an attitude that appreciates their dialectical interdependence and sees the analyst as "always in a position of some uncertainty as to the nature of what has emerged in the patient and in himself or herself as wellsprings for action."

Hoffman argues that sustaining the analytic ideals of perfect

Irwin Hoffman's article, published originally in *The Psychoanalytic Quarterly*, Volume 65, No. 1, will appear in a forthcoming book and cannot be reprinted in this volume.

empathy and neutrality not only leads to the growth of inappropriate ego ideals and, in turn, defensive illusions, but also perpetuates an "institutionalized avoidance of actuality," which he links to the pervasive avoidance of death throughout the discipline ("There is never any hurry in psychoanalysis").

Analysis is emphatically not some kind of "sanctuary from the world of choice," Hoffman contends. For instance, the process of affirmation is, inescapably, selective; similarly, the decision not to offer any overt suggestion can be a silent source of influence. Constructivism in the social sciences and in psychoanalysis in particular has special implications, because people, unlike physical objects, are shaped by how they are regarded and what is expected of them.

Finally, Hoffman takes the position that we cannot "wash our hands of responsibility at that juncture where neurotic suffering and normal human misery meet." After all, analytic work can never create "fully enlightened grounds for action." Our commitment requires that we be partners with our patients as they struggle with both neurotic conflicts and existential predicaments.

Hoffman supports his argument with a persuasive clinical vignette.

7

THE ANALYST'S AUTHORITY IN THE PSYCHOANALYTIC SITUATION

THE ANALYST'S AUTHORITY IN THE PSYCHOANALYTIC SITUATION

BY OTTO F. KERNBERG, M.D.

QUESTIONING TRADITIONAL AUTHORITY

A significant trend in the development of the theory of psychoanalytic technique during the last two decades, present throughout the entire psychoanalytic community but particularly accentuated in the United States, has been the questioning of the authority of the psychoanalyst to formulate interpretations based upon "facts" in the psychoanalytic situation. From different psychoanalytic viewpoints with different theoretical underpinnings, a commonly shared question has been raised: To what extent is the analyst's stance toward the patient at risk of becoming an authoritarian imposition of the analyst's viewpoints? Or, to what extent is a highly desirable, respectful empathy with a patient's experiences brushed aside when the analyst treats divergences between the analyst's views and those of the patient as "resistances"? The analyst's assumed professional authority, in short, may contain authoritarian elements that run counter to the spirit of analytic work, and may perpetuate or even strengthen the emotional difficulties and pathology of the patient.

A major related critique has been the questioning of the "anonymity" of the psychoanalyst: the analytic emphasis on avoiding the patient's acquiring any realistic knowledge of the analyst's life and personality. It has been suggested that this may, in fact, cause the perpetuation of idealizations in the psychoanalytic relationship, transforming the analyst from a "person without personality" into an image of perfection that reinforces idealizations and the splitting off of the negative transference toward other authority figures.

119

Within the Lacanian school, the image of the analyst as the "subject of supposed knowledge" has been questioned as an expression of the acting out of the oedipal situation that potentially remains unchallenged by the analyst's authoritative interpretations (Etchegoyen, 1991, pp. 127-146). Bion's (1967) critique of the categorical formulation of interpretations within the Kleinian school, expressed in his recommendations to interpret "without memory or desire," reflects his major concern regarding the risk of the analyst's imposing preset theories on the developments in each session. Within ego psychology, Gill and Hoffman's (Gill, 1982; Gill and Hoffman, 1982) research on analysts' contributions to the transference, their observation of analysts' tendency to deny aspects of the immediate reality of their own behavior that triggers patients' transference responses, has led to the concept of transference as a compromise formation between the patient's transference dispositions and the analyst's contributions to transference enactment. Thomä and Kächele (1987) have elaborated this concept, pointing to the intimate connection between transference and countertransference developments, and to the unique nature of each psychoanalytic process derived from the personality of both participants.

The interpersonal psychoanalytic approach also underlines the intimate interaction between transference and countertransference: countertransference reactions are viewed as central in understanding the patient's unconscious conflicts enacted in the present dyadic psychoanalytic relationship (Epstein and Feiner, 1979; Greenberg, 1991; Mitchell, 1988). Self psychologists have affirmed the need to tolerate the patient's idealizing transferences, particularly in the treatment of narcissistic personalities. Their focus on traumatic experiences that may disrupt the optimal self-selfobject relationship in the transference also implies a particular attention to the analyst's contribution to such traumatic disruptions of the idealized relationship (Kohut, 1977). Without adopting the theoretical framework of self psychology, Schwaber (1983, 1990), in careful, clinically documented work, illustrates that behind what may appear at first as transference reactions derived from the patient's past are the patient's realistic reactions to the analyst's behaviors—behaviors that need to be explored systematically in the psychoanalytic situation.

From a different vantage point, Laplanche (1992) has suggested that unconscious messages stemming from the analyst's own unconscious are an unavoidable aspect of the psychoanalytic interaction, and, by this very fact, constitute a repetition of the earliest experience in the mother-infant relationship: mother's unconscious fantasies are expressed in the interaction with her infant and experienced by the infant as "enigmatic" messages that profoundly influence the development of the original unconscious fantasies in the infant's mind.

One of the most interesting developments in recent years has been the gradual increase in communication among psychoanalysts of different theoretical approaches. At times, this has led to what might seem a rather loose eclecticism, but it has often been the creative stimulus for new formulations and research (Kernberg, 1993a). One major consequence of such nonadversarial discourse has been the awareness that the same psychoanalytic material may be subject to very different viewpoints, to interpretations along alternative lines, and that, even within each particular psychoanalytic orientation, analysts perceive and interpret quite differently from each other.

As a result, there has been a major philosophical shift in the field, a questioning of the traditional assurance in describing "facts" in the patient's material, an emphasis on the conceptual frame and perceptive sensitivities of the analyst, and the acknowledgment of the unavoidable importance of the analyst's theoretical model in organizing his or her observations. Carried to an extreme, such a questioning attitude may lead to nihilistic denial of the possibility that an analyst can acquire any "objective" information and knowledge regarding the patient's unconscious motivation and psychic past other than the unconscious meanings derived from the present interpersonal psychoanalytic situation. A radical questioning of the professional "authority" of the psychoanalyst is a natural consequence of these developments.

Powerful cultural influences have contributed to these self-questioning professional developments regarding psychoanalytic technique. The feminist critique of the patriarchal power relations in the treatment of female patients by male analysts; the Marxist critique of the imposition of the analyst's ideological commitments under the guise of technical neutrality; the questioning of traditional assumptions about sexual orientation; awareness of the prevalence of physical and sexual abuse (in contrast to infantile sexual fantasies); and research in psychiatry pointing to the actual past victimization of patients, particularly women, who enter psychotherapeutic treatment: all these have combined to raise questions about the psychoanalytic assumption of unconscious intrapsychic conflicts in contrast to reality determined deficits, and to emphasize the need to validate patients' experiences in contrast to the analysis of their resistances against the awareness of unconscious conflict. The tribulations of psychoanalysis in countries suffering from dictatorships and totalitarian regimes have highlighted the extent to which an apparent position of technical neutrality may correspond to the cultural and political orientations of patient and analyst, thus strengthening the question regarding the authority and related cultural and ideological "blind spots" of the analyst.

All of these currents and developments, then, have raised questions regarding the traditional authority of the psychoanalyst as a "blank screen" and his or her role as participant observer of the patient's psychopathology. The traditional view, from that perspective, would reflect an outdated "one-person psychology" that does not correspond to the reality of the "two-person psychology" or even the interpersonal network psychology that evolves as a consequence of these critical approaches.

Extreme manifestations of these recent trends include treating transference and countertransference almost as if they were symmetrical, the assumption that analysts have no specific knowledge other than what evolves jointly in their exploration with patients, the neglect of unconscious intrapsychic conflict in contrast to the focus on deficits, distortions, and fixation derived from past trauma, and a stress on the curative aspects of the present interpersonal psychoanalytic relationship in contrast to the curative effects of interpretation of past unconscious conflicts. At the theoretical level, such trends are usually matched by a type of object relations theory that underemphasizes or denies drives, that questions technical neutrality together with the anonymity of the analyst, and that proposes a relatively free communication of the analyst's emotional reactions and viewpoints to the patient in an atmosphere that stresses an egalitarian, nonhierarchical interchange.

THE EMERGENCE OF A NEW SYNTHESIS

Obviously, in describing the confluence of multiple theoretical, clinical, and cultural developments in the questioning of the analyst's authority, I have not been able to do justice to the complexity of all the arguments involved. In what follows, I shall take up various aspects of these arguments and attempt to clarify some of their strengths and weaknesses. In the process, I shall propose a certain view of the psychoanalytic situation and the psychoanalyst's responsibilities and functions within it.

To begin, the concept of authority itself needs to be clarified further: often authority and authoritarianism are confused, and this may also happen with the concepts of authority and the exercise of power: insofar as authority refers to the exercise of power in a social situation, it is easy to confuse these concepts. Power refers to the capacity to carry out a task, and in the social realm, the capacity to influence or control others; authority refers to the adequate application of power to the task, and, in the social realm, to the adequate and legitimate exercise of power in order to carry out a socially desirable task (Kernberg, 1978, 1979, 1991, 1993b). Authority, in short, refers to the "functional" aspects of the exercise of power; it is the legitimate authority vested in leadership and involves the requirements for carrying out leadership functions. Authoritarianism, in contrast, refers to the exercise of power beyond that required to carry out the task, and, in the social realm, the illegitimate use of power beyond what is justified by the socially sanctioned task.

All task performance implies the exercise of power and authority. In the social realm, the exercise of authority without adequate power leads to impotence, paralysis, failure of leadership, and chaos. In fact, while authoritarianism usually brings about a petrification in the social realm, the consequent negation of the authority of others whose function would be central in the decision-making process may also induce chaos at some steps removed from the authoritarian leadership: chaos and petrification may coexist rather than simply alternate when authoritarianism is followed by total breakdown in the leadership function (Kernberg, 1994b).

I apply this concept of authority to the nature of the psychoanalytic relationship because I believe that the psychoanalyst's authority is legitimate and, in fact, an indispensable and central aspect of his or her work. The psychoanalyst's professional function is based upon specific training and knowledge, upon the legitimization of such training and knowledge by the social and cultural structures that provide psychoanalytic education, and upon the acknowledgment of the scientific status of psychoanalysis. In setting up the frame of psychoanalytic treatment, in explaining to the patient the rule of free association and the function of the analyst to provide the patient with knowledge about the unconscious by means of interpretation, the analyst exercises, I believe, legitimate authority—that is, adequate power required by his or her professional functions.

Thus, the analyst carries out a leadership function in a collaborative process in which part of his or her authority is delegated to the patient, while the patient, in turn, delegates to the analyst aspects of the patient's authority for work during the treatment.

Perhaps this description sounds trivial or obvious, but in practice, as we know, the analyst's realistic authority defined by the treatment contract may be rapidly transformed by transference developments into the patient's perception of an idealized, omniscient, and omnipotent authority to whom the patient can delegate total responsibility for his or her life. Or the analyst may be perceived as an arbitrary, oppressive authoritarian who demands submission and attempts to exercise total control over the patient (Kernberg, 1995). If the patient were *not* to assume that the analyst has some legitimate authority and that in entering psychoanalysis, the patient has to accept the leadership authority of an analyst trained to carry out such a treatment, the psychoanalytic relationship would become absurd. There is no reason why the patient should give any credence, respect, or money to a psychoanalyst who has no specific professional authority—to a questionable professional person who has nothing to contribute to the situation that the patient would not also be able to contribute.

In my view, the concept of technical neutrality assures the functional authority of the psychoanalyst and protects the patient from an authoritarian imposition of the analyst's views or desires. Technical neutrality, as Anna Freud (1936) defined it and as Freud originally clarified in a letter to Pfister (E. Freud and Meng, 1963, pp. 117-121), does not consist of "disgruntled indifference," but is an objective, concerned stance regarding the patient's problems, an unwavering effort to help the patient clarify the nature of these problems, and a position equidistant between the contradictory forces operating in the patient's mind. Technical neutrality implies an equidistance between the patient's id, superego, acting ego, and external reality, and a position of closeness to, or alliance with, the observing part of the patient's ego.

Undoubtedly, such a position of technical neutrality may be considered an ideal position from which analysts tend to be torn away again and again by countertransference developments, a position that analysts must attempt to reinstate again and again by self-analytic working through of the countertransference.

Analysts' use of their understanding of countertransference as part of the material entering into the interpretive work needs to be matched by their willingness to acknowledge any "acting out" of their countertransference disposition that may occur in the heat of the sessions; this enables analysts to acknowledge their humanity to the patient without undue self-revelation, atonement for guilt, or defensive rationalization of behavior (Kernberg, 1994a). Technical neutrality, however, needs to be clearly differentiated from the concept of analytic "anonymity" which involves concerted efforts to avoid letting patients acquire any information about analysts as individuals apart from their interpretive function. At an extreme, aspiring to anonymity may lead to artificial, non-natural behavior on the part of analysts, a phobic avoidance of even ordinary social courtesy within the professional relationship, let alone any contacts with patients outside the analytic situation.

I believe that the concept of anonymity that strongly influenced the teaching and practice of psychoanalytic work from the 1940's through the 1960's, perhaps especially within the Kleinian and ego psychological schools, contributed to exaggerating the idealization processes in the transference to an extent that interfered with the full analysis of the transference. It fostered splitting and displacement of the negative transference and a nonanalyzed submission of the patient to the idealized analyst. This problem was particularly marked in the context of psychoanalytic education, an issue I have explored elsewhere (Kernberg, 1986). Such unanalyzed idealizations in training analyses of candidates lead, I believe, to an unconscious identification with their own idealized training analyst, the adoption of an "anonymous" role, and a contamination of technical neutrality with an authoritative and categorical stance in the interpretive process. From this viewpoint, I believe, anonymity distorted technical neutrality, and fostered a categorical style of interpretation as well as a lack of full examination of subtle countertransference acting out in the psychoanalytic situation. Stone's

(1961) concern over this development was an early reaction to this trend.

In the course of every psychoanalytic treatment, the analyst's way of formulating interpretations, of exploring open questions with the patient, the analyst's demeanor, and the decor of his or her office provide the patient with powerful clues about the reality of the analyst's personality. Active efforts on the part of the analyst to deny the reality of the patient's observations or to ignore them would be in sharp contrast to the technical requirement that the analyst pay careful attention to the patient's perception of him or her in order to explore in great detail the reality of the stimuli that motivate transference developments. A position of technical neutrality is eminently compatible with a nonphobic, full exploration of both the patient's realistic and unrealistic perceptions of the analyst.

The analyst's curiosity about the patient and the analytic material is naturally selective; it is dependent upon the analyst's theoretical approach, technical preferences, countertransference reactions, and, of course, on the patient's conscious and unconscious stimulation of the direction of the analyst's curiosity. As long as such curiosity determines questions formulated from a position of technical neutrality, it can only help the psychoanalytic work. Interdictions against the analyst's raising questions, against indicating his/her particular interest, or against all comments that are not interpretations may foster an artificial picture of the psychoanalyst as the perfect interpreting machine. This fits the concept of anonymity (and unchallenged idealization) and reflects, I believe, a remnant of the 1950's and 1960's tradition.

The psychoanalyst, in my view, should behave as naturally as possible, without any self-revelation or gratifying of the patient's curiosity and transference demands. Outside of his or her specific technical function, the analyst should behave within the ordinary norms of social interaction. Being natural, however, must be matched by the analyst's specific role, that is, a position of technical neutrality that, by definition, also implies the analyst's not revealing his/her own preferences, commitments, desires, and fears, in order to provide maximum freedom for the patient to develop transference dispositions and the patient's own solutions to intrapsychic conflicts (Kennedy, 1993). The position of a "blank screen," from that viewpoint, does not imply invisibility of the analyst's personality, but rather a naturalness and authentic respect for the patient's freedom to arrive at his or her own decisions.

Technical neutrality, in short, does not imply anonymity, and natural behavior does not imply that the analyst is not in a consistent, stable professional role relationship with the patient. Nor does technical neutrality imply that the psychoanalyst's personality will not influence the patient, in the same way as the patient necessarily will influence the analyst through countertransference reactions. The reality of the analyst as a professional person concerned with understanding the patient, empathic with the patient's suffering, alert to the patient's destructive and self-destructive temptations, cannot but provide, in the long run, a uniquely helpful human experience. Some patients may never before have had any human experience of such a positive nature in their lives. The positive influence of the analyst's personality, however, will necessarily be undermined by the patient's distortions of the analyst as part of transference developments: under ideal circumstances, the systematic analysis and resolution of the transference will permit a sublimatory internalization of realistic aspects of the analyst's personality as part of the reorganization of the patient's personality throughout the treatment.

In contrast, the analyst's bypassing, deterring, or overriding transference developments by actively utilizing his or her own personality clearly implies an abandonment of technical neutrality, which is detrimental to the patient's autonomous growth. By the same token, the analyst's full exploration of his or her countertransference reactions and the psychoanalytic use of countertransference understanding in the formulation of interpretations strongly increase the focus on the interpersonal nature of the psychoanalytic situation. Such an approach clearly reflects a conception of a "two-person psychology" as an essential frame for the understanding of the patient's unconscious conflicts and an understanding of the countertransference as a major channel of communication (together with the other "channels" of the content of the patient's free associations and the patient's verbal style and nonverbal behavior in the hours.)

Given the concern about the analyst's authoritarian behavior within recent psychoanalytic literature, I feel it needs to be restated that every analysis that penetrates to the depth of unconscious conflicts will face the patient with unavoidable anxiety, guilt, and pain. If the function of defensive structures is to avoid the anxiety over unconscious conflict, the interpretation of such defensive structures, even while pointing to their irrational motivational sources, cannot avoid bringing about anxiety and pain. In their wake come strong efforts to defeat this exploration from that part of the patient which is opposed to change and to self-exploration—namely, the defensive operations and structures that necessarily oppose the analyst's efforts to uncover unconscious conflict. Beyond such unavoidable conflicts in the transference derived from the very nature of impulse-defense configurations, the destructive unconscious forces at work, particularly the self-destructive tendencies of patients with severe psychopathology, will inevitably become activated in an adversarial stance toward the concerned and helping analyst.

Under such conditions, sharp discrepancies between the view of the patient and that of the analyst may evolve in the sessions, and the analyst may be tempted to avoid such clashes by reducing or postponing efforts to face the patient with painful aspects of intrapsychic conflicts. The assumption that any painful experience of the patient in response to an intervention from the analyst requires a recognition of the analyst's authoritarian assertion of his or her views creates the risk of slowing down or paralyzing the interpretive work. To put it differently, an analyst's excessive concern with the effects of authority on the patient—with the patient's "vulnerability" to any viewpoint different from the patient's own—may bring about a masochistic submission to the patient's pathology and a loss of the psychoanalytic perspective, rather than the analytic resolution of the origins of this vulnerability as a defense. By the same token, the patient's conscious and unconscious efforts to seduce the analyst into accepting the patient's conscious view about him/herself may bring about temporary improvements in the patient's condition as part of the supportive effects of such a collusion, but it will inhibit the psychoanalytic work in the long run.

A related danger in analytic work is that of analyzing an unconscious conflict at the more superficial levels at which the patient can tolerate it, such as the unconscious meanings in the "here and now" only, while bypassing the deeper, more primitive levels of the same conflict that might trigger a patient's primitive anxieties and guilt. Thus, for example, direct manifestations of primitive destructive wishes and fantasies, of conflicts around sadomasochism and threatening erotic longings, may not be explored fully. One of the immediate effects of an effort to maintain a "positive emotional relationship" in the transference at all costs is the fostering of repression, splitting, dissociation and/or projection of the aggressive aspects of ambivalent transference relationships onto third parties.

A related issue concerning authority and authoritarianism is the psychoanalytic work with patients who have been severely traumatized in the past. In such cases, the patient's unconscious identification with both victim and victimizer may be enacted in the transference, with particular anxiety of both participants over the enactment of the patient's unconscious identification with the traumatizing agent. Under these circumstances, the psychoanalyst may be seduced by the patient into focusing on the aggressive conflict between the patient and the original traumatizing object: the enactment of the patient as victimizer in the transference, in contrast, would lead to immediate activation of a hostile interaction, of violent accusations against the psychoanalyst as part of a rationalization of the patient's effort to exercise omnipotent control. If the analyst fears that any assertion of his/her authority means an authoritarian attitude, the analyst may be quite relieved by the displacement or split-off activation of the patient's sadomasochistic relationship outside the transference.

In practice, interpretations under conditions of positive transference and those under conditions of strong negative transference may require a different style and emphasis. The maintenance of an unwavering calm and friendly style of communication on the part of the analyst may become an unconscious provocation under conditions of intense negative transference. And an occasional firm statement of the analyst's view may become an appropriate communication of the analyst's "indestructibility" in the face of the patient's onslaught, thus reassuring the patient that the aggression is not so dangerous as he/she had feared. More generally, wording interpretations along a broad spectrum of certainty, from tentative questions and casual comments to emphatic statements, may reflect both the stages of the interpretive elaboration and the emotional atmosphere of the sessions.

This brings me to the major issues of "what are psychoanalytic facts," the unavoidable influence of the analyst's theoretical assumptions on his/her perceptions and interpretive work, and the questioning of the "objective" nature of interpretations. Obviously, all interpretations are "subjective" in the sense of reflecting the analyst's understanding of what the "selected fact" is. There is no doubt that patients express themselves through multiple channels of communication—free associations, slips of the tongue, dreams, nonverbal behavior, affect displays, and condensations, contiguities, and metaphors in their discourse—and that the psychoanalyst will necessarily have to select the data that he or she believes most relevant at the moment (Levy and Inderbitzin, 1990). Such selections, however, if carried out within a broad observational basis while tolerating necessary periods of nonunderstanding, should eventually reflect what is actually dominant in patients' experience.

A position of technical neutrality, an openness to what patients bring in every hour, and, particularly, an openness to what appears to be affectively dominant throughout all these channels should help psychoanalysts integrate their observations into a "selected fact" and minimize the danger of an artificial distortion—or straightjacketing—of the analytic material. Psychoanalysts' legitimate authority does not imply that they understand all the time what is going on, or that in their understanding and interventions, they are always doing "the right thing." Just as there are multiple surfaces of the psychoanalytic material leading to a common issue at the depth beneath such surfaces, there are multiple ways of formulating the material that, by means of patients' reactions to them, may gradually help to orient psychoanalysts to where the center of presently activated unconscious conflict lies.

In other words, the conception of the interpretive process as one of trial and error, of gradual approximation to the material, which includes periods of nonunderstanding as well as of tentative explorations of the material by the analyst, should counteract the temptations to make categorical, authoritarian interpretations that force the patient's material into the analyst's theoretical frame of reference. The formulation of interpretations in an "unsaturated" way—that is, avoiding technical language and the theoretical concepts that are part of the psychoanalyst's frame of reference and presenting a formulation that lends itself to an open-ended spectrum of responses—should orient the psychoanalyst gradually to a better understanding, and counteract the risk of authoritarian interpretations.

There are unavoidable moments, particularly with patients presenting severe psychopathology, when what the analyst interprets as a transference regression will appear to such patients as a reasonable reaction to the analyst's behavior. Under these conditions, the first step is to examine the extent to which the patients may be observing realistically certain aspects of the analyst's behavior that the analyst has been blind to. (Schwaber's critique in this regard is pertinent.) However, after the limits of the patients' realistic perceptions have been established in the analytic exploration, and the analyst clearly perceives the repetition of unconscious patterns from the past in the present relationship, it is important to analyze them, and to analyze them not only to a point where the patients are able to acknowledge their distortion of the reality of the analyst's behavior in the light of their own unconscious conflicts in the "here and now," but to continue this exploratory process to the deeper levels of the past.

In my experience, one of the problems of analyzing the unconscious meanings only in the "here and now" in the resolution of intense negative transferences is that the decrease of the adversary relationship between patient and analyst has such a seductive effect on both participants that the analyst may fail to pursue the problem further into the patient's past.

There is no doubt that psychoanalytic work is influenced by the personality as well as the communicative style of psychoanalysts. Psychoanalysts' ongoing exploration of their own contribution to the relationships established in the transference, from patient to patient, should convey to them, over time, what their strengths and weak spots are. Ongoing peer supervision is probably the most important, potentially corrective experience for problems in analysts' functioning, and an important contribution to continuous growth and self-knowledge in their work. Continuous self-education should become a much more prevalent part of psychoanalytic education than it is at this time. In particular, senior analysts should present their clinical work to groups of junior analysts. The custom now is that the most junior clinicians present their work to the most senior ones, which may tend to perpetuate theoretical biases as well as personality-derived rigidities in the technical work of some senior colleagues.

In any particular analytic experience, it is important that analysts be aware of the risks of imposing a "conventional" frame on the patient's experience. To be "unconventional"—not in the sense of countertransference acting out by identification with a patient's antisocial conflicts, but through an openness to alternative solutions to challenges in life—is an important corrective to the observation that technical neutrality is based upon a collusion of cultural viewpoints between patient and analyst.

A CLINICAL ILLUSTRATION

The problems and conflicts around authority are illustrated, I believe, in my treatment of a patient with an obsessive personality disorder; in the course of his analysis, he reproduced in the transference his submissive and rebellious relationship to his extremely dominant, now deceased father. The patient's obsessive doubts, depression, and inhibition in work, as well as his difficulties with sexual potency, had developed after the death, in rapid succession, of his father and of an older sister whose controlling behavior had replicated that of the father, and whose envy of and competition with her successful younger brother had been a source of my patient's fear and resentment in the past. He was a mental health professional with an administrative responsibility in a health delivery organization. His conflicts with subordinates whose rebellious behavior, as he saw it, was a challenge to his authority, were matched by his authoritarian attitude toward his wife and daughters. He had intense relationships with a few male friends who represented wise and supportive father figures for him, and whom he would insistently and repeatedly ask for advice when his own obsessive doubts paralyzed his actions.

In the transference, during an extended period of time he attempted to seduce me into "telling him what to do," and much time was spent analyzing how he was trying to read into my comments what my preferred solutions to his conflicts in reality might be, thus escaping from his sadistic superego's attack on whatever decision he would aspire to make. This patient had rebelled against his father in his early childhood by failing miserably at school in spite of high intelligence; his father's impotent efforts to improve the patient's functioning at school represented a major problem throughout his entire childhood. Father, a creative, "self-made" man, seemed successful in all aspects of his life except in dealing with his son's difficulties. The mother always remained somewhat in the background. Eventually, it turned out that she supported her son only in the absence of his father, using him as a companion and as an object for others to admire, but immediately dropping her support for the boy as soon as his father initiated punishments because of the failures at school.

At one point in his treatment, after many months of elaborating his unconscious submission to, rebellion against, and identification with his father and his struggle against homosexual feelings related to the oedipal submission to father and to early dependency needs frustrated by his teasing and rejecting mother, the patient's symptoms worsened again. He could not decide on how to reorganize the administrative structure of his institution, which endangered his own position within it; he was unable to decide what actions to take with one of his daughters whose difficulties in school seemed to replicate his own childhood difficulties; he was again fearful of "justifying" his sexual wishes in the relationship with his wife, who he felt was unresponsive to his needs but whom he dared not confront with his dissatisfaction; and he could not tolerate the idea of enjoying himself at a forthcoming vacation. In the middle of this symptomatic worsening, the patient complained that I was not helping him, that all the understanding he had gained had a purely intellectual quality, that nothing had changed. He appealed to me to tell him what I thought about this situation, and whether an alternative treatment might be indicated at this point. He harbored the strong conviction that if he ended his psychoanalysis now, it would restore him to the independence he had achieved throughout these years, which was now undermined by continuing in this hopeless and restrictive treatment situation.

In thus summarizing the developments over many weeks of treatment, I cannot do justice to the intensity of this patient's plea for me to take action in helping him to arrive at decisions about how to deal with the various conflicts in his life. It seemed very clear to me that in response to major triumphs in his professional life and improvement in his relationship with his wife and children, his unconscious guilt over assuming the role of a strong and loving father had brought about the regression both in his behavior and in the transference. He made enormous efforts to seduce me into what I could only interpret as advice giving, while protesting strongly against my "rigid" maintenance of an analytic relationship. At the same time, he was convinced that he would be able to resolve his difficulties if he freed himself from me.

This patient had ended a previous psychoanalytic treatment with a premature termination; in response to the patient's request, his first analyst had agreed to the termination, apparently convinced of the patient's capacity to function much better by himself. It was only two or three years after the end of this first analytic experience that the return of his major symptomatology brought him back into treatment. I now pointed out to him that he was tempted to carry out the same rebellious "disruption" of his analysis with me; that he was simultaneously expecting advice and counsel from me while disregarding all self-exploration of the issues that we had examined over an extended period of time in the psychoanalysis.

The patient then accused me of arbitrarily exercising my authority by imposing "self-reflection" on him as a way of resolving his conflicts. I pointed out that this reminded me of the experience he had had with his father whose "forcing him" to go to school seemed a brutal restriction of his freedom. I suggested that the patient was enacting a fantasy: he must either submit to an irrational authority such as I represented at this point or rebel against it by rejecting everything that came from me—with the self-destructive effect of renouncing either his autonomy or his learning in the psychoanalytic process. I pointed out that his categorical demand that I provide him with guidelines for "better behavior" or he would end the relationship with me reflected an identification with what he had perceived as the arbitrary authority of his father: he was attempting now to force me into submission to his view of treatment. In this identification with pathological aspects of his father, he denied to himself, out of guilt, identification with the creative aspects of his father that would permit him to use what he was learning in the analytic situation and to become more independent and assertive in his life. Eventually, the working through of this level of unconscious conflict in the transference led to a deeper level of the same conflict: his rage and resentment at being "force-fed" by an indifferent yet controlling mother.

I hope I have illustrated how I maintained a position of technical neutrality as opposed to the patient's complaints that I was not helping him and that I was leaving him alone. While I analyzed various transferential implications of this demand—such as the angry request for love from a cold and ungiving mother (and the enraged refusal to be force-fed) and the protective authorization from a dominant and otherwise guilt-inducing father, I felt that maintaining my firm stance represented a position of technical neutrality in spite of the patient's assumption that I was insisting in an authoritarian way on my treating him. In the process, I analyzed his conflicts with the oedipal authority without either being seduced into a supportive stance or agreeing to what I interpreted as a premature, rebellious acting out in his threat of disrupting his treatment. I believe I was able to resist his seductive efforts to draw me into interventions that would have meant my taking a stance regarding the educational problems of his daughter, the sexual difficulties with his wife, the reorganization of his institution, and his management of vacations. In all these areas he attempted to elicit information from me that would help him know how to deal with them, and he experienced my resistance to his efforts as authoritarian control. At the same time, throughout that entire period of his analysis, he experienced my interpretations as a condensation of his father's authoritarian control and his mother's force-feeding him, all of which I attempted to work through interpretively.

In conclusion, I believe that the exercise of functional authority in the psychoanalytic situation is a necessary aspect of the psychoanalyst's work, that such functional authority is facilitated by a position of technical neutrality, that technical neutrality implies a combination of naturalness and remaining in one's psychoanalytic role, but not anonymity, and that the current appropriately increasing emphasis on analysis of countertransference does not imply a symmetry of transference and countertransference. I believe that the influence of the personality of the analyst on the psychoanalytic treatment is unavoidable. However, it should be significantly and adequately reduced by the very position of technical neutrality. Such a stance entails the understanding that the gradual working through and resolution of the transference will permit the patient eventually to identify in a sublimatory way with aspects of the personality of the analyst which the patient will unavoidably become acquainted with. I think that a "nonconventional" attitude in the sessions may protect the analyst to some extent against the limitations of technical neutrality derived from the common cultural background of patient and analyst. Above all, I believe that the maintenance of technical neutrality and the noncommunication of the analyst's own value system and life experience best protects the patient's freedom to arrive at his or her own conclusions through the understanding and resolution of unconscious conflicts.

REFERENCES

BION, W. R. (1967). Notes on memory and desire. *Psychoanal. Forum*, 2:272-273, 279-280.

EPSTEIN, L. & FEINER, A. H., Editors (1979). *Countertransference*. New York: Aronson.

ETCHEGOYEN, R. H. (1991). *Fundamentals of Psychoanalytic Technique*. London: Karnac Books.

FREUD, A. (1936). *The Ego and the Mechanisms of Defense. The Writings of Anna Freud*, Vol. 2. New York: Int. Univ. Press, 1966.

FREUD, E. L. & MENG, H., Editors (1963). *Sigmund Freud-Oskar Pfister Briefe 1909-1939*. Frankfurt-am-Main: Fischer Verlag.

GILL, M. M. (1982). *Analysis of Transference, Vol. 1. Theory and Technique*. New York: Int. Univ. Press.

————& HOFFMAN, I. Z. (1982). *Analysis of Transference, Vol. 2. Studies of Nine Audio-Recorded Psychoanalytic Sessions*. New York: Int. Univ. Press.

GREENBERG, J. (1991). *Oedipus and Beyond. A Clinical Theory*. Cambridge, MA/London: Harvard Univ. Press.

KENNEDY, R. (1993). *Freedom To Relate Psychoanalytic Explorations*. London: Free Association Books.

KERNBERG, O. (1978). Leadership and organizational functioning: organizational regression. *Int. J. Group Psychother.*, 28:3-25.

———— (1979). Regression in organizational leadership. *Psychiat.*, 42:24-39.

———— (1986). Institutional problems of psychoanalytic education. *J. Amer. Psychoanal. Assn.*, 34:799-834.

———— (1991). The moral dimension of leadership. In *Psychoanalytic Group Theory and Therapy: Essays in Honor of Saul Scheidlinger*, ed. S. Tuttman. Madison, CT: Int. Univ. Press, pp. 87-112.

———— (1993a). Convergences and divergences in contemporary psychoanalytic technique. *Int. J. Psychoanal.*, 74:659-673.

———— (1993b). Paranoiagenesis in organizations. In *Comprehensive Textbook of Group Psychotherapy*, 3rd Edition, ed. H. I. Kaplan & B. J. Sadock. Baltimore: Williams & Wilkins, pp. 47-57.

———— (1994a). Acute and chronic countertransference reactions. *Rev. Franç. Psychanalyse*, 5:1563-1579.

———— (1994b). Ideology and bureaucracy as social defenses against aggression. Unpublished.

———— (1995). Omnipotence in the transference and in the countertransference. *Scandinavian Psychoanal. Rev.*, 18:2-21.

KOHUT, H. (1977). *The Restoration of the Self*. New York: Int. Univ. Press.

LAPLANCHE, J. (1992). *Seduction, Translation, Drives*. Edited by J. Fletcher & M. Stanton. London: Institute of Contemporary Arts.

LEVY, S. T. & INDERBITZIN, L. B. (1990). The analytic surface and the theory of technique. *J. Amer. Psychoanal. Assn.*, 38:371-391.

MITCHELL, S. A. (1988). *Relational Concepts in Psychoanalysis. An Integration*. Cambridge, MA/London: Harvard Univ. Press.

SCHWABER, E. A. (1983). Psychoanalytic listening and psychic reality. *Int. Rev. Psychoanal.*, 10:379-392.

———— (1990). Interpretation and the therapeutic action of psychoanalysis. *Int. J. Psychoanal.*, 71:229-240.

STONE, L. (1961). *The Psychoanalytic Situation. An Examination of Its Development and Essential Nature*. New York: Int. Univ. Press.

THOMÄ, H. & KÄCHELE, H. (1987). *Psychoanalytic Practice: Vol. 1: Principles*. New York: Springer-Verlag.

8

CHANGES IN SCIENCE AND CHANGING IDEAS ABOUT KNOWLEDGE AND AUTHORITY IN PSYCHOANALYSIS

CHANGES IN SCIENCE AND CHANGING IDEAS ABOUT KNOWLEDGE AND AUTHORITY IN PSYCHOANALYSIS

BY ELIZABETH LLOYD MAYER, PH.D.

> The violent reaction to the recent develop-
> ment of modern physics can only be un-
> derstood when one realizes that here the
> foundations of physics have started mov-
> ing, and that this motion has caused the
> feeling that the ground would be cut from
> science.
>
> WERNER HEISENBERG (1958, p. 167)

Said the Sun to the Moon—'When you are but a lonely white crone,
And I, a dead King in my golden armor somewhere in a dark wood,
Remember only this of our hopeless love:
That never till Time is done
Will the fire of the heart and the fire of the mind be one.'

> EDITH SITWELL (*Heart and Mind*)

One way to describe what we do in psychoanalysis might be that
we work to marry the fire of the heart and the fire of the mind.
We try to make them one—at least in glimpses, for moments at
a time. Unlike Sitwell, who says it can't be done (not, anyway,
until some inconceivable and poetic future in which Time itself
is done), psychoanalysts make it their daily business.

Also unlike Sitwell, psychoanalysts live firmly lodged in time.

I am grateful to Charles McMillan, Ph.D., of Lawrence Livermore Laboratories
for his thoughtful guidance regarding contemporary physics, and to Kim Chernin
and Carol Gilligan, Ph.D., for our ongoing conversations.

We live in the dailiness of seeing patients, and we confront daily questions about how we can help the fire of each patient's heart meet the fire of that patient's mind in new and generative ways. That is one kind of meeting between heart and mind in psychoanalysis, and it's one kind we work to facilitate. But there are other kinds as well. The patient's heart meets the analyst's mind, the analyst's heart meets the patient's mind, and the analyst's heart must regularly meet that analyst's own mind. It is the fire in each of those meetings—the fire of each heart meeting the fire of each mind—that makes for the intensity of analytic work.

Our theories of technique are attempts to organize our experience of that intensity into something which helps our patients. At their best, those theories help us negotiate how the fire of each heart meets the fire of each mind in something we call the best interests of the patient. At their worst, our theories derail us from that task. In recent years, questions about whether and how our familiar theories of technique derail us have inundated our literature. The authors raising those questions proceed from myriad points of view, and they make various diagnoses about what is wrong. But despite their differences, they all converge around a central and common issue. They all question longstanding assumptions about the relation between knowledge and authority in the analytic encounter, whether in the handling of moment-to-moment dialogues between analyst and patient or in the theoretical matrix within which a psychoanalytic process is conceptualized.

In what follows, I will suggest that we may be able to gain some insight into current challenges to concepts of psychoanalytic knowledge and psychoanalytic authority by examining recent changes in science, along with contemporary changes in our scientific world-view. I will suggest that those changes in world-view have affected psychoanalysis directly, as reflected in our published literature, but that they have also affected analysis indirectly and implicitly, by infiltrating the private thinking of practicing psychoanalysts in subtle and often unarticulated ways. I will propose that one consequence of that infiltration has been to exacerbate discontinuities between analysts' private views and public theories about how they practice: discontinuities between what analysts really do and what they say they do. To the extent that such discontinuities remain unarticulated, I will suggest that they are destructive both for psychoanalytic practice and for the development of theory. And I will propose that looking to recent changes in science may help us articulate at least some of what has tended to remain unarticulated. Finally, I will go back to Heisenberg with whom I began, and suggest ways in which analysts' fear that the ground could be cut out from psychoanalysis as science may help explain their reluctance to permit what they really do and really think to enter the realm of public and explicitly articulated discourse.

I started with Heisenberg, but also with Sitwell. I began with her for several reasons. First, I find her imagery evocative with regard to an overall issue that I think is central in our current controversies concerning technique: the state of the relation (especially the passionate, fiery portion of the relation) between each heart and each mind in the analytic dyad. In addition, I think that same imagery may capture something which speaks to the troubling discontinuities which can arise between analysts' private and public theories: the ways in which personal, private and ultimately heartfelt knowing can seem, to some analysts, irrevocably split off from their intellectual loyalties—loyalties to official theories of analytic technique which look at least something like what we are used to calling science. Finally, as we try to avoid the many reductionistic pitfalls that beset an examination of how changes in science may inform psychoanalysis, I think it may prove useful to keep poetry in mind. We are accustomed to drawing on poetry for its metaphoric function, with all its evocative potential. Science may inform us best about psychoanalysis if we draw on science in a way that is not so different. Just as poetry evokes and enlivens our perceptions, science may do the same—no less figuratively, no more authoritatively.

Redefining Knowledge and the Authority with Which We Know

I have suggested that the many authors who are currently raising questions about our widely accepted theories of technique converge, whatever their differences, around a central issue: the need to redefine psychoanalytic knowledge, psychoanalytic authority, and the relation between them in the psychoanalytic situation. For example, McLaughlin (1981, 1982, 1991, 1995) has suggested that the strict dichotomy we have traditionally enunciated between transference and countertransference is an arbitrarily hierarchical distinction, designed to protect the analyst from having to recognize that he or she has no greater claim to objectivity, reality, or truth than does the patient. Hoffman (1983, 1992, 1994) has emphasized that the analyst's interpretation of reality is never authoritative, nor is the analyst in a position to judge what constitutes transference distortion in the patient's perceptions of the analyst. Gill (1982, 1993) believes that the very term "distortion" in relation to transference implies that the analyst knows what undistorted truth would be, an idea which flies in the face of the indeterminate nature of truth. Aron (1991) suggests that the analyst cannot claim to judge the accuracy of the patient's perception of the analyst; therefore, the idea that analysts "validate" or "confirm" patients' perceptions is both presumptuous and wrong. Cooper (1993), echoing Bollas, states that the era of "official psychoanalytic decoding" is over; the analyst can no longer be viewed as a reasonably objective and authoritative translator and interpreter of the patient's experience. Stolorow (1995) suggests that the concept of analytic neutrality is a defensively grandiose illusion, protecting the analyst from recognizing the nature of his or her knowledge, and from recognizing that interpretations are always suggestions, analysts are never objective, and the transference is always "contaminated" by the person of the analyst. Ehrenberg (1992) argues that the idea of the analyst as a dispassionate observer survives simply to serve the analyst's need to be valued as an authority. And Mitchell (1992) states that the unquestioned authority claimed by earlier generations of psychoanalysts for their own knowledge is outmoded and on the face of it inconceivable, given the climate of our present-day world. Roughton (1994) believes that we have shifted from emphasizing the analyst's knowledge and authority to acknowledging that patients, ultimately, know more about themselves for psychoanalytic purposes than we do. Spezzano (1993, 1995) suggests that we know psychoanalytic truth to the extent that we recognize the most useful statements regarding evidence of the unconscious that a given patient and a given analyst can, struggling out loud together, agree upon in the moment. Renik (1993, 1995) questions what he views as our longstanding reliance on the analyst's implicit authority, stating that what the analyst knows about analytic events is always irreducibly subjective, and that the analyst should therefore seek to explain his or her thinking as fully as possible to patients, rather than abstaining from explanation in a stance that amounts to reliance on implicit authority. Psychoanalytic knowledge is a frankly consensual achievement which privileges neither the analyst's nor the patient's authority to know.

So concepts of knowledge and authority are significantly up for grabs in contemporary theories of psychoanalytic technique. That should not surprise us, since concepts of knowledge and authority are up for major reconsideration in most fields these days (Dossey, 1982; Edelglass, et al., 1992; Harman and Clark, 1994; Tarnas, 1991; Wheatley, 1992). Centrally propelling all these reconsiderations are far-reaching and fundamental shifts in the premises which underlie science. *There has been a sea change in our scientific world-view which makes certain questions about knowledge and authority not only possible but necessary for any enterprise that orients itself, no matter how loosely, toward what we call science.* As a result, psychoanalysis is in ferment—but so is every other field of scientific endeavor.

On the other hand, psychoanalysis is one particular kind of scientific endeavor, and it is worth looking at exactly how a shift in scientific world-view has specific implications for psychoanalysis and for the unique methodology that constitutes psychoanalytic technique. The fact that knowledge and authority are being globally reconsidered by psychoanalysts may be significantly explained by our placement in a wider scientific *Weltanschauung*, but there remains the question of how changes in that *Weltanschauung* are translated into explicitly *psychoanalytic* effects.

It has become, for example, routine for analytic authors to bow in the direction of Heisenberg and his Uncertainty Principle when raising questions about the analyst's capacity for objective knowledge in the analytic situation. The argument tends to run that, given the Uncertainty Principle, it is no longer plausible for us to assume that the analyst can operate as an objective observer whose participation is without effect on whatever he or she is observing in the analytic engagement.

However, this use of Heisenberg's argument actually misses the essential issue that Heisenberg was trying to elucidate in his Uncertainty Principle: the fact that our knowledge of nature is *fundamentally limited*. (Not only does nature *prohibit* simultaneously knowing both the position and the momentum of subatomic particles in any given experiment; to measure one is actually to erase the property of the other. Any attempt on the part of the observer to determine what is fundamentally unknowable leads to radical alterations in the outcome of the experiment.) The fact that nature imposes fundamental limits on knowledge is rarely the point being bolstered when Heisenberg is cited in our literature.[1]

I think there is an interesting irony here. Useful analytic thinking has proceeded from application of a physical principle that misses the point of the principle itself. A principle from physics has been employed to justify an argument which has

---

[1] Schwartz (1995) has recently made a similar point and has in fact suggested: "The story that Heisenberg created in an attempt to give physical meaning to a difficult abstract narrative has achieved currency only *outside*, not *inside*, the field [of physics]. . . . In fact, most physicists prefer Max Born's . . . more direct interpretation in which the probabilistic structure of the theory is accepted as given without elaboration" (p. 48, italics added).

radically and powerfully challenged the privileged knowledge and authority ascribed to the analyst as objective observer in psychoanalysis—yet, from the standpoint of physics, the argument misses the central issue. The irony is interesting, I think, because it helps clarify precisely how we can expect changes in scientific world-view to have implications for psychoanalytic thinking, and points to both the caution and the enthusiasm with which we should entertain those implications.

I will address the caution first. As we attempt even remotely literal application of changing concepts in science to the ultimately idiosyncratic data of psychoanalysis, we encounter multiple problems. Levels of inference beg to be confused, temptations to category errors abound, and we run the risk of losing track of precisely the awareness that makes our particular brand of empiricism possible: the awareness that psychoanalytic data, observation, and purpose are unique and particular to psychoanalysis, just as the data, observation, and purpose that belong to any branch of science have their own distinct and specific characteristics.[2]

But having expressed that caution, we can also recognize that changes in scientific world-view have an extraordinary capacity to galvanize thinking. As concepts like uncertainty, complexity, and chaos revolutionize conceptions of physical reality, they function as a kind of template for questions about every other aspect of reality. As psychoanalysts grasp even the rudiments of what those changes mean for physics, longstanding analytic assumptions suddenly seem worth challenging, new lines of question get legitimized, and novel hypotheses become conceivable. Perhaps most important, changes in scientific world-view liberate a crucial ingredient of scientific investigation, identified by Polanyi as "heuristic passion." "Heuristic passion," he says, "is . . . the mainspring of originality—the force which impels us to

---

[2] Polanyi (1974) has devoted a good deal of attention to discussing the scientific reductionism that results from ignoring this specificity, or what he calls the quality of disjunction among various branches of science.

abandon an accepted framework of interpretation and commit ourselves, by the crossing of a logical gap, to the use of a new framework" (1958, p. 159).

Current changes in scientific world-view seem to me to be stimulating experiences of precisely that heuristic passion among contemporary psychoanalysts. There is a barely contained excitement that is palpable in the writings of analysts who are starting to consider various ways in which new scientific ideas may carry import for psychoanalysis (Fogel, 1990; Furman, 1993; Godwin, 1991; L. Hoffman, 1992; Moran, 1991; Mosher, 1990; Spruiell, 1993). We have a lot to gain by drawing on that excitement. The physicist Frank Oppenheimer put it casually but incisively: "If one has a new way of thinking, why not apply it wherever one's thought leads to? It is certainly entertaining to let oneself do so, but it is also often very illuminating and capable of leading to new and deep insights" (Cole, 1985, p. 2). Oppenheimer suggests an associative and even metaphoric use of science which allows us to consider that new developments in, say, physics, can jog our consensual view of what matters and how things work in ways that are useful— maybe even transforming—for fields as far removed from physics as psychoanalysis. He does not suggest that we interpret science lightly or loosely, but he does suggest that the impulse to play freely and across disciplines with implications of new scientific ideas can lead to highly creative results.

The idea that new ways of thinking in science could be, in Oppenheimer's words, "very illuminating" for psychoanalysis was an idea anticipated and eagerly embraced by early psychoanalysts. In 1921, Freud conjectured that the tenets of science might someday change to contain, but also to kindle, the thinking of psychoanalysts better than could the physics and chemistry of his day. "Analysts," he wrote, ". . . cannot repudiate their descent from exact science . . . . Instead of waiting for the moment when they will be able to escape from the constraint of the familiar laws of physics and chemistry, they hope for the emergence of more extensive and deeper-reaching natural laws. . ."

(pp. 178-179). By 1941, Siegfried Bernfeld asserted that the familiar laws which Freud found constraining had indeed been supplanted, and that psychoanalysts recognized the obsolete nature of science defined "in terms of atoms, cells, and brain-parts, between which physical forces carried on their trade . . . . [W]e [psychoanalysts]," he announced, "have shifted our emphasis to agreeing with our fellow scientists on an intersubjective body of knowledge" (pp. 342-343). (Fifty-five years later, as we watch the proliferation of articles asserting the radical import of intersubjectivity for theories of technique in psychoanalysis, it is clear that the consensus Bernfeld proclaimed with such conviction has not entirely arrived. That's no surprise: changes in worldview take a long time to filter into working theory, and their implications are hotly debated even as new organizing paradigms are being massively and consensually adopted [Kuhn, 1962, 1977]. Besides, as Bruner [1993] says, we're never done fighting the closet positivist in each of us.)[3]

By and large, changes in the realm of physics are the changes that have been most explicitly considered by psychoanalysts. Spruiell summarized some of the most recent ones in his Plenary Address to the American Psychoanalytic Association in 1991, putting them in perspective for psychoanalysts as follows:

A major scientific revolution is underway. . . . Psychoanalysts have been in its midst, although few have recognized that fact. . . . The revolution will have enormous effects on our

---

[3] The extent to which Bernfeld's 1941 paper did actually anticipate certain rudiments of contemporary thinking regarding intersubjectivity is striking. Spezzano (1996) has identified three levels of discourse on which an intersubjective paradigm is currently and controversially reframing psychoanalytic thinking: the ontological (regarding the essentials of human nature), the epistemological (regarding how we can claim to know about the unconscious), and the developmental (regarding the origins of self and object representations). Both the ontological and the epistemological levels were addressed by Bernfeld, with attention particularly to the latter and to the way in which psychoanalysis makes use of a two-person conversation and "a process of actively influencing the object observed," in order to devise a uniquely psychoanalytic method of scientific observation.

long-range aims and expectations, both for development as a
special discipline and . . . integration with other intellectual
disciplines (1993, p. 4).

The idealizations of what was thought to constitute science
have been almost totally cast aside by a growing body of the
best educated contemporary scientists, especially physicists (p.
10).

On the basis of his reading of current work in both physics and
mathematics, Spruiell goes on to articulate what he sees as the
broad range of assumptions that have been thrown open to
question by recent changes in science:

> . . . the belief that the rational capacity to predict events is
> theoretically unlimited; the pretense that scientific studies are
> public in nature; that there is a necessity, if the intention is to
> achieve scientific veridicality, to reduce variables and study
> large numbers statistically; that certain assumptions about
> what constitutes valid experimentation, verification, and the
> nature of "truths" can be codified as the "canons of science,"
> which define the "scientific method"; that scientific progress
> occurs in small increments; and that it is justified to have in-
> creasing confidence in the near-omniscience of measuring de-
> vices (pp. 7-8).

If we leap from Spruiell's articulation of specifics to extrapolat-
ing one broad and simple principle governing scientific investigation, the principle might be that *we need fundamentally to rethink
ways in which we have imagined the existence of authoritative, certain,
absolute, objective, causal, or predictive knowledge.* That's the kind of
global template suggested by ways in which physics is shifting its
definition of physical reality. As such, I believe it is one of the
templates helping to organize current questions in psychoanalysis: questions not just about how we formulate conceptual principles and design research methods, but also questions with
pragmatic import for day-to-day matters like what we say to our

patients, how we listen to them, and how we organize our reactions to what we hear.[4]

A similarly global template, extracted from an equally revolutionary sea change in the definition of science, is currently emerging from biology. It has been less explicitly discussed by psychoanalysts, but I believe it has also helped organize the kinds of questions currently under consideration by analysts. It is a shift which asserts that *we need fundamentally to redefine the states of mind which facilitate scientific knowing and to re-examine the observer's position of authority in relation to both the object of knowing and the process of knowing itself.* Philosopher of science and biophysicist Evelyn Fox Keller, in her reflections on the brilliantly original work of Barbara McClintock, the Nobel Prize-winning cytogeneticist, has described McClintock's version of this shift:

> McClintock offers a vision of science premised not on the domination of nature, but on [what she calls] "a feeling for the organism." For her, a "feeling for the organism" is simultaneously a state of mind and a resource for knowledge: for the day-to-day work of conducting experiments, observing and interpreting their outcomes—in short, for the "doing" of science . . . her conception of the work of science is more consonant with that of exhibiting nature's "capacities" and multiple forms of order, than with pursuing the "laws of nature." Her alternative view invites the perception of nature as an active partner in a more reciprocal relation to an observer, equally active, but neither omniscient nor omnipotent (1992, p. 32).

McClintock revolutionized genetics, and her discoveries regarding the transposition of genes were the product of her par-

---

[4] In conjunction with this kind of rethinking, ongoing debates about whether psychoanalysis belongs in the category of "science" seem to me (Mayer, 1996) and also to Renik (1994) to lose their punch. The hermeneutics versus science argument usually sets up a definition of science to which few contemporary scientists would adhere, and tends not to take into account the revolution in assumptions about the nature of "science" that Spruiell summarizes.

ticular vision of science, a vision viewed as wildly dissident by most of her peers. Her refusal to adopt a conventional objectifying attitude toward the plants she studied was captured in the following comment which Keller cites (though Keller notes it as an "uncharacteristic lapse into hyperbole" for McClintock). "Every time I walk on grass," said McClintock, "I feel sorry because I know the grass is screaming at me" (Keller, 1983, p. 200). The hyperbole may have been uncharacteristic, but Keller quotes the remark as expressive of McClintock's insistence that original discoveries in science are the product of a state of profound "feeling" for that which is being studied, a quality of empathy usually reserved for intimate human relationships and certainly outside the purview of what's typically considered requisite in defining a scientific attitude. In a similar vein, Maturana and Varela (1992), in their study of the biological basis of cognition, argue that our portrayals of how human beings know about anything at all—science included—have profoundly underemphasized the "unbroken coincidence of our being, our thinking and our knowing" (p. 25).

Current Changes in Scientific World-View: Public Versus Private Effects

I want now to examine our current ferment regarding psychoanalytic technique and how current changes in scientific world-view are, I think, contributing to that ferment.[5] I believe

---

[5] Changes in science are, I believe, contributing to that ferment directly but also indirectly, insofar as the broad influence of science has profound effects on the general intellectual climate within which we think. However, it seems likely that the underlying impetus for the questions that are currently redefining science originate not only in science itself, but in general trends that are affecting science just as much as psychoanalysis. The question of where the underlying impetus actually begins raises the much larger issue of how and why a culture's overall epistemology shifts, an issue which I will not address here, except to note that even when not directly *causal*, there is at least a strong *correlative* relation between current changes in scientific world-view and changes in the way psychoanalysts are

we can observe one way they are contributing in the contemporary papers on technique I cited earlier, papers which are centrally concerned with redefining knowledge, authority, and the relation between them in psychoanalysis. Directly reflecting issues in contemporary science, those papers assert that the analyst can no longer be envisioned as an objective or authoritative observer—no longer, even, a participant-observer whose effects are in principle determinable. They suggest that psychoanalytic observations are never theory-free; nor, therefore, is psychoanalytic knowledge. They do not focus on whether a clinical hypothesis can be confirmed or disconfirmed but on whether it proves useful. Ambiguity, far from representing unfortunate evidence of our limited claim to authoritative knowledge, is taken to be inevitable and more basic than the complexity contained in concepts like multiple function or overdetermination (see especially Renik, 1993). By regarding these reassessments as at least partially determined by a shift in scientific world-view, I believe we can come to understand something of their common impetus as well as the shared intention and ultimate direction they represent.

So the papers that contain these reassessments represent one way in which we can examine how changes in scientific worldview have found their way into affecting psychoanalytic thought. As published articles, these papers have a public function. They declare the authors' interest in reconsidering public theories about what analysts do. They are public attempts not only to integrate changes in scientific world-view with psychoanalytic theories of technique, but, at the same time, they represent attempts to bring public theories of technique more closely in line with analysts' private experience of what they actually do. And there is an interesting linkage there. As changes in world-view invite fresh questions about what we do,

---

thinking. So whether we are looking at changes in psychoanalysis which are directly caused by changes in science or at changes in psychoanalysis that are simply coinciding with changes in science, looking to science is, I think, likely to help us articulate what is going on in psychoanalytic thinking.

they alter private perspectives on old habits. To that extent, they encourage analysts to become aware of *discontinuities between theory and practice, ways in which what analysts actually do in their offices may not conform to what accepted analytic theories say they do. Published papers render those discontinuities explicit, such that private effects of changes in world-view can become subjects of public discourse.*

But I do not think published papers represent the only, or even the major, way changes in scientific world-view affect psychoanalysts and their work. Changes in world-view tend to sneak up on us. They become part of our intellectual surround, ordering and defining our actual experience as well as our ideas.[6] The questions that point up discontinuities between theory and practice are questions which inform the way analysts start considering their work long before papers assessing the importance of those discontinuities become accepted contributions to theory. The questions which alter private perspectives on old habits start to affect practice long before they end up being written about. To that extent, published papers represent a kind of tell-tale: indices which formally articulate the way shifts in scientific world-view have been infiltrating the way we think.

So that leaves us with a question: what happens to all the unofficial infiltrations, all the subtle, inchoate ways that changes in world-view permeate the daily clinical assessments, formulations, and concerns of practicing analysts? Those infiltrations remain not only unofficial but implicit. *Because they are implicit, I believe they have a particular and important consequence: they start to exacerbate the discontinuities I pointed to earlier, contributing to a widening rift between what analysts say they do and what analysts really do.*

Sandler, in 1983, described the ubiquity of such rifts in psychoanalysis, suggesting that there is an essentially conservative

---

[6] Philosopher of science Lynn Nelson points out: "Scientists . . . are granted and exercise cognitive authority to shape the larger community's understanding of (all) nature, including human nature" (1990, p. 140).

trend in psychoanalytic theorizing which, when matched with various political and institutional constraints, leads many analysts to feel they would not be viewed as "proper" analysts, were they to reveal to their colleagues the many ways in which they diverge from "standard" technique. Sandler's focus is on our reluctance to alter theory in the light of new or challenging or inconsistent observations. In his view, we deal with conflicting observations by developing private theories which describe actual clinical practice but which we do not bring face-to-face with public theory. Dissonance and discomfort are thereby avoided.

> With increasing clinical experience the analyst, as he grows more competent, will preconsciously (descriptively speaking, unconsciously) construct a whole variety of theoretical segments which relate directly to his clinical work. They are the products of unconscious thinking, are very much partial theories, models or schemata, which have the quality of being available in reserve, so to speak, to be called upon whenever necessary. That they may contradict one another is no problem. They coexist happily as long as they are unconscious. They do not appear in consciousness unless they are consonant with what I have called official or public theory (p. 38).

While Sandler expresses concern over what is lost to public theorizing by the extent to which analysts are disinclined to talk about what they actually do, he sees analysts' ability to transcend theory as an essentially good thing, indicative of clinical flexibility and sensitivity to the needs of patients. He regards private theories as an adaptive response to the useful but constraining nature of our public theory; thus he is able to argue that contradictions between private and public theory can and do "coexist happily" in the minds of analysts, as long as they remain unconscious (or preconscious).

I want to suggest a different view. I am not impressed that contradictions between private and public theories coexist as happily as Sandler suggests. And I think they tend to coexist *least* happily when they remain, in Sandler's terms, unconscious or preconscious in the minds of the analysts who adhere to them. In fact, I think those contradictions often encourage a corrosive and destructive state of affairs in which, as time goes on, many analysts start to feel less and less like "real" analysts doing "real" analysis. As they honestly examine how they actually work, those analysts develop an increasing and often uncomfortable sense that much of how they think they help their patients doesn't fit with the model of analytic technique to which they in principle adhere. They begin to dissociate the analysis they practice from the analysis they publicly espouse, write about, and even teach. They start to feel fraudulent and outside the rules as they lose the experience of having an integrated and acceptable public identity, a public identity that conforms to their private psychoanalytic experience. The dissociation of what *is* from what's *supposed to be* opens the door to familiar dangers: private conduct becomes more and more isolated from the potentially modulating influence of collegial scrutiny and public discussion and, even worse, that modulating influence may be sacrificed on an internal level as well. A variety of consequences can follow—ranging from an insistent muddiness of thinking which is required to prevent contradictory ideas from encountering each other, to severe and disturbing lapses in conscience.

So how to understand the widely divergent implications that Sandler and I have suggested? *I believe the divergence may be partly explained by a differing context within which each of us places the split between private and public theory, including the extent to which we view that split as evidence of what I earlier described as implicit and unofficial infiltrations of changing scientific world-views.*

In Sandler's approach, I think we can hear echoes of what Kuhn and others have described as the pursuit of normal science. Inconsistent or contradictory observations are assimilated by making plenty of room for anomalies, such that an original and overarching paradigm can be retained, while it stretches to incorporate as many new observations as possible: "conceptual categories are adjusted until the initially anomalous has become the anticipated" (Kuhn, 1962, p. 64). The emphasis is on fitting into the reigning paradigm and adapting to accepted theory in whatever way works. Sandler (1983) makes the adaptation work by suggesting that the "partial private schemata," developed by individual analysts in contradiction to public theory, actually reflect appropriate and useful accommodations to the demands of individual clinical situations. "[T]he so-called parameters that one introduces often lead to or reflect a better fit of the analyst's developing intrinsic private preconscious theory with the material of the patient than the official public theories to which the analyst may consciously subscribe" (p. 38). Eventually, Sandler suggests, public theory adjusts to incorporate the most valuable bits and pieces of private preconscious theories, and in that way, incrementally and gradually, psychoanalytic theory is advanced.

This is normal science, and it portrays one view of how our field, like any other, can and does develop. But there is another route. It's the one that happens when normal science is disrupted and the process of incorporation fails to work, when anomalies stubbornly resist assimilation and start to tear at the fabric of theory rather than heading in the direction of eventual absorption. If the private schemata by which analysts operate constitute anomalies which fall into this latter category, I think that the happy coexistence between private and public theory described by Sandler becomes less and less feasible. Rather than happy coexistence, we start to see evidence of the more troubling consequences I proposed. Private schemata become harder and harder either to sequester or absorb.

I suggested earlier that we can view published controversies over technique as indicative of the way the wind is blowing with regard to identifying certain fundamental issues up for consideration by most practicing analysts. I also suggested that the central preoccupation of our current published controversies is the redefinition of knowledge and authority in the psychoanalytic situation, a redefinition which coincides with sweeping ways in which knowledge and authority are being redefined in science. I believe it may be precisely those redefinitions which constitute the essential content of analysts' private schemata that are *not* currently adapting to happy preconscious coexistence with public theories of technique. If this is true, we can add that we should not be surprised: to the extent that those redefinitions have challenged the pursuit of normal science *outside* psychoanalysis—as they certainly have—we should expect them to challenge the pursuit of normal science *within* psychoanalysis as well. We are unlikely to find that they represent private schemata which can be readily absorbed into so-called public theory.

What Happens When Public and Private Theory Diverge: A Case Example

A case example may be illuminating. I was recently consulted by a colleague who found himself developing a set of private ideas about how he was helping a patient which he could not readily integrate with his public theory of analytic technique. As we talked, it became clear that we could come up with plenty of factors predisposing to the disjunction this analyst was experiencing—in his character, in what sounded like problems with his own analysis, in limitations of his theoretical understanding, etc. However, this analyst was in many ways motivated to help his patient, and it became increasingly apparent that the mere *fact* of a severe disjunction between his private and public views about how analysis worked had exerted an enormously destructive effect on his ability to do well by his patient. It was only as his private ideas—in Sandler's terms, his "partial private schemata"—were, over the course of our consultation, finally brought face-to-face with his public theory, that he could start consciously to consider how he understood the contradictions between them, and at that point start to redress some of what had gone wrong with his patient.

Our consultation began with my colleague's telling me that he had been feeling increasingly attracted to a female patient. He admitted he was now disturbed and frightened by the extent to which he was starting to allow himself to become physically involved with her. As I listened to him, I was struck by a number of paradoxical elements in his presentation. On the one hand, he described two years of rather impressive analytic work with her. He had a good understanding of her dynamics which he had channeled into insightful interpretive work. She had responded well, with behavioral changes, but also with important changes in her sense of herself. The picture that initially emerged was of a thoughtful (if inhibited and rather rigid) analyst, describing an analytic process which was thoroughly in line with a public theory of analytic technique that has characterized mainstream American psychoanalysis for many years. He, as analyst, viewed his analytic function primarily in terms of facilitating his patient's transferences and interpreting both her transferences and resistances to them. He had maintained a conventionally neutral and abstinent stance in the service of accomplishing both these tasks. He had learned a good deal about the infantile framework within which his patient's problems had appeared to develop, and he had been able to convey his understanding to her with considerable skill. His rendition of all this was more than just dogma; he described plenty of convincing clinical instances in which he appeared to have conducted himself according to exactly the standard theory of technique to which he adhered.

On the other hand, there was a subtext. As I began to hear more about how this analyst's attraction to his patient had finally started to develop into sexual involvement, another thread in his view of the treatment started to appear, a thread which we might view as one of Sandler's "partial private schemata." From the beginning, the analyst had felt a strong liking for this patient and a particular wish to help her. As I questioned him about these feelings, he admitted that he had, all along, cared a lot about her—more than was usual in the way he felt about patients. And, he added with some confusion, he felt that the unusual extent of his caring had been very good for her. He thought it had translated into her feeling understood—and into his actually understanding her—in ways that had been peculiarly good for the analysis, though quite outside what he viewed as the analytic work. Equally outside, he hesitantly suggested that even the sexual aspects of their relationship had seemed to aid her in working on issues that were central to the analysis.

The extent to which this subtext was dissociated from the analyst's view of the official analysis he had been conducting was extreme: indeed, stunning. It was as though he had been conducting two different treatments—one about insight and the other about a caring, "real" relationship. One was analysis, and one was outside analysis. One was about the analyst's ability to convey knowledge interpretively while revealing very little of himself; the other was about mutual feeling and the mutual expression of those feelings.

Now it is certainly true that the degree of his dissociation sets this analyst apart from many of his analytic peers and makes him dismissable as a frankly bad example of the theory of technique to which he subscribed. For plenty of reasons (I began to be able to identify just a few of them), his interpretation of theory was especially rigid and unbending; to that extent, he was indeed a bad example of his particular theory of technique. Many analysts have managed to operate with a public theory in which abstinence and neutrality are viewed as central to the analytic task, but they are able nonetheless to incorporate a deeply empathic, caring attitude as an essential background to their work, meanwhile negotiating awareness of intense feelings toward their patients.[7]

So it would be possible to understand the derailment of this particular analysis in terms of this analyst's idiosyncratic limitations in applying a widely accepted theory of technique with which many analysts have done much better. But I think it may be useful to think of this analyst not as a *bad* example but instead

---

[7] I believe our frequent solution of attributing such feelings to "countertransference," and then distinguishing countertransference from Sandler's "private theories," draws an ultimately arbitrary distinction, designed to exempt certain aspects of private functioning from direct and disturbing confrontation with public theory.

as a *good* one—not of technique but of the failure of a public theory of technique happily to coexist with a private, barely articulated "partial schema" regarding what helps patients and how analysis works. In fact, it *may actually be that bad examples of public theory are especially worth examining as good examples of what can happen when public and private theories diverge, since part of what may show up most baldly in those cases are discrepancies which are masked when native therapeutic ability permits public theory to be applied less faithfully.*

In this analyst's mind, adherence to public theory required a stance of cordial, engaged, but distant authority on his part, facilitating his analytic function as interpreter of the patient's experience. His understanding of public theory made a sharp distinction between what was "analytic" versus "therapeutic." What had thrown him in the analysis he presented to me was that this distinction had fallen apart. When he encountered a patient who particularly challenged his ability to clothe his feelings in an official guise of neutrality and abstinence, he found what he viewed as "non-analytic" experiences and communications starting to dominate his sense not only of what was helping his patient, but more disturbingly, his sense of what was helping the analysis. He began to feel more and more uncomfortable, not just with the frank betrayal of ethical guidelines he thought he believed in, but also with what felt like a betrayal of the theory of technique he thought he believed in. The latter betrayal had, in a certain sense, facilitated the former. Once he felt himself to be operating outside his model of how analysis was supposed to work, he found himself unable to turn to that model for help in managing the intensity of any of his feelings about his patient. He already felt outside the rules; eventual physical contact left him, to his own bewilderment, feeling only marginally further outside.

This analyst, by the time he came to talk to me, was one of those analysts who had ceased to feel like a "real" analyst practicing "real" analysis. He was filled with shame and a sense of fraudulence. I say shame rather than guilt because he didn't feel primarily guilty. Despite his qualms of conscience over the physical involvement which had led him to consult me, he actually thought he had helped and was helping his patient. (The patient thought so as well, and part of the analyst's eventual comfort in revealing the status of their relationship to me resulted from his relief at my letting him know that I, too, thought he had been helpful—though I also told him I thought his confusion about *how* he'd been helpful was significantly responsible for the very destructive turn the treatment had taken and was likely to keep taking.)

But if not primarily guilty, he *was* ashamed. He was not just ashamed of his physical contact with his patient; he was equally ashamed of the way his private sense of how he had helped his patient led to all kinds of ideas that challenged his official theory of how analysis helps people. The mere fact that he had those questions led him to feel like a failed analyst. He imagined that other analysts—"real" analysts—could make public theory work in ways he couldn't; he blamed his interpretive skills and his capacity for neutrality, but he did not question either his public theory or his understanding of it. To the extent that he became conscious of feeling that a nonneutral, nonabstinent stance had actually been helpful to his patient and her analysis, he was stuck with a "partial, private schema" which refused to coexist happily with his public theory of technique.

So I am suggesting that this analyst can be viewed as one kind of casualty resulting from a divergence between public and private theory. There were many things (about his character, his own analysis, his training, etc.) which predisposed him to become such a casualty, but those are not my point—my point is that he describes a disturbing version of the consequence that can follow when analysts start to operate according to private theories that do not coincide with their public theories. And if we turn our attention to the actual *content* of what this analyst found so dismayingly contradictory to his public theory, I believe we find ourselves looking at a muddled, ill-considered version of exactly the issues I have described as the central and organizing themes in current published controversies over technique.

In brief, this analyst's version of public theory placed the capacity to interpret a patient's experience knowledgeably, from a position of benign implicit authority, at the center of what made for being a good analyst. As he became aware that his intense noninterpretive engagement with his patient, along with his unaccustomed disclosure of himself and his feelings, seemed not just to help his patient, but actually to aid her in her exploration of herself, he found himself at sea. He found himself raising silent but fundamental questions, questions concerned particularly with the nature and place of his own knowledge and authority in defining his psychoanalytic role. To the extent that those questions remained unacknowledged and sequestered from his official view of how he practiced analysis, they (along with the attitudes and behaviors they engendered) went underground: partial private schemata that were unincorporable into his public theory. But they did not go unexpressed. They were increasingly expressed in action, in the developing physical relationship he was having with his patient. It was only as those private schemata were finally, over the course of our consultation, brought face-to-face with his public theory, that this analyst could start consciously to consider how he understood the contradictions between his private experience and his public theory. (And I should add that he began at the same time to gain enough perspective on his sexual involvement with his patient to terminate his relationship with her, refer her to another analyst, and take up further treatment for himself.)

The Current Failure of Normal Science Solutions: Lipton and Sandler

In 1977, Lipton suggested that modern psychoanalytic technique was headed in a direction which he viewed as untenable. He proposed that modern "classical" technique had lost track of a distinction which was essential to the original technique outlined by Freud. In a sense, I think we can view Lipton as trying to reroute the course of normal science as applied to the development of a psychoanalytic theory of technique. Lipton suggested that modern theory had taken a wrong turn in expanding the purview of technique to include aspects of the analyst-patient relationship which Freud had specifically excluded from technical consideration. Courtesy, spontaneity, cordiality, and warmth were, for Freud, in the nature of assumptions: part of the personal human context within which a psychoanalytic relationship, like any other, might unfold, and within which all aspects of the analyst-patient relationship could eventually be subject to analysis. Thus, Freud [1909, p. 303] could casually remark that his patient, the Rat Man, "was hungry and was fed" upon arrival for an analytic session, with none of the technical implications described by subsequent analysts, who called the event, as Zetzel [1966, p. 129] did, "an intervention which must be defined as unanalytic."

Lipton (1977) suggests that, partly in reaction against the corrective emotional experience concept, modern theory began to identify every aspect of the personal relationship with a patient—including the expression of human involvement and concern—as a matter of technique, resulting in a serious distortion of the analyst's function.

> Paradoxically, modern technique can produce just what it may have been designed to avoid, a corrective emotional experience, by exposing the patient to a hypothetically ideally correct, ideally unobstrusive, ideally silent, encompassing technical instrumentality rather than the presence of the analyst as a person with whom the patient can establish a personal relationship. In addition, modern technique also incurs the danger of fostering iatrogenic narcissistic disorders by establishing an ambience in which the patient has little opportunity to establish an object relationship (p. 272).

> The complaint that 'psychoanalysis is becoming dehumanized' ... may be connected with just this tendency to substitute an

encompassing technical instrumentality for a person (p. 266).[8]

Lipton was aware that this modern portrayal of the ideal analyst was doing psychoanalysis a significant disservice. Simultaneously and as a corollary, he saw that contemporary theories of psychoanalytic technique were straining. He responded in the best tradition of normal science: by carefully re-examining original theory, he was able to argue that current flaws and current strains resulted from *misguided development of original theory*, not problems with the theory itself. This is normal science, and to that extent it is in line with Sandler's approach (though Lipton differs with Sandler by placing many of Sandler's "partial, private schemata of technique" firmly outside the realm of technique). *Both Lipton and Sandler salvaged public theory by establishing a separate and legitimate category for all the anomalies that are encompassed by ways in which analysts' noninterpretive engagement is necessary to analytic work—a category that includes exactly those same anomalies which, I have suggested, are currently challenging traditional conceptualizations of knowledge and authority in psychoanalytic theories of technique.*

Lipton's effort at normal science did, in my view, accomplish something very useful. He elegantly explicated how Freud's original theory actually worked: at its best, and in the hands of its early practitioners and those who, like Lipton himself, closely followed them.

However, the problem with normal science is not that it doesn't work to explain things. It does. The problem is that the explanations which work so well for explaining one group of events start to seem less and less suited to explaining others, or even to explaining new versions of the old ones. Newtonian physics hasn't stopped explaining some things brilliantly (like,

---

[8] Lipton acknowledged that modern technique had developed a way around this problem with the concept of a therapeutic alliance, but he suggested that this apparent solution was no solution at all, since it fostered artificiality by making human concern a technical prescription, and it exempted from analytic attention elements of the transference which required handling *within* the realm of technique.

say, the path of billiard balls shot across a billiard table). It just doesn't explain other things quite so well, if well at all (billiard balls, for example, moving close to the speed of light). Even the things Newtonian physics explains best turn out to be things that are not explained nearly so well once the parameters within which those things are defined or observed become altered.

But now back to the analyst who consulted with me. His view of what an analyst should be coincided exactly with Lipton's portrait of the ideal analyst in modern classical technique. In Lipton's terms, he might have been seen as an example of the failure of modern theory. Leaving aside the need to deal with this analyst's character problems, failures of his own analysis, and consequences of the actual boundary violation with his patient, Lipton's remedy for this analyst as a clinician might have been to try to return him to something approximating Freud's original theory of technique (or at any rate, to something approximating Lipton's rendering of it). That's a normal science remedy and I think it remains a very common one in psychoanalytic institutes. Many supervisors of overly rigid and abstinent candidates make it their aim to constitute a humanizing influence that frees up candidates' "courtesy, spontaneity, cordiality and warmth," as matters outside technique, but as nonetheless crucial features of what it takes to be a good analyst.

And as with Newtonian physics, it is not that this approach doesn't work. In an approximate, pragmatic way, if we don't take things too much apart or look too closely at why they are happening, it often works just fine (and so does Newtonian physics). But I think it is an approach and a remedy which avoids the explanatory precision that would allow us to see the limits of how it works. It solves the problem of things we cannot explain by making their influence an assumption, by placing them outside the realm of what we *try* to explain. It is therefore an approach that significantly restricts our potential knowledge about how *all* the myriad ingredients that make for effective psychoanalysis fit together and facilitate each other.

So it is an approach that strikes me as in principle limiting.

More to the point, however, I don't think it actually works as well as it used to. These days, it seems to me that at least some of our candidates—among them some of the brightest and the best—are raising significant questions about the utility of an abstinent, authoritative, and neutral stance. Such questions are not settled for very long by supervisory encouragement to establish a personal relationship with patients that falls outside the realm of technique (Lipton's solution) or to become more comfortable with the use of parameters (Sandler's "partial private schemata"). The questions troubling those candidates represent concerns that are more insistent and more fundamental. They are not questions about how to handle anomalous moments. Instead—when those candidates are able to be explicit about how and what they are thinking—I believe their questions tend to constitute shorthand for far-reaching questions about the nature of analysis, the definition of analytic work, and the essential features of the analyst's role. They are questions about how we know what we know, questions about what we are in fact able to know, and questions about how we employ our authority in furthering our attempts to know. They are questions about knowledge and authority in psychoanalysis, and they, like the questions of the analyst who consulted me, imply that something fundamental has shifted regarding what we are willing to take as given and what we hold as inviolable in our theories.

I suggested earlier that current published controversies over technique represent a set of indices that can help us recognize ways in which our fundamental psychoanalytic assumptions may indeed be shifting, specifically in conjunction with overall changes in our contemporary scientific world-view. I suggested that the central concerns of our published controversies entail exactly the shifting assumptions about knowledge and authority which are currently redefining science. I also suggested that, like most indices, our published papers do not tell the whole story. For the rest of the story we have to look outside our official literature, to the subtle, unofficial, and inchoate ways that, implicitly and over time, changes in scientific world-view have started to infiltrate the daily thinking of practicing psycho-analysts. The analyst who came to consult me exemplified, I proposed, one way in which that gradual infiltration can be manifested, while the candidates whose questions are not satis-fied by normal science recommendations exemplify another. In both instances, I believe we can see versions of how, returning to Sandler's language, certain partial private schemata are having trouble happily coexisting with our consensual public theory of technique. And in both instances the schemata causing trouble turn out to be—as in our published controversies over tech-nique—centrally concerned with the nature of psychoanalytic knowledge and the nature of the psychoanalyst's authority to know.

Where Are We Heading? Some Speculations

It seems likely that other partial private schemata will also show up as worth examining if we want further to understand the ways changing scientific world-views are affecting psycho-analytic thinking. And it is my guess that a significant number of those schemata will suggest revisions of public theory far more radical than our published controversies have yet considered. If analysts' partial private schemata do indeed reflect changes in scientific world-view, some of them are likely to rock the foun-dations of analytic thinking as thoroughly as science itself has been rocked.[9]

---

[9] And science, along with the definition of scientific knowledge and authority, has, of course, been rocked. I started with Heisenberg's comment regarding the violent reaction caused by the development of modern physics which led to "a feeling that the ground would be cut from science." Einstein put it this way: "All my attempts to adapt the theoretical foundation of physics to this [new type of] knowledge failed completely. It was as if the ground had been pulled out from under one, with no firm foundation to be seen anywhere, upon which one could have built" (in Capra, 1983, p. 77). And Niels Bohr remarked: "Anyone who is not shocked by quantum theory has not understood it" (in Gribbin, 1984, p. 5).

We might try some speculations. For example, if we take seriously McClintock's vision of the state of mind that permits
scientific discovery, how radically might we come to revise our
definition of what makes for a scientific attitude, and might that
revision have some startling implications for the sorts of mental
capacities which we would consider helpful in furthering the
growth of scientific knowledge—including psychoanalytic
knowledge? Or if we turn to physics and take seriously a development such as Bell's theorem,[10] how will we start to come to
terms with its shockingly counterintuitive implications regarding causality: the fact that atomic particles which were once
contiguous and are then separated over great distances, continue to remain in apparently instantaneous contact, capable of
mutual influence? Does taking either McClintock or Bell seriously require that we begin to grasp something like the concept
of what physicist David Bohm has termed as "implicate order" to
the universe, such that (however minimally and clumsily we
grasp it), we become permanently and irrevocably skeptical of
our perceptions of things as separate and separable, and start
genuinely to recognize those perceptions as reflections of the

[10] In 1935, Einstein, Podolsky, and Rosen developed a mathematical argument
which they imagined would defeat quantum theory; it proposed that, if quantum
theory were correct, "then a change in the spin of one particle in a two-particle
system would affect its twin simultaneously, even if the two had been widely separated in the meantime" (Einstein, Podolsky, and Rosen, p. 777). Almost thirty years
later, John Bell devised a theorem which showed that the EPR prediction of instantaneous nonlocal action (EPR for Einstein, Podolsky, and Rosen) could in fact occur.
A few years later, the quantum mechanical predictions of Bell's theorem that Einstein had deemed impossible were effectively confirmed. Henry Stapp, a physicist at
Berkeley and an authority on Bell's theorem, has called it the most important discovery in the history of science. He summarizes it thus: "If the statistical predictions
of quantum theory are true, an objective universe is incompatible with the law of
local causes" (by local causes, Stapp means causal relationships which depend on
information communicated at a rate not exceeding the speed of light, thereby ruling
out the instantaneous response predicted by Bell's theorem). In Stapp's view, the
implications of Bell's theorem are not limited to atomic particles, but are of major
significance in their translation to our macroscopic existence (in Dossey, 1982, pp.
98, 101).

limited, explicate nature of how we currently think, not of anything more fundamental?[11] And if we start to recognize *that*, how surprisingly may new evidence of connection and inseparability start to creep up on us, disrupting, among other things, our habitual distinctions between knower and known, to an extent barely hinted at in contemporary controversies about the place of intersubjectivity in psychoanalytic technique?

So we can start with McClintock or with Bell and we can, as Oppenheimer suggested, consider how extraordinary new ideas from outside psychoanalysis may have implications for psychoanalysis itself. Keeping in mind all the cautions I enumerated earlier about applying new ideas in science to psychoanalysis, it is crucial to be careful about how we undertake that consideration—but I think there is one application which we can safely expect will be, in Oppenheimer's words, "very illuminating." And that involves the simple recognition that a scientific development such as Bell's identification of the possibility of nonlocal action means that *an entirely new set of questions about causality has become conceivable for us.* The fact that those questions have become conceivable reflects a reorganization of our collective minds, including a reorganization of what attracts our interest and our attention. As the original gestalt psychologists demonstrated, we do not see without a framework for seeing. Once we have a new framework, we see all kinds of new things. And once certain questions become conceivable, we find them arising in all kinds of unexpected places.[12]

The question is not how we can apply McClintock's findings or Bell's theorem directly to psychoanalysis. The question is how the questions opened up by McClintock and Bell may affect the

[11] Bohm (1980) uses the term "implicate order" to describe the quantum potential and fundamental organization of unbroken wholeness which underlies our perceived world of separateness and fragmentation; he is describing an "enfolded" order to every aspect of the universe, in which all parts "implicate" the whole.

[12] Scientific knowledge is in this sense socially constructed, without implications (despite a history of controversy on the subject) for the degree to which it is also constrained by evidence.

questions we find conceivable—perhaps, eventually, crucial and organizing —*in relation to distinctly psychoanalytic events and hypotheses.*

We might, for example, consider physicist Arthur Zajonc's argument that the quantum mechanical predictions of Bell's theorem raise crucial questions for a scientific definition of rationality. In his words, "something in Einstein's view of rationality must be given up. The question remains, what? The EPR-Bell archetypal experiment urges on us the possibility of a more flexible form for rationality than that of traditional science. We need not give up rationality, but rather must broaden its meaning" (1993, p. 311).

What might such a broadened definition of rationality look like for psychoanalysts? We're certainly very far from being able to answer that question, but I think Zajonc is suggesting that we, along with investigators in every field of science, might consider Bell's theorem as a basis on which we can start to entertain the question in new ways.

For example, as analysts, we have given enormous credit to the power of irrationality in the unconscious, but our view of rationality has not altered much since Freud's early theories. Might certain aspects of what we have termed irrational edge into the category of whatever a broadened rationality might contain? Might that broadened rationality lead us to question time-honored distinctions between primary process and secondary process, or between conscious and unconscious, in ways that may alter our ideas about thought and thinking? Might the idea of nonlocal effects help articulate a host of new questions about the essential qualities and ultimate limits of human intuition? Or about the nature of human communication—communication, certainly, between analyst and analysand, but even, perhaps, communication between human beings who "were once contiguous and are then separated over great distances"? We have, at this point, no basis on which to assume Bell's theorem *has* macroscopic implications for human communication—but equally, we do not have a basis on which to assume it does *not*. And the mere fact of asking whether it does or doesn't, may help us articulate profoundly important questions about what human communication really entails. (For a more elaborated review of both these questions and a growing body of relevant research, see Mayer [1996].)

Some of the questions I am raising imply possibilities that we psychoanalysts, along with our fellow scientists, have in the past firmly relegated to the realm of the irrational. Will they remain quite so firmly placed there if we start to broaden our definition of rationality in the ways Zajonc and his colleagues are calling on scientists to do? More to my particular point, are questions like these—questions that I believe are insistently emerging from our contemporary scientific *Weltanschauung*—*already* informing the partial private schemata of practicing analysts in ways that radically undercut conventional public analytic theories about *how* we know and *what* we know?

We could look to McClintock as well. She helped focus questions currently being raised in various branches of science about the state of mind that permits scientific knowing—the state of mind that permits, especially, *new* knowing or discovery. She suggested that work according to the so-called scientific method is useful insofar as it provides a framework for communication among scientists, but she is emphatic that it never provided her with the state of mind from which she made her discoveries. This hardly makes her unique among scientists, but I believe she was unusual in the extent to which she spelled out possible implications of her own state of mind for formal research methodology and design. In her search to know more about *how* she knew what she knew, McClintock turned increasingly to a fascination with the discipline of mind developed in Tibetan Buddhism. As she puts it, she "had the idea that the Tibetans understood this *how* you know" (in Keller, 1983, p. 203). Central to what she felt the Tibetans understood was something she viewed as essential to scientific discovery-making: a relation to the object of investigation in which the investigator's wholehearted attention and receptivity are maximized. Her "feeling for the organism" was something she suggested the Tibetans knew how to achieve, and she anticipated that their methods might be of crucial interest to contemporary scientists in our current scientific revolution, a revolution which she imagined would "reorganize the way we look at things, the way we do research" (Keller, 1983, p. 207).

McClintock's questions about how we know what we know are very close to questions articulated by numerous physicists, who have also suggested that states of mind systematically developed in various Eastern traditions may teach us something about states of mind useful for comprehending current developments in science. Schrödinger wrote: "Our science—Greek science—is based on objectification. . . . But I do believe that this is precisely the point where our present way of thinking does need to be amended, perhaps by a bit of blood-transfusion from Eastern thought" (1945, p. 140). These days it is almost a truism to comment on the mystical bent of various pioneers in modern physics, but it is nonetheless striking how many of them have written explicitly about the value of a meditative or mystic state in relation to scientific knowing (to cite a few: Heisenberg, Einstein, de Broglie, Jeans, Planck, Pauli, Eddington, Bohr, and Robert Oppenheimer).[13] Zajonc, concluding his recent massive study of the history of light, asks, "What should be the nature of future knowledge; how will we see light tomorrow?" (1993, p. 338). As part of his answer, he suggests that we look in the direction of monks, who know "that through *a disciplined practice* they can internalize nature so they can realize *new capacities of mind*" (p. 341, italics added).

So what about these disciplined practices and these new capacities of mind that scientists are recommending to us? Are they of any relevance to the way we sit in our offices, listen to our patients, attend to their associations, and interact with their

---

[13] I am in no sense suggesting that these physicists took physics to "prove" mysticism, as some authors have argued in a logic that significantly confuses levels of discourse and which has been cogently criticized by Wilber (1984, Preface).

experiences? Do they have anything to do with knowledge in psychoanalysis? Or with the nature and place of authority in achieving psychoanalytic knowledge? Do they, once again, have anything to do with the questions that are *already* informing the partial private schemata which are bumping up against analysts' public theories?

I think perhaps they do.

A study group was recently formed by some members of the American Psychoanalytic Association to discuss these sorts of questions. The group formed in the way many study groups do: informal conversations led a number of analysts to discover that others shared interests which never got talked about at official meetings. The questions that interested these analysts arose from particular personal experiences which had disconcertingly bumped up against their individual versions of official clinical theory. In response, each had developed more or less articulated partial private schemata about crucial aspects of how we know what we know in analysis. Some of those schemata have been frankly disturbing to the analysts describing them and are based on experiences they have found exceedingly unsettling to disclose among colleagues. When spelled out, they suggest possible implications for psychoanalytic knowledge which are as potentially radical as the questions I have just enumerated.

For example, one analyst has described a certain frame of mind that he views as similar to meditation, in which he thinks he tends to be at his most insightful about his patients. Most recently, in working to develop the quality of experience that characterizes this state, he finds that the mental state is accompanied by a consistent perception of a band of light around a patient's head and body, a perception that vanishes as soon as his own mental state shifts, even very subtly. He is of course fascinated; what is he seeing and why? The perception of light has a particular interest for him because it is so closely associated with the mental state in which he feels he is doing his best analytic work. It has led him to question whether that mental state enables perceptions of his patients which may be different in kind from the perceptions he has always associated with "analytic listening." He has started to wonder whether, in that state, his insights are actually less a function of "listening," but more a function of perceiving something on a level he is calling "energetic"—which manifests both in the light he is seeing, but also in the intuitions about his patients which that particular mental state seems to facilitate. He finds these questions disturbing but engrossing. What is most disturbing to him is the extent to which both his experience and the questions he is starting to articulate lead him to feel more and more removed from what he is used to calling science and used to calling rational.

Another member has described a growing conviction that his habitual understanding of concepts like empathy and projective identification, while adequate to describe many aspects of how he feels he knows about his patients, fails fully to capture the extent of the intuition he experiences at certain moments when, in his words, he is aware of a subjectively unusual state of consciousness in which he feels himself "go inside" the patient's experience. In those moments he knows things and anticipates things which he feels are simply not knowable by any means we call rational: he says he knows literal details of past events he has never heard about, and he has even anticipated future ones (correctly, he later finds out). Other members of the group have echoed versions (albeit less dramatic ones) of feeling that they sometimes know about patients in ways that seem to challenge conventional definitions of what we are able to know about other people. Discussions have consolidated around a central question: when does the data of our experience with patients start to require that we reach beyond what we can comfortably include within our usual definition of rationally based intuition in psychoanalysis?

Another member has also used the phrase "going inside" a patient's experience to describe an unusually profound state of feeling connected to a patient. He, however, has focused less on what he *knows* about his patients in that state, and more on how that state appears to further his own ability to communicate with patients in a way which seems to him outside his usual capacities—leading him, then, to wonder about how human beings in general affect each other for healing purposes, and to wonder how, ultimately, healing happens at all. Two members of the group became especially interested in these questions following personal experiences in which terminal disease conditions suddenly and dramatically disappeared, thoroughly challenging the analysts' medical understandings of what is physiologically possible and how the mind affects the body. These analysts report being deeply shaken in their basic assumptions about reality and about the mind—in the assumptions that have grounded their years of psychoanalytic practice. They find themselves questioning much that our public and official psychoanalytic theories take for granted, both about how the mind works and, in a corollary way, how the analytic relationship works.

These are the kinds of questions being considered by the study group. They are questions that, I think, have quite a lot in common with questions being opened up by contemporary redefinitions of science: particularly with those questions which are reframing the nature of our connection to the objects of our knowing, while redefining our understanding of how that connection permits us to know. The analysts considering them are deeply committed to what Freud called our origins in science. But they are, I would say, equally interested in joining psychoanalysis to the revolution in science that Spruiell described and the revolution in biology that McClintock represented. Their discussions about how to accomplish that joining remain on a rudimentary and highly speculative level. Their concerns about retaining a rational and scientific orientation are profound—in the midst of experiences that seem to defy the science and the rationality with which they grew up. At the same time, their discussions have been strikingly infused with the quality that Polanyi called heuristic passion. There is a strong sense that, however disturbing, the questions with which these analysts are struggling are, for them, very much at the heart of things and potentially transformative for their understanding of what constitutes effective psychoanalytic work.

I believe there is a great deal more of that heuristic passion waiting to galvanize our field if we let it. And, as in the study group I described, I think much of that passion resides in the way certain newly conceivable questions emerging from changes in our contemporary scientific world-view may be helping to articulate—maybe even helping to stimulate—aspects of analysts' personal analytic experiences that do not fit comfortably into our familiar psychoanalytic theories. As a result, I think our field is seeing the development of some profoundly challenging "partial private schemata" about how analysis works.

Physicist David Bohm has defined science as "a means of establishing new kinds of contact with the world, in new domains, on new levels" (1965, p. 230). Perhaps we can view analysts' partial private schemata as attempts at science in Bohm's sense: individual attempts to establish new kinds and domains and levels of contact with the world of psychoanalytic events. Those attempts range from the muddled rethinking that the analyst who consulted me was struggling with, to the basic questions being considered by the study group I described. To the extent that we do not invite the full range of analysts' current partial private schemata into our contemporary public discourse—particularly, perhaps, the most startling and disquieting ones among them—we have a lot to lose. Radical new sensibilities about what makes for knowledge, and about how we know what we know, are very much in the air. They are currently furthering developments in every branch of science (Harman and Clark, 1994; Jahn and Dunne, 1987). They will either be harnessed for psychoanalytic purposes or they will not. If they are not, they are likely to do one of two things. They may become partial private schemata that go underground, with all the potentially destructive consequences both for thinking and for conscience which I described earlier. Or they may simply go elsewhere, and drain our liveliest dialogues away from dialogues that concern official theory in psychoanalysis, In either event, we stand to lose a great deal.

The essential goal of psychoanalysis—understanding human experience within the unique crucible of a relationship between analyst and analysand—retains, I believe, its excitement and ultimate value. The crucial question facing us is how freely we will allow new possibilities to inform the ways we go after that goal. I have suggested that, if we stick with the empiricism that is immediately available to us through the data of analysts' currently operative partial private schemata, we will find evidence that the newly conceivable questions which are arising in science have already started significantly to influence some psychoanalysts. As we pursue the articulation of those schemata—many of them ill-defined and still embryonic—our ideas about knowledge and authority in psychoanalysis will probably be mightily altered. But my guess is that psychoanalysis will be mightily enriched.

• • • • • •

I began with Sitwell's *Heart and Mind,* and with the suggestion that her imagery is evocative of our current dilemmas, both in psychoanalysis itself and in our attempts to know about it. She speaks of the fire of the heart, the fire of the mind, and the state of their relation to each other. The analyst who consulted me was unable to negotiate that relation in anything like a viable meeting. Our contemporary controversies over technique emphasize the importance of acknowledging multiple versions of how those meetings happen, the fire of both hearts in the analytic dyad meeting the fire of both minds, no single conjunction of one with another privileged as more significant, organizing, or authoritative than any other.

It seems to me that Sitwell's imagery captures as well a running theme which characterizes the changing scientific worldview I have described. Increasingly we are acknowledging that the fire of the heart is no less a part of what makes for science and scientific discovery than is the fire of the mind. As we attempt to articulate some of the discontinuities between analysts' private and public theories that are presently troubling our field, I think we will find that the best of analysts' partial private schemata—the ones most likely to enhance psychoanalysis—may be quintessentially distinguished by the way they join the fire of the heart with the fire of the mind, in a union akin to what Polanyi (1958) called personal knowledge:

> . . . this personal co-efficient, which shapes all factual knowledge, bridges in doing so the disjunction between subjectivity and objectivity . . . (p. 17).

> It commits us, passionately and far beyond our comprehension, to a vision of reality . . . we live in it as in the garment of our own skin. Like love, to which it is akin, this commitment is a "shirt of flame," blazing with passion and, also like love, consumed by . . . obligations to universal standards. . . . such is the true sense of objectivity in science (p. 64).

As psychoanalysts struggle not only to retain their roots in science, but also to incorporate implications of the radical redefinition science itself is undergoing, I think we will find Polanyi's personal knowledge crucial in helping us develop the imaginative capacities that will be required of us. Zajonc (1994) writes of the need for those capacities in relation to other branches of science.

> The intellectual current of atomic thinking, of analysis, still runs fast and deep. . . . Yet if quantum theory is any guide, it is only our imagination that is limited. Nature, and even our mathematical descriptions of her, are unambiguous in their indications. Atomism and localism are only impoverished, limiting cases of a far richer and more subtle order to the universe. . . . Behind each [of these] statement[s] is an experiment. . . . I have done these experiments, as have hundreds of other physicists in laboratories around the globe. To these investigators the experimental results are routine—no surprises; but the demands they place on our imaginations are enor-

mous. It is to this aspect that I appeal, to the need for a renewal of thinking, the birth of a richer imagination. Like demands are being made on us by biology, ecology, cognitive science, medicine, and a myriad of other fields. We are at a threshold (p. 323).

Psychoanalysts stand at that same threshold. And it seems to me that precisely the things we know most about as psychoanalysts—rendering conscious what has been unconscious, and investigating mental resistance to change—will assist our access to the richer imagination we will be needing. As we strive to join the rest of science, that richer imagination promises to enliven both our theory and our practice enormously.

REFERENCES

ARON, L. (1991). The patient's experience of the analyst's subjectivity. *Psychoanal. Dialogues*, 1:29-51.
BERNFELD, S. (1941). The facts of observation in psychoanalysis. *Int. Rev. Psychoanal.*, 1985, 12:342-351.
BOHM, D. (1965). *Special Theory of Relativity.* New York: Benjamin Books.
———(1980). *Wholeness and the Implicate Order.* London: Routledge & Kegan Paul.
BRUNER, J. (1993). Loyal opposition and the clarity of dissent. *Psychoanal. Dialogues*, 3:11-19.
CAPRA, F. (1983). *The Turning Point: Science, Society and the Rising Culture.* New York: Bantam Books.
COLE, K. C. (1985). *Sympathetic Vibrations: Reflections on Physics as a Way of Life.* New York: Bantam Books.
COOPER, S. (1993). Introduction: hermeneutics and you. *Psychoanal. Dialogues*, 3: 169-176.
DOSSEY, L. (1982). *Space, Time and Medicine.* Boston: Shambhala Publ.
EDELGLASS, E., MAIER, G., GEBERT, H. & DAVY, J. (1992). *Matter and Mind: Imaginative Participation in Science.* New York: Lindisfarne Press.
EHRENBERG, D. B. (1992). *The Intimate Edge. Extending the Reach of Psychoanalytic Interaction.* New York/London: Norton.
EINSTEIN, A., PODOLSKY, B. & ROSEN, N. (1935). Can quantum mechanical description of reality be considered complete? *Physical Review*, 47:777-780.
FOGEL, G. I. (1990). Review of *Chaos: Making a New Science* by J. Gleick. *Bull. Assn. Psychoanal. Med.*, 29:95-96.

FREUD, S. (1909). Notes upon a case of obsessional neurosis. *S.E.*, 10.
———(1921). Psycho-analysis and telepathy. *S.E.*, 18.
FURMAN, R. (1993). Kuhn, chaos and psychoanalysis: an introduction. *Child Anal.*, 4:133-150.
GILL, M. M. (1982). *Analysis of Transference, Vol. 1: Theory and Technique.* New York: Int. Univ. Press.
———(1993). Interaction and interpretation. *Psychoanal. Dialogues*, 3:111-122.
GODWIN, R. (1991). Wilfred Bion and David Bohm: toward a quantum metapsychology. *Psychoanal. Contemp. Thought*, 14:625-654.
GRIBBIN, J. (1984). *In Search of Schrödinger's Cat: Quantum Physics and Reality.* New York: Bantam Books.
HARMAN, W. & CLARK, J. (1994). *New Metaphysical Foundations of Modern Science.* Sausalito, CA: Inst. of Noetic Sciences.
HEISENBERG, W. (1958). *Physics and Philosophy.* New York: Harper Torchbooks.
HOFFMAN, I. Z. (1983). The patient as interpreter of the analyst's experience. *Contemp. Psychoanal.*, 19:389-422.
———(1992). Some practical implications of a social constructivist view of the psychoanalytic situation. *Psychoanal. Dialogues*, 2:287-304.
———(1994). Dialectical thinking and therapeutic action in psychoanalysis. *Psychoanal. Q.*, 63:187-218.
HOFFMAN, L. (1992). Review of *Chaos: Making a New Science* by J. Gleick. *J. Amer. Psychoanal. Assn.*, 40:880-885.
JAHN, R. & DUNNE, B. (1987). *Margins of Reality: The Role of Consciousness in the Physical World.* New York: Harcourt Brace.
KELLER, E. (1983). *A Feeling for the Organism: The Life and Work of Barbara McClintock.* New York: W. H. Freeman.
———(1992). *Secrets of Life, Secrets of Death: Essays on Language, Gender and Science.* New York: Routledge.
KUHN, T. S. (1962). *The Structure of Scientific Revolutions.* Chicago: Univ. of Chicago Press.
———(1977). *The Essential Tension: Selected Studies in Scientific Tradition and Change.* Chicago: Univ. of Chicago Press.
LIPTON, S. D. (1977). The advantages of Freud's technique as shown in his analysis of the Rat Man. *Int. J. Psychoanal.*, 58:255-273.
MATURANA, H. & VARELA, F. (1992). *The Tree of Knowledge: The Biological Roots of Human Understanding.* Boston: Shambhala Press.
MAYER, E. L. (1996). The essential subjectivity and intersubjectivity of clinical facts and some speculations regarding the relevance of research concerning anomalous mental effects. *Int. J. Psychoanal.* In press.
MCLAUGHLIN, J. T. (1981). Transference, psychic reality, and countertransference. *Psychoanal. Q.*, 50:639-664.
———(1982). Issues stimulated by the 32nd Congress. *Int. J. Psychoanal.*, 63:229-240.
———(1991). Clinical and theoretical aspects of enactment. *J. Amer. Psychoanal. Assn.*, 39:595-614.

————(1995). Touching limits in the analytic dyad. *Psychoanal. Q.*, 64:433-465.

MITCHELL, S. A. (1992). Introduction to symposium: What does the analyst know? *Psychoanal. Dialogues*, 2:279-287.

MORAN, M. G. (1991). Chaos and psychoanalysis: the fluidic nature of mind. *Int. Rev. Psychoanal.*, 18:211-221.

MOSHER, P. (1990). Review of *Chaos: Making a New Science* by J. Gleick. *Bull. Assn. Psychoanal. Med.*, 29:95-96.

NELSON, L. (1990). *Who Knows? From Quine to a Feminist Empiricism.* Philadelphia: Temple Univ. Press.

POLANYI, M. (1958). *Personal Knowledge: Towards a Post-Critical Philosophy.* Chicago: Univ. of Chicago Press.

————(1974). *Scientific Thought and Social Reality*, ed. F. Schwartz, *Psychol. Issues*, Monogr. 32. New York: Int. Univ. Press.

RENIK, O. (1993). Analytic interaction: conceptualizing technique in light of the analyst's irreducible subjectivity. *Psychoanal. Q.*, 62:553-571.

————(1994). Publication of clinical facts. *Int. J. Psychoanal.*, 75:1245-1250.

————(1995). The ideal of the anonymous analyst and the problem of self-disclosure. *Psychoanal. Q.*, 64:466-495.

ROUGHTON, R. E. (1994). Repetition and interaction in the analytic process: enactment, acting out, and collusion. *Annual Psychoanal.*, 22:271-286.

SANDLER, J. (1983). Reflections on some relations between psychoanalytic concepts and psychoanalytic practice. *Int. J. Psychoanal.*, 64:35-45.

SCHRÖDINGER, E. (1945). *What Is Life—Mind and Matter?* London: Cambridge Univ. Press.

SCHWARTZ, J. (1995). What does the physicist know? Thraldom and insecurity in the relationship of psychoanalysis to physics. *Psychoanal. Dialogues*, 5:45-62.

SITWELL, E. (1968). *The Collected Poems of Edith Sitwell.* New York: Vanguard.

SPEZZANO, C. (1993). A relational model of inquiry and truth: the place of psychoanalysis in human conversation. *Psychoanal. Dialogues*, 3:177-208.

————(1995). "Classical" versus "contemporary" theory: the differences that matter clinically. *Contemp. Psychoanal.*, 31:20-46.

————(1996). The three faces of two-person psychology: the meanings and clinical implications of the one-person versus the two-person dichotomy at the developmental, ontological and epistemological levels of psychoanalytic discourse. *Psychoanal. Dialogues*, 6, in press.

SPRUIELL, V. (1994). Deterministic chaos and the sciences of complexity: psychoanalysis in the midst of a general scientific revolution. *J. Amer. Psychoanal. Assn.*, 41:3-44.

STOLOROW, R. D. (1995). Deconstructing the myth of the neutral analyst: an alternative from intersubjective systems theory. Unpublished.

TARNAS, R. (1991). *The Passion of the Western Mind: Understanding the Ideas That Have Shaped Our World View.* New York: Harmony Books.

WHEATLEY, M. (1992). *Leadership and the New Science: Learning about Organization from an Orderly Universe.* San Francisco: Berrett-Koehler Publ.

WILBER, K., Editor (1984). *Quantum Questions.* Boston: Shambhala Publ.

ZAJONC, A. (1993). *Catching the Light. The Entwined History of Light and Mind.* New York: Oxford Univ. Press.

———(1994). New wine in what kind of wineskins? Metaphysics in the twenty-first century. In *New Metaphysical Foundations of Modern Science*, ed. W. Harman & J. Clark. Sausalito, CA: Inst. of Noetic Sciences, pp. 321-343.

ZETZEL, E. (1966). 1965: Additional notes upon a case of obsessional neurosis. *Int. J. Psychoanal.*, 47:123-129.

9

Power, Authority, and Influence in the Analytic Dyad

POWER, AUTHORITY, AND INFLUENCE IN THE ANALYTIC DYAD

BY JAMES T. McLAUGHLIN, M.D.

> Intercourse between individuals and between social groups takes one of two forms: force or persuasion.
>
> ALFRED NORTH WHITEHEAD (1949, p. 105)

Psychoanalysis has struggled with issues of power and influence in the analytic relationship since Freud first attempted to separate his new science from its beginnings in hypnotic suggestion. That he was unsuccessful then in disclaiming power and influence, and we since then as well, has been our collective rue and challenge to this day.

First seeking to deny the existence of the analyst's influence, then attempting to eliminate it, we have only gradually come to acknowledge and cope with its being an inescapable component of the interplay of the dynamics of power between the analytic pair.

I first make some observations regarding certain dynamic, and perhaps inherent factors upon which this relational inevitability is based. I then offer reasons and clinical data to support my technical preferences for working analytically within the quiet band of asserted influence. I will try to show how this mode of working serves to sharpen our awareness of our proclivities toward undue assertion of power, to provide a safeguard against our excesses, and to enhance the place and power of the patient in the accomplishing of mutative analytic work.

I shall be using the word influence as an inclusive term to refer to a specifiable portion of the broader spectrum of the

189

usages of power. It connotes "the quiet, insensible or gradual exertion of power, often arising from strength of intellect, force of character, eminent position, and the like." (This and the remaining definitions come from *Webster's*, 1959.)

These allusions to more subtle deployments of power point to what I see as the analyst's most effective, and genuinely analytic, use of influence. They differentiate influence from the stance of "authority," which "implies the formal, legal, or overt exercise of power by virtue of some office, jurisdiction or special title." They make a little clearer the distinction between influence and "persuasion," the latter to be understood as "the act of influencing the mind by arguments or reasons offered, by entreaty or expostulation."

The term *suggestion*, of course, most annoyingly overlaps the span of influence in its range of meanings: i.e., from "the evocation of new ideas by association" to "a hint"; to "the act of putting something into someone's mind"; to "the uncritical acceptance of a statement, idea or purpose when made by a person to whom a person is docile and submissive." With this last we are into the thick of hypnotic suggestion and our best analytic efforts to press the patient to see what he or she may wish not to see. We are ill-poised to meet the challenges to the scientific objectivity and authority that we would wish to claim for our discipline.

There are further and compelling tendencies innate to how the mind works, and in how minds communicate, that should persuade us to relinquish all hope of an influence-free analytic position.

A fundamental way in which the mind works is evident in the reflections of a bisexual patient about whom I shall say more later. While describing a vivid visual image in his mind of a woman's vagina, Mr. Q suddenly sees, equally closeup and compelling, the erect penis of a recent homosexual partner. He remarks that this sequencing invariably happens to him, even during his actual encounters with partners of either sex. He is bothered that he must exert considerable concentration to blot out the inner opposite to what he actually is facing.

Hegel (1821) made much of this oppositional tendency, indeed put it central to his philosophy: that man's mind is such that he cannot think about anything without some inner reference to its opposite. The Scottish philosopher, Alexander Bain, emphasized this essential relativity of all knowledge, thought, or consciousness, so that even our language reveals the two-sided referencing in all that we know (cited by Freud [1910] in his paper on the antithetical meaning of primal words).

Freud from the beginning attributed dynamic significance to such phenomena, postulating the emergence of a "counter-will" in the hysteric (1892-1893, pp. 126-127). He eventually made its dynamic intent central to his theories of resistance, repression, and conflict. Freud in a way returned to Hegel's view in his eventual emphasis upon the innate conservatism of the dynamic unconscious, whose intrapsychic processes were to be viewed as a struggle of old insistences opposing the challenges of new developmental urgencies.

Hegel made this natural oppositionalism central in his dialectics. He saw the best attempts by two minds to find understanding as a never-ending oscillation between efforts to resolve negations by agreements, attempts leading to yet new negations, and in turn fresh efforts to share new understanding, ad infinitum. Otherwise, as he saw it: when the intent of one is to compel the other, as so often it is in families and society, the collaboration of mutual influencing must give way to force.

So, following the reasoning of Freud and Hegel, we may expect that in our efforts to communicate we may be ready to engage and receive, but we also carry within us this inherent stubbornness which resists the new that confronts us. The natural history of interpersonal relationships speaks eloquently of the dynamic complexities that amass out of this basic trait; how prone we are to opposition when thrust and counterthrust are driven by anxieties over inequalities of power and authority between individuals, between individual and family/society, and so forth.

From these tensions, both within the individual and between the individual and the rest of the world, come three needs and tendencies that infuse most if not all of our communicating in the domain of human relationships.

These are, in sum: *the intention or wish to influence, the feeling of being influenced, and the conviction that one has influenced.* As background tendencies these come into play from the beginning of analytic work, then become highlighted and hyperbolized, for both patient and analyst, in the dyadic intensities of the analytic process. In some respects these tendencies can be looked upon simply as manifestations of transference. But there are data from fields beyond that of psychoanalysis which suggest that these inherently conservative, oppositional ways can, in some very basic way, empower the workings of transference itself.[1]

The first tendency is the wish, need, and intention to influence, persuade, or force the other to respond in accord with our wish(es).[2] This first tendency is so pervasive and accepted as to require little expansion here. The second and third tendencies are less easily observed, perhaps, in the outside world, but become central to deepening the experiential dimensions of the analytic work.

The second tendency involves *the conviction of the one that his/her behaviors are necessary responses to the behaviors of the other.* Put

---

[1] The cognitive psychologist, Wegner (1994) has found neurophysiologic research support for the concept of "ironic processes of mental control." His findings demonstrate that intentional thinking is accompanied by a nonvolitional background monitoring that consistently intrudes into the foreground both contrary and antithetic thoughts.

[2] Child and infant observational research has provided a convincing picture of the child as engaging, perhaps before but surely from birth and thereafter, in reciprocal communicative interaction with the mother (Brazelton, 1982; Stern, 1985). The behaviors of both infant and mother, from wherever and whenever the start may be, speak eloquently of the urgency and power of the efforts of the one to evoke and shape those behaviors desired of the other. The back-and-forth sequencing, as well as simultaneity, of this interplay during early development create what truly is a matrix of shared impetus and response; a mix so entwined as to blur any clarity over who wants (or does not want) what from whom.

differently, each, out of wish or fear, experiences himself/herself as being influenced by the other, and his/her own reactions as being caused by that other.

This conviction is well known in our analytic theory and technical usages. It is manifest in the analyst-centered concept of countertransference, and maximized in our concept of projective identification. The ready acceptance by the analyst of this essentially projectional assumption matches the patient's equal readiness to attribute incitement to the analyst. As I see this symmetry, it can be understood as part of the inevitable regression occurring to both parties in the course of meaningful work. The analytic interaction revives the interactive subtleties of early child-mother relating, wherein boundaries and differences are only beginning to be established, and the qualities of thinking are still pervaded with primary process.

The third tendency is this: *one of the pair believes that his or her behaviors are the occasion and reason for the (re)actions of the other.* This belief is a paradoxical reversal of the second and speaks to the primary process nature of both, and to their early developmental roots (Emde, 1988). When manifest in the child or in a primitive culture or in a couple in love, we define this third tendency as magical, animistic, or moonstruck. Yet it emerges alive and well in the analytic situation.

In the clinical fragment that follows we will come upon commonplace enactments between Mr. Q and me which point to the immanence and power in each of these tendencies, even as we were just beginning to engage in our work. They begin immediately to shape the experiences of influencing and being influenced that become central to the enhancement of effective analytic work, as well as to the destructiveness of analysis gone awry.

These sensitivities around the issues of whose power, whose influence is being asserted, have steadily challenged our theory and shaped our technique.

Indeed, the history of the evolution of analytic technique reflects a remarkable shift: in the early years, dogged denial of the analyst's influence, while at the same time trying to maximize and stabilize its deployment; then the reluctant acceptance of mutual influence, and more recently the current preoccupation with the significance of the analyst's influence.

A brief review of these historical shifts will help me make my case.

With the beginnings of analysis based in the medical model of Western European science, it was probably inevitable that the analyst would be placed in a superior position. As the one who was presumed to have healing powers to heal the patient's hurting, the analyst assumed a mantle of influence connoting parent, teacher, god-figure, physician.

At the same time, because Freud wished to claim scientific objectivity, to downplay any resemblance between analysis and hypnosis, and to curb the excesses of his fellow analysts, he attempted, in his papers on technique, to impose powerful constraints and idealizations about how analysis was to be carried out (Freud, 1911, 1912, 1915). Every aspect of what he there prescribed, the aggregate of which lives on in what we refer to as the "analytic frame," can be construed as an effort to modulate and/or exploit the interplay of reciprocal influence. Stipulated by the analyst, the various rituals around couch, fee, time, and attendance, the disparity between who is to speak, and about what, all reflect regulatory efforts aimed at containing both parties while supporting a privileged position for the analyst.

The Fundamental Rule has long epitomized these weighty prescriptions, even as it has served as a sensitive indicator of our shifting attitudes. It endures as the primary clinical tool and indicator in the contemporary practices of many among us, even as its stipulation and use as the essential focus of analytic inquiry have been increasingly refined and diluted.

The Rule, whether forcefully enjoined or tentatively suggested, presses the patient toward a divided mind-set that fosters a joining with the observational perspective of the analyst. The patient is encouraged to share the analyst's commitment to an objectifying preoccupation with the patient's verbal content while invoking the license of free association to permit access to the patient's emotional depths.

This shared objective attempts to keep both parties focused not so much upon each other but upon the workings of the patient's mind. This prescribed stratagem can be seen as an attempt to reduce the impact and immediacy of the analyst's personal need to exercise authority over, and to modulate his becoming overinvolved with, the patient. It supports the need of the analyst to be screened from the full force of the patient's own needs, including the latter's reluctance to comply with the needs of the analyst. In brief, it is aimed at creating a protected context for both, in which neither looks directly at the other, and each is thereby presumed to be better able to cling to the safety of the analyst's assigned objectivity of detachment.

The inability of either of the pair to make analysis work like this provides, of course, the heart and substance of what we have come to find analysis to be about.

For the patient, in seeking to satisfy his or her own needs, is vulnerable to the felt necessity to assert more of his or her accustomed adaptive efforts, anything to offset his/her lesser power to influence the response of the analyst. The patient struggles to evoke the giving of what he or she needs while warding off the pressures of the analyst to satisfy the analytic requirements.

Offsetting the presumed imbalance of power favoring the analyst are the analyst's own vulnerabilities of need that derive from the motivations for doing analytic work in the first place. To the extent that the analyst has the healer's impulse to be devoted to a sufferer, the analyst is liable to be caught up in idiosyncratic or shared regressive transference states. If the analyst has the conquistador's yen to name and master the unknown, he or she is liable to the need to dominate and lead, to elicit behaviors from the patient that assure the analyst that his or her ambitions are being realized. Under the pressure of these needs it will be the analyst who courts and cues the patient, and now is vulnerable to the influence and power of the patient. The analyst, like the patient, will be moved to assert his or her necessities to determine the course this new relationship will take.

These schemata may serve to connote the stage now set for the playing out of often remarkable transformations and transcendence for one and often both in the dyad. What was prescribed to be a quiet and decorous inquiry into the workings of one mind becomes a tumultuous engagement of two minds, of two individuals who have risked opening themselves to the pressures of the other. In a relationship neither one alone has sufficient power to direct, it remains the dilemma of the analyst, the responsibility and task, to try to keep it ethically and technically righted.

I hope to make a strong case for the proposition that we analysts do best when we openly and consistently acknowledge this ubiquity of mutual influence and do what we can to monitor the preferred position that we cling to. For we may then find better ways to modulate the hazards and liabilities of what influence we may possess and optimally direct its impingements. There is nothing novel about this position. Much of the effort to advance and refine analytic technique over the past seventy years has been directed at least implicitly toward assessing the optimal stance of the analyst.

The analyst's influence was downplayed in the early years by assigning to it an unobjectionable facilitating function. In theory the analyst's physicianly benignity would evoke transference resonances of supportive parental others of the infantile past. This facilitation would encourage patient compliance with the exploratory aims of the analyst and enhance the analyst's pedagogic function, an influence seen as unobjectionable when put to the good purpose of helping the patient be done with immature behaviors (Freud, 1912).

The patient's right to influence with *her* view of things seems to have been regarded by Freud, and the rest of us for long thereafter, mainly as "resistance," judged to be essentially an interference, necessary for the patient, to be put up with until it could be understood, worn down, or outgrown.

The espousal of the analyst's superior knowing and the obligation to assert it against a resisting patient who must be pressed to see things realistically remained a dominant position in American psychoanalysis well into the fifties, at least. This position is reflected in a standard dictionary definition of resistance in those times: "In Psychoanalysis: Opposition displayed by the patient to attempts of the analyst to penetrate the unconscious" (*Webster's*).

Over the past fifty years many have wrestled with the liabilities of the authoritarian assumptions in this early model. Some found ways to make this austere mode work, through subtle technical modulations and personal revamping of meanings. Others broke entirely with the mode. Many of us have changed in how we think about and do our work, to a degree that no two of us are likely to see analysis and our work from identical perspectives. A few have done their utmost to spell out the nature of these changes (Gill, 1982; Schafer, 1983). Far more have kept our altered ways to ourselves.

Many of the differences among us still lie in issues of power allocation. The relative significance we attribute to theory versus clinical evidence; the value we place upon interpretation versus relationship; how much we see ourselves as a detached watcher, or as a participant observer whose transference potential approximates that of the patient; how much we see our role from Freud's dominant perspective as the authoritative conveyor of analytic truth, or how much, from his subordinated view, as a seeker of unknown truth latent in the patient; whether we see ourselves as arbiter and teacher of a reality that must be taught, or as a teacher of ways by which the patient may come upon his or her own reality.

One trend I believe to be common has been to humanize the analytic relationship. This trend has tended to reduce the tilt between the analytic pair, and to acknowledge the fallibility of the analyst (Cooper, 1993). This has been a salubrious development overall, excepting where it has fostered the illusion that the playing field has thereby been leveled, and democracy is triumphant. For there remains our natural ineluctible push to assert our point of view as the preferable way to understand and to try to persuade the other that ours indeed is the Way.

So, naturally, I want now to assert my way of seeing the analytic situation and its phenomena, to do my persuasive best to influence you to consider its possible advantages. It is more than likely that many will find in my position little that is novel to their experience. I will be ready to agree, while wishing there were ways we really could consider the significance of our small differences.

Since the late seventies I have tried to experience analytic work from a position that acknowledges the relativism of knowing, and I have tried to explore the question: whose knowing is to give direction and focus to the analytic quest: the patient's, the analyst's, or both?

Driven by this question, I found much that intrigued me in centering my work in the psychic reality of the patient. I came to think of the patient's manifest concerns and perspectives as the analytic surface, to be taken seriously as the primary focus of exploration. I found I did best when I could put into the background, except as generic guides, my acquired expectations about meaning and relevance. I came to find in this reining in of my own perspectives neither constraint nor constriction of my analytic powers; instead a greater freedom to question and follow trends in the patient wherever these might take us. Whatever particular meanings might eventually be assigned in the data provided by the patient were best worked out between us. When my stance became reliably expectable between us, it was possible for the patient to trust and I to dare. I was surprised how far the patient might go in his or her freedom to come upon new data and insight of his or her own, and I in my freedom to bring attention to behaviors, phrasing, and idiom of the patient that he or she might find worthwhile to attend to.

From this base we could often entwine our two separate reality views in ways at times collaborative, at times clashing. I was struck by what was obvious: in our each assuming the validity of our view, we increasingly made manifest the idiosyncratic shaping of the reality that each lived by. In the details of those shapings could be seen the power of our separate pasts.

So I argued for a return to Freud's earlier views of psychic reality and transference as general psychological principles to be applied to patient and analyst alike. I urged that we espouse a relativistic stance to counter the traditional tilt that stressed the infantile aspects of the reality view of the neurotic patient measured against the enlightened perspective of the analyst (McLaughlin, 1981).

I have been seeking, ever since, for ways both to act upon and to convey a more truly collaborative clinical stance of less knowing and more seeking to be informed of and to grasp how the patient perceives things, including the impact of my efforts to understand.

For want of a better term for this technical emphasis, I think of it as *analysis based in the psychic reality of the patient.*

It is a way of acknowledging how the reality view of each of us *is* our psychic reality, compounded out of all that we have experienced in the sum and transformations of our growing up. Psychic reality includes how one sees things through those primitive and preverbal modes that Freud referred to exclusively as primary process; yet it includes all later acquisitions of perception and responses that come with the maturing of these primary modes and their entwinement with secondary process capabilities (McLaughlin, 1978).

This expanded view of psychic reality accepts as a given that the past is indeed active in some fashion in the present reality-view of each of us, and we call it transference, as a consequence of the essentially conservative modes of survival of our psychophysical being.

My emphasis upon the centrality of transference in shaping the psychic reality of each of us is part of my conviction that the analytic quest is more than a story-making carried out for the illusionary comfort of the two participants. It is a quest for the stuff that carries through and from the roots and trunks of our developmental past to give individual shape, color, and vitality to our unique experiential present.

Hence I believe that the fundamental task of the analyst *is to use his or her powers primarily to lead and guide the patient toward HOW he or she will discover rather than to WHAT*; to help the patient grasp *how* he or she can contemplate the inner world of self and others, rather than toward *what* specific experiences and shapings will be found in the search.

The use of the Fundamental Rule, I suspect, was intended to accomplish just this. But, like any other special focus or emphasis, including my own particular attention to the patient's reality view, the analyst's need to further his or her own view will inevitably nudge him/her to provide answers for the reasons the patient associates or behaves as he or she does.

I have found that for me this focus upon the patient's viewpoint, his or her analytic surface, provides a counter to my tendency to provide answers and closures. To keep returning to and trying to sustain a stance of exploratory openness to be informed has served me well in my seeking to expand and deepen the patient's own search for fresh knowing. Working in such fashion provides experientially a model and base by which the patient may find the comfort and incentive to explore his or her surface-to-depth personal view of the world through the shared refraction of another's gaze.

My own stance, similar to Gill's (1982) but more closely aligned with that of Schwaber (1983), yet inevitably not identical with either, can be put like this: "I will listen to whatever you may wish to say, attempting to understand your meaning and viewpoint with the least imposition of my own view or meaning as I can manage. Since I do not presume to know, I shall often need to question and to ask for illumination. I will be alert to and inquire about your nonverbal behaviors and shifts of affect, in order that I may help you sense the many levels of meaning that you have connected with what you are speaking about. I will listen for allusions to how you perceive and react to my behaviors, out of my aim to help you articulate the validity and logic of how you have come to see your world, and me in it. Through looking at how you see me I will try to help you see yourself, at surface and depth, hoping thereby to strengthen your capacities to find even more of yourself to authenticate and own."

I believe this stance is consistent with Freud's subordinated view of the not-knowing analyst, and consonant with his early notion of the primacy of addressing the analytic surface through making contact with the patient's own concerns and states of being (Freud, 1905; McLaughlin, 1990; Smith, 1990).

This stance obviously includes being alert for verbal and behavioral clues that might indicate that the patients are reacting emotionally to what they perceive both within and around them, at levels both at and beyond their conscious awareness. Importantly, it includes seeking to detail and clarify patients' reading of the significance of my behaviors, readings often perceptive of my emotions, attitudes, and behaviors that lie beyond *my* conscious awareness.

The therapeutic rationale for this stance lies in what experience has taught me to expect: that this authentication of patients' perceptual powers and viewpoints strengthens their capacities to look further into themselves and bring forth conflicted content in recovering their own developmental antecedents.

This expectation has a venerable history in psychoanalysis, beginning with Freud's (1915) closing paper of his technique series, "Observations on Transference-Love," wherein he enjoins the analyst to respect fully the patient's perceptions of the reality of her love, and not to override or repudiate her view. The analyst must hold fast to the half-truth that such feelings reflect resistances, never to be responded to in kind. Freud promises the steadfast analyst that the patient will then feel safe enough to allow all her preconditions for loving, all her desires and fantasies, to come to light; "and from these she will herself open the way to the infantile roots of her love" (p. 166).

Bernfeld, in his classic "Facts of Observation in Psychoanalysis" (1941), observed that the patient's divulging of a secret tended to follow a comment of the analyst that conveyed acceptance and thereby diminished in the patient obstacles of internal shame or distrust. The psychotherapy research of Sampson and Weiss (1986) has independently confirmed and expanded upon Bernfeld's perception.

Schwaber (1983, 1986, 1990) has provided a continuing series of contributions that attest to the therapeutic impetus for the patient that lies in the analyst's persistent seeking to be informed of the patient's perceptual experiences and their inner historical determinants.

This stance of the seeking analyst reflects and supports a considerable shift in the power gradient between patient and analyst. It is a shift that enhances the patient's place in the dyad, with the relative subordination and redistribution of the analyst's knowledge and authority. It includes acceptance of and acting upon the idea that one can be the source and reason for the behavior of the other. This assumption recognizes that the patient, rather than the analyst, is at times the primary source and guide for what can become known between the analytic pair.

Sustaining this deliberate acknowledgment of the patient as primary source requires that the analyst must become committed to the effort, however faltering, to learn from the patient the surface-to-depth nuances of how the patient has perceived and reacted to his or her world, including all of the analyst's behaviors. This commitment to be, like the patient, the object of scrutiny requires a temperamental openness in the analyst to the cogency of this view; both view and commitment then must be consolidated by the analyst's accumulating clinical experience that attests to their validity. Such openness serves as a powerful and continuing stimulus for self-scrutiny on the part of the analyst.

This sustained quality of listening affords the patient the fundamental experience of being believed. (I am indebted to my colleague, Murray Charlson [personal communication, 1994] for putting it in this epigrammatic fashion, and for his pointing to the transformative power this can hold for the patient.)

"Believing" here connotes multiple levels of meaning. It starts with a commonplace analytic acceptance of patients' stated views as indeed a reflection of something of themselves that they need to convey. It adds an essential dimension: responding to the need of the patients to know that what they are offering is being received as it is. This is *not* a listening mode of naïve acceptance of received and final truth. It *is* a face value acknowledgment of the impact and value of patients' views, lived out through the analyst's sustained commitment to exploring and expanding the further significance that patients can come to see in what they have said, in the light of their shared quest.

Where this stance can differ from accepted analytic lore is in the analyst's continuing effort to minimize his or her tendencies to translate or shape the developing nature of the meanings on the basis of that accumulated lore, whether his/her own or shared with his/her field.

It is this effort at forbearing acceptance which in turn fosters patients' willingness to gamble on the integrity of the analyst's invitation to the opportunity for a deep and collaborative exploration of the patients' psychic life, in the patients' own idioms and from their points of view.

In this core experience there is a moving power, by and for the two participants, that I do not fully fathom.

A possible clue to a central ingredient may lie in the archaic quality of the belief, particularly when acknowledged, that one can indeed be the cause of the behaviors of the other, that one can indeed have such significance as to evoke the behaviors of the other. This way of experiencing the interplay of mutual influence and power is prominent in the closeness of baby and mother (Stern, 1985). The utter absence of this belief, in early development, can stunt or kill. It is a belief that pervades the entwinement of lovers, and colors every intense relationship throughout life. As I see it, the analyst's feeling and timely conveying the impact of the patient upon him or her, and the analyst upon the patient, can evoke in both parties powerful resonances of those oscillations of mutual influence and confluence that were central to our early relating. Such evocations lend particular intensities of immediacy and realness to the experiences of being touched and touching, seen and seeing, moved and moving, influenced and influencing in the analytic dyad.

I have found it no easy task to sustain this mode of putting aside one's life-view for the sake of learning that of the other. I must try deliberately to constrain and internally monitor my tendency to determine, to decipher, to interpret, the patient's meaning and thrust.

Tracking the patients' responses to my interventions has led me through a series of expansions from my once-minimalist analytic stance. I have come to prefer, in both my analytic and consultative work, a tentative and questioning style of voicing my ideas and observations. I float ideas before the patient, rather than declaiming them in a way that the patient too easily can feel as fastening them to him or her. I do not presume to know the meaning of silence between us.

I feel less burdened by the presumption that I must articulate my interventions just so, and freer to give voice to my own preconscious stirrings as tentative, sometimes playful stuff that the patient might reject, play with, or revise.

This collaborative mode of looking *with* the patient at what might be seen fosters a mutual receptivity in the work field between us, which allows both of us to say and hear much more of each other's view than had been possible when my declamatory style put me in the role of arbiter. I do not wish to suggest that this mode invariably surmounts all obstacles. What it does is reduce unnecessary burdens of my shaping that make it harder for the patient and me to do our work; and it allows access to content that neither of us could have anticipated.

Working in this fashion tends to open us to active self-inquiry. Attending seriously to observations from the patient about our ways of relating continually challenges us to observe and inquire into our motives for what we do. Both the wish to influence and the wish not to do so become highlighted as constant tensions.

As one small instance: often in the past, after I had spoken with what I thought had been commendable objectivity, the patient would tell me that I sounded flat and disinterested, even dead. In retrospect, or in subsequent listening, I, too, could detect these qualities that sounded alien to what I was actually feeling. Conversely, I could hear at times in my voice an earnestness and declarative insistence when I felt I was just trying to say things as clearly as I could, and with no awareness of a need to persuade. Frequently, I would relate both these styles to my fear that the patient would repudiate what I was about to say, as though my behavior were provoked by the patient.

But there proved to be more to it. I caught surges of irritation when my patient reduced my best ideas to chopped liver. I would press my point, say it more persuasively. What this was about fell into focus when I stumbled upon fresh memories having to do with groping in a childhood world fogged with astigmatism. I came upon old shame over being proved wrong in my speaking of what I was only vaguely seeing. And how I took refuge in the world of books where there were fine words to go with the story images I could see more clearly in my imagination. Awareness of fresh aspects of this old history and reworking of its miseries allowed me to become more comfortable in having my words repudiated. But more important, I could now listen more receptively to what lay in the patient's refutations. The patient's "yes, but . . ." along with the emendations and alternatives that might follow, struck me far less as resistance and more as the inherent tensions inevitable to intense collaborative effort.

The seeking mode requires that we school ourselves to enter the patient's view and remain there for much of the work; that we become accustomed to being in a perceptual state that is not our own. It is then that we most experience a topsy-turvy unsettling that comes with renouncing our own familiar outlook. Awash in fogs of ambiguity, we yearn to claim the guide and gleam of our own knowing.

But if we can remain steady, we are open to the surprise of fresh seeing, once we "get it." I have put this last in quotes, for this is how I hear myself and others speak laconically of the affective richness that lies in finally grasping what the patient and analyst have been groping for. When the getting is achieved, it carries the excitement of our having grasped an authentic aspect of the patient's experience.

Here is a case sampling whose details may speak for the approach I have just sketched.

Clinical Vignette: Mr. Q

Mr. Q and I had begun our work in the early eighties when I was finding my way into these modes of intervening. A successful businessman then in his mid-forties and unmarried, he sought relief from low-level depression, fluctuating self-esteem, and inability to take pleasure from his work, or to find comfort in his relationships with either sex.

He came to the analytic work with the unstated wish that I would ignore his homosexual cruising as holding no significance for his preferred stance as an urbane and exemplary gentleman. For a long time his impeccable behavior toward me conveyed only a hint of the insistence behind his politeness, an insistence that I see him so, and accept him as such. I felt no particular sense of this initially, and found his good manners an easement to our getting the analysis under way. From his side he found my usual courtesies sufficient for his initial expectations and he was able to settle in.

This most mundane interaction, early on between us, could on its surface seem devoid of significant desire or need to influence, on the part of either of us. Instead, of course, it was loaded with concerns and expectancies, positive and negative, for both of us.

From my side I was interested in engaging Mr. Q as effectively as I knew how, for myriad reasons, many of which were not specific to this individual about whom I yet knew so little. My new patient, as he only later told me, was minutely assessing my every move, reassured enough by what he saw to allow him to overcome his anxious readiness to quit had my reception been otherwise. In a very essential way, each of us had persuaded or at least influenced the other to feel that we could find it worthwhile to keep going.

He casually noted that he dated various women with some pleasurable arousal, rarely attempting more than genital fondling. He preferred the anonymity and quick relief of men's room sex with strangers, and was emotionally close to no one. His offhandedness barely concealed his bravado and wariness in this early disclosure of his bisexuality. It took several years of analysis to get into the chronic bleakness of his early years, and to learn a little of how he had developed his façade of outward compliance and niceness.

Mr. Q was the fifth son in a family that already had the first son they wanted but kept gambling for the daughter of their dreams. She arrived on the scene when he was barely two. He felt that his mother had little regard for him thereafter, despite his best efforts to be a good little boy who adored his little sister. The nature of their failed relationship was captured in a screen memory recounted affectlessly in the first year of our work. Mother, as she fed little sister at her breast, ridiculed him before his brothers for having tugged at her blouse, begging to be allowed to nurse.

It took several years to piece together how he had pulled back into himself in pain and rage over such slights while still a preschool child, squelching his anger and outward show of aggression to the extent that he could only rarely feel his rage, or sexual and tender feelings. For a very long time, when he allowed me to see a glimpse of these he would abruptly cut them off with a slicing gesture of his left hand across his mid-abdomen, describe them as residing near his genitals but now outside his awareness.

He surveyed his world with cold vigilance and opaque eyes, just as he had kept score of where his parents bestowed their preferences. For almost a year I was unaware of this, for he smiled readily in greeting and leaving and was dutifully still on the couch. Not until we became engaged in the struggles that I will now describe did I become acquainted with the cold remoteness of his unblinking stare.

As he began to speak a bit more about his sexual preoccupations he would at times suddenly spin upward to a sitting position, to glare at me with slitted eyes for the rest of the session. He was anxious to observe my face, see what really was there, for he could not trust my voice; he had to be sure that I was not about to do something bad to him. I found early on that any pressure, however gently expressed, to have him resume lying down or to tell what he was experiencing led only to even more malevolent grimaces and spit-flying, gasping rage. These episodes would slowly subside into dulled states that he dismissed as devoid of content as were the "fits" like these, fits that he recalled having had since his preschool years. His behavior was such that I wondered for awhile about a low level temporal lobe dysfunction.

Gradually, he began to reveal fragments of what was going on in his mind during his spells and their sequelae.

He felt utterly like a small child, helpless and overwhelmed by bits and pieces of memories of endless guerrilla warfare with both parents around two major issues. He rejected the possibility that these recollections might now be stirred by the quieter battles in which we were engaged.

With his mother it had been a power struggle around his bouts of constipation, spoken of and played out now with me in his masterful hinting at and withholding of any emotional significance. It took much labor before he could call forth from behind his great divide the hot defiance that went with flatly recalled occasions when he was repeatedly enticed into mother's reach with promises of food treats that included Exlax, and snugglings that grabbed him. Once captured, he was swiftly given an enema by mother and the maid.

Mr. Q had turned to his reserved and chronically overworked father, first flirting for attention like his little sister, until father's shaming stopped him. Then he strained to be macho, like big brother Ben, to garner some leftovers from food and attention lavished on eldest brother and the rest. He imitated Ben, but made not a dent. He attempted sex as best he could as a four-year-old, in the fashion of his brothers, and with the same neighbor girl of their age and choice. They got away with it, perhaps even chuckled over by dad. He was caught by his mother and turned over to his father for repeated thrashings.

In these same years Mr. Q shadowed his next older brother by day, and snuggled close to him at night, sharing a bed until well into their adolescence. As adults they became distanced, yet Mr. Q clung with gratitude and muted yearning to memories of those times with his brother, his only times of physical closeness and at least casual acceptance into the family.

I will tease out only a few strands of persisting dynamic themes that tell of struggles between us as the above story took shape.

A most conspicuous repetition centered in Mr. Q's becoming excitedly absorbed in an idea or word from me that he felt to be a beacon that "lit things up" for him, a key that opened a sense of understanding and filled him with relief. Yet, in beginning the next hour, he would revert to his stolid reserve, speak of having resumed his familiar "auto-pilot" detachment, and show only vague sadness at having thought no more about the previous hour. What had been good had now turned bad.

In one telling instance: I had reflected aloud upon a need I sensed in him for comforting, a need he seemed to have come to feel ashamed of; and my sense of his yearning for "shame-free comfort." He responded animatedly, repeating the phrase while alluding to the pleasure he could feel in allowing himself to imagine being fed and comforted now. There was a quality of expectant excitement in his manner. He spoke in general terms of how different this was from the old grudging giving and having to settle for less as a child. I asked if he were having any specific images or memories as he talked. None, he reported flatly. He was aware of "feeling just like that little boy right now," but he was unable to go further. He left speaking of his pleasure with what had been amplified in the hour, and declared his determination to "stay with it" over the weekend break.

The following Monday he glumly reported that he had done nothing on his own and now had only flat recall of the "shame-free comfort" theme. The magic of it was gone. He was sure it was like the ways he had gone dead as a child when he came sadly to the conviction that there was no good place for him in the family once his sister had arrived. He was wistful about having lost touch with the good feelings of last Friday's hour.

Sustaining the more actively inquiring mode that I had begun to explore, I remarked on his glumness; he grunted acknowledgment. Then I asked if there had been anything in our working last Friday that had bothered him. I had found that raising such a question in this fashion, after first seeking a shared perception of his emotional state, was a sequence that had begun to induce between us a feeling, however tentative, of working together. After first demurring, Mr. Q grudgingly revealed that my asking for specific detail had taken over and broken into his sheer enjoyment of how good he was feeling. He had felt mild irritation that I was asking for more, was not satisfied with what he was producing. Sensing a resemblance here to old issues between patient and both parents around not being able to engage or be pleasing to them, I was tempted to speak of this old tension now made real with me, or to ask him to expand on what he had just told me.

Luckily, a touch of analytic tact kept me from the request for more. I held back from pointing to the historical connection, out of a conviction that I could not be sure of the validity of what I saw as a pattern. I had best stick to speaking about what I right now knew with and through him: that he was glum. I wondered if his glumness had to do with his still being irritated?

Mr. Q visibly relaxed just a little, told me plaintively that he had wanted me just to be there as he reveled; silent probably, or maybe letting him know, somehow, that I knew how he felt. But then (his voice became crisp and declamatory as it had been when he was leaving on Friday), he should know better. Why would anything ever be different! I spoke of my regret that I had hurt and disappointed him on Friday, in my behaving in the way that he had described. And perhaps he had felt no certainty that I would even know how I had hurt him? Mr. Q fell into open-mouthed gasping and near-choking for more than a minute as he groped for words. He pulled himself together to point out in coldly objective tones that he had by now told me clearly enough how it was between him and his family. He never had been able to make a dent and was long through with the pain of trying. He hoped it might be different with me, and sometimes it was. But nothing that was good between him and others ever lasted.

My apology, which clearly had a powerful effect upon Mr. Q, can be viewed variously. I would at one time have thought of it as most unanalytic. But my experiences with such honestly felt and expressed regret had shown me how, for both parties, such an acknowledgment can be a really corrective emotional experience, often more fruitful to further analytic work than some of my more objectifying efforts had been (McLaughlin, 1992).

One consequence of my apology was to set in motion innumerable enactments of this "it was once good, but now it's gone" theme. We came upon seemingly endless ways in which I had let him down by not responding to his unvoiced wishes; and now needed to do reparative work of the sort just described. Some were linked to the old struggles of autonomy versus submission to mother, as when Mr. Q went through a week of bland flatness and withdrawal. He finally let me know that I had shown too much enthusiasm over a hard-won insight that he had come upon. I had robbed him of his personal triumph over something that should have been his alone to enjoy. He by now could speak more clearly, and I could grasp more clearly how I had deprived him; so it was easy and right for me to acknowledge my affronting him through my failure to sense his needs.

As we worked in this seeking fashion through many variations, I had a growing sense that a kind of retribution was being exacted. What my apology had set in motion, what I elected to live out rather than to bring to his attention at the time, seemed a kind of righting of old wrongs that had to run its course. This extended enactment of my compliance with the patient's wishes can rightly be seen as a surrender of my authoritative stance of analytic abstinence. Yet it served as a positive force in the progress of the analysis at this point, which later we could look back upon and explore for its manifold and shifting transference meanings.

Mr. Q clearly began to show more comfort in experiencing, in small and shaky increments, first rage and disappointment, then strongly positive emotions around dependency and yearning, and to falter his way to their quite articulate and detailed expression. His stretches of alienation and withdrawal gradually shortened from weeks, even months, to days and even to recovery during the same hour.

Now he could find words for the inexpressible state that had left him literally gasping for words a year earlier. He told me how his shock that Monday had been triggered by my semi-apology for what I had done to deprive him of his pleasure the previous Friday. This was an experience totally new and unsettling. No one in his family, his parents especially, ever had admitted being at fault or doing any wrong to him. He was accustomed to being the one to be blamed. He had no way to handle the contradictory feelings of anxious hate and gratitude set off by my response.

A second dynamic issue, even more obviously loaded with matters of authority and influence, was played out in concurrence with the above. This involved the continuing vicissitudes of Mr. Q's sexual encounters in men's rooms. When we began our work, these brief, anonymous fellating and mutual masturbatory transactions were the highlight of his sexual contacts. They supplemented his own busy masturbation, accompanied by barely acknowledged fantasies of nonpenetrative mutual genital touching with others of either sex.

Mr. Q's shame and defiance when he began to acquaint me with these matters had been extreme. It took more than a year before he told me that my lack of apparent rejection of him, and particularly my accepting his parting handshake, had allowed him some hope that I would not find him disgusting and untouchable. Over the ensuing years he had been alert for indications that I was scornful of him and really wanted him to commit himself to heterosexuality.

I truly could remain comfortable with these continuing and ego-syntonic behaviors, until the threat of AIDS became a Pittsburgh reality. Mr. Q, who maintained a bland detachment toward his acting out as part of his habitual façade of nonchalance, seemed oblivious to the risks of oral sex.

And so we entered into a prolonged, quiet tension prompted by my questioning him in a physicianly fashion regarding his awareness of the risks he faced. He quickly informed me that he, of course, knew far more than I about the matter; and he would take precautions when he felt the need to do so.

Mr. Q increased both his cruising and his forays into dating women. Professing to find petting with women far more exciting than sex with men, he went through a succession of brief and ill-fated affairs with ill-chosen women. As each encounter with waif or predator left him burdened or depleted, he made it wordlessly evident that these were the expectable results of my interfering ways, even as he disclaimed any connection.

During these misadventures he dropped details about his intensified homosexual encounters, such as allusions to bleeding gums or cracked lips. I felt some tug to intervene or counsel, which I tried not to convey. But I am sure that I became more active in looking for clues that might strengthen my efforts to help him see the provoking and reproachful vengefulness toward me that I felt his behaviors conveyed.

My stumbling efforts to recover the quest for the feel and texture of his viewpoint led initially to a minimal acknowledgment by Mr. Q that I had bothered him with my unnecessary questions about his handling of his AIDS precautions. Then came his rage over his conviction that I was indeed trying to manipulate him into giving up the sexual behaviors that had become his enduring defense against the risks of intimacy with either sex.

In these recurring enactments between us he/we came upon the details of the layering of true and false selves made familiar to us by Winnicott (1960), Modell (1990), and others. Mr. Q's façade of docile compliance and painfully perfected social skills hid, even from himself, the rage and contempt with which by the age of four he regarded the world. He came to share my deep respect for the adaptive and protective capacities his detachment and avoidance of feeling had provided him, especially during his developing years when they served to secure his dogged efforts to cling to a masculine identity and core sense of self.

I would like to close this clinical vignette with excerpts from two hours of the last year of our work, consecutive hours with a five-day break between them occasioned by one of Mr. Q's frequent business trips. The quoted material is as close to verbatim as I could excerpt.

In the hour preceding the break he had dwelt with enthusiasm upon his increasing grasp of "my basic self, my gutsy kid-self that would never give in, even if it meant I had to hide all of my life. I love him! He's real, and he's mine! He's me!" His voice dropped in vigor and insistence. "Even as I say this I'm fading, losing hold."

ANALYST: Such strength and conviction in your voice as you held him, and now sound sad and weak and giving him up?
PATIENT: [sits up halfway as he replies] Are you putting me on? You know we've just again been talking about how saying anything I really mean means I give it up. It's not mine. It's yours. It's nothing! [sinks back onto the couch] But I know that's not really so, I could hear your voice. No teasing in it. I *will* hold onto this base self regardless! [pause of several moments] This is harder to say, to stick with. When I feel this me that seems real I'm also feeling something about you that feels real. I'd like to say it feels good. But that would mean giving you something. And I can't give anything that's real, that's worthwhile. Something goes wrong. [patient sounds perplexed, heavy]
ANALYST: It's something more than turning good stuff over to me?
PATIENT: Yeah, but I don't think of words for it; don't want to. Makes me think of some stuff you were going on about awhile back. When I was talking about how good it felt between Little Ben [patient's lovable young nephew] and me. You said something about the generosity of loving back. I didn't get it. I know it's time to go now. I'm going to try to hold onto this base feeling. *That* I feel I'm getting!

Mr. Q bustled into the next hour, quick to inform me that "I've held onto me all this time. Now I can tell you I wasn't giving it to you quite straight. Underneath that base me is the *real* me." [Here his voice becomes deeper, almost raspy.] "I've hated and despised everyone most of my life, like that was the only way I knew to feel, to stay safe, to not care. Like I'm hating you right now!"

ANALYST: Your voice sounds heavy, harsh; this is your hatred now?
PATIENT: I have to hate you! Yet I keep telling you, without really telling you, that it is only in here, with you, that I can really feel this real me. Why must I hate you? Is that all I am? I know by now you don't hate me, don't despise me like I've

done to you. [patient is here on the verge of rare tears] I'm remembering something you said to me, said years ago. About how you kept getting glimpses of a real person in me that I had to keep hiding. I thought you were nuts, or kidding. But I thought I heard feeling in your voice, maybe sadness. I think I felt love for you for that. I know I wanted to reach out and hug you. But you'd have seen that as my homosexual stuff. I've been letting you know long enough how angry I have been that you told me you couldn't let me have sex with you; how that was your problem, not mine. But it's made me want to withhold everything from you.

ANALYST: That's still the way it stands?

PATIENT: No, that's changing, too. I can feel you've had a lot of caring for me, respect me. And say! I think I've got it, about that generosity of loving back. I *have* felt it with Ben. I'm feeling it now with you. That my loving you for your loving me makes me feel I do have something good to give back! It feels safe here. Will it be safe out there? I've been slow to get there, but I'm going to give it my best try! [the hour is ending and Mr. Q about to rise]

ANALYST: I'm proud for you!

He suddenly hugs me as he passes, and I return his hug. There were two more such brief hugs by the time the work ended. We did considerable analytic work upon them, after the fact.

Hours like these marked the progress he was able to make in the latter half of the work. He gave up his cruising to enter into a sequence of intermittent yet satisfyingly intimate affairs in other cities with men of his own caliber. In our hometown he sought and sustained in sequence two fully sexual and coitally satisfying relations with women able to afford him a compatible long-term relationship. Transference resonances were evident in all of these, eventually openly admitted and worked upon.

But he could not bring himself to make permanent ties to either a man or a woman during the time of our work. He has occasionally checked in with me to report his continuing enjoyment of his noncommitted bisexuality in relationships that tend to be mutually gratifying, until a partner presses too insistently for an acknowledged commitment. Then he moves on.

DISCUSSION

To what extent do these clinical sequences demonstrate what I have described about my mode of working? What vicissitudes of power and influence are to be seen?

I see this mode as striving to help Mr. Q locate and authenticate his individual ways of seeing and experiencing his world, to find affirmation of being believed in his fundamental perceptions. Mr. Q had had precious little of this beyond infancy. He warily repudiated such affirmation in his adult social relationships. The supportive and releasing power of being perceived and believed, recurring in myriad configurations, evoked in my patient sufficient trust in how and why I work, and growing confidence in his own capacities to see what he had before striven not to see. Then, gradually, he could reveal, to himself as well as to me, his hidden self, whose surges of love and rage both delighted and frightened him, and also find value in the highly adaptive social abilities of his façade self that he previously scorned for its shameful submission to those he hated and needed.

And, as his own words say clearly enough, when he could trust me enough to feel loved and believed in, he found in himself capacities to trust and claim his own positive as well as negative feelings toward himself and others.

I see the changes in Mr. Q as reflecting the effectiveness of my basing my efforts to work in the softer dimensions of influence quietly asserted. Without these easements, I doubt that we could have achieved a productive working alliance. Yet it is evident enough that I was often pressing him to attend to something, even if it were a shift of affect, or nonverbal accompaniment, or his own viewpoint about which I hoped to learn more. Even my most tentatively offered subjective responses could not remain free of some nudge of directing imposed by me/perceived by him.

Of such pointings I would say that at their best they directed his attention to some behavior or topic which might serve him as a clue to an emotionally significant concern outside his awareness. This I see as helping him with the "how" of his analytic search, *relatively* unweighted of authoritative pressure for him to accept any "why" explanation of mine.

In this renunciation of knowing why lies what has been a significant shift in my analytic position. I still can see, beneath the manifest concerns that are the patient's "surface," many possible motives and dynamic configurations that my experience and lore have sensitized me to expect. These surmisings are inevitably there in me, as cumulative shapings comprising my transference expectancies, my reality view. I would not wish to be without the richness of context with which they inform my view.

Yet I find that these premises have little of the appeal they formerly had when I presumed that it was my task to provide authoritative answers that would direct the patient away from his or her erroneous and infantile perspective. I have some confidence that this old stance, in my use, too often invalidated the patient's view, and left him or her without this core sense of being believed.

My conviction about this, and my preference for the more subordinated analytic stance somehow convey to the patient the dynamic actuality of my third postulate about influence; i.e., that it is the belief of the one that his or her behaviors are the reason and occasion for the actions of the other.

With Mr. Q, my expressing the idea that I might have done something to make for tensions between us initially repelled him, made him wary and anxious. That I might act from the position of having been wrong was utterly foreign to his experience. It was he who glumly assumed himself to be the reason for the indifference of his family. So I might just be ensnaring him with sweet talk. Played out over time, my stance powerfully influenced basic aspects of his reality view, among these his coming to feel that his fierce defensiveness and bland façade were acceptable but no longer needed.

When my concern for the potential self-destructiveness of his homosexual cruising led me to press him, I fed into his fears that I was attempting to interfere with or proscribe his sexual activities. This realized and brought to the fore his transference expectancies based in the shaming and disciplining of him by father. Eventually, from this heat there emerged his awareness of a different and positive side which he could feel in my concern: that I was not indifferent to him, nor disgustedly turning away from him as had been his father.

Each of us was steadily monitoring our impact upon the other. So long as the patient found convincing clues that I was indeed secretly intent on having him stop his cruising, he felt driven to even more risky and provocatively described encounters in rebellious counterforce. In turn I could not sustain the detached neutrality that to me would have been akin to true indifference.

Our show of force was fed on both sides by the second tendency noted above: a conviction that the behavior of one was a necessary response to the actions of the other. I believed that the counterforce of my urging was required by the liabilities of Mr. Q's insistent behaviors, while he felt himself to be rebelling as a necessary counter to my proscriptive pressure.

What eased this circular reaction was first our recognizing his fear that I was covertly intent on rejecting him for good. He then made it clear that my dissembling was driving him to anxious rebellion. I should be out in the open where he would know what to do. Acknowledging that I could see his point, and could see how I was making difficult matters more hurtful for him, I was able then to speak about the dilemma of my wish to urge him to do the sensible thing, countered by my concern for his need for autonomy.

In our collaborative effort to clarify these dynamic issues can be seen the interworking of both the second and third tendencies.

The second: that one assumes one is responding to the behavior of the other, is manifest both in Mr. Q's conviction that my intrusion had triggered his defiance, and in my accounting for my intervening as a response to his risky cruising.

The emergence of the third tendency: that one believes one's behaviors to have incited the behaviors of the other, came (implicitly) into focus as the result of close and shared exploratory work between us around this second tendency. Mr. Q could openly challenge me directly about my attempting to dissemble my critical concern over his risky cruising. He was right, and my acceptance became an endorsement of the logic of his viewpoint. This third tendency became explicit with my acknowledging his view that my behavior was a provocation for his actions. His responses to this were striking, positive, and eventually analyzable. Quite important was that these led eventually to his self-reflections upon how *his* provocations had provoked *my* countering behaviors, then to see how his old expectations had led him to try to provoke the very rejection that he so feared.

This particular exchange around the acknowledgment of mutual influence marked the beginning of Mr. Q's relinquishing the cruising and of his addressing more directly the nature of his bisexual yearnings toward me.

I have come to feel that the recognition and acknowledgment of the workings of this third tendency, expressed either by the analyst or patient—and eventually by both—denotes the context in which moments and periods of deeply analytic work can be collaboratively engaged in. Such mutual recognition of influencing and being influenced provides vantage points rich in empathic potential. From these, one or both in the dyad can look at the interplay between them, at the part each has played in creating the happening, and at the very personal, inner expectancies of hope and fear that each has brought to bear in influencing what transpires.

I am convinced that these mutative happenings are central to the best analytic work that each of us does, in whatever individual style and mode may be our preference.

The struggle entailed for the analyst in my preferred mode

can be looked upon as the analyst's applying his or her separate and different mind and self to seek and provide information about the uniqueness of that other mind and self, to the goal that both may gain understanding, primarily of the patient yet inevitably of both.

I stress here the working of two separate minds in order to make clear that the central focus upon the patient's reality view does not mean the seeking of unbroken agreement and oneness in the dyad. It does not call for the abnegation of the analyst's use of his or her professional capacities and views, but rather the active redeployment of these in the particular ways I have tried to convey.

What is sought is a more subtle and endlessly negotiated seeking for a shared understanding of the patient's view, a mode of influence made acceptable and reliable through prolonged testing and validation.

In closing, I want to emphasize once more the potential for mutative analytic progress that lies in the working through of the experiences of mutual influence in this manner. Over time and bit by bit, the significance and value that both parties find in the words and actions of the other, the power and meaning of one for the other, the trust and belief in what is discovered between self and other, become experienced, articulated, and assimilated.

Putting the matter thusly suddenly brings to the fore the realization of a clinical observation alive in the background of my experience for now many years. The words of appreciation I have heard from my patients in their taking leave, like the parting words of their patients my colleagues have told me about, spoke very little or not at all of the analyst's towering intellect or analytic prowess. Instead semi-articulate phrases allude to small analytic happenings, still resonant in these patients, that provided core perceptions of their having felt stood by, their pain and joy recognized, their personal value affirmed, something essential in them believed.

Much of this close attention to the patient's view of reality truly addresses small matters. But, singly and cumulatively, their exploration amasses a moving force in the working dyad. It is a force that has been built up through the patient's trust in and acceptance of the analyst's influence. Won in this manner, the analyst's optimal influence can indeed find its mode and basis well approximated in those dictionary words now a half-century old: "the quiet, insensible, or gradual exertion of power, often arising from strength of intellect, force of character, eminent position. . . ."

REFERENCES

BERNFELD S. (1941). The facts of observation in psychoanalysis. *J. Psychol.*, 12:289-305. Reprinted in *Int. Rev. Psychoanal.*, 1985, 12:342-351.
BRAZELTON, T. B. (1982). Joint regulation of neonate-parent behavior. In *Social Interchange in Infancy*, ed. E. Tronick. Baltimore: Univ. Park Press, pp. 137-154.
COOPER, S. H. (1993). Interpretive fallibility and the psychoanalytic dialogue. *J. Amer. Psychoanal. Assn.*, 41:95-126.
EMDE, R. N. (1988). Development terminable and interminable. I. Innate and motivational factors from infancy. *Int. J. Psychoanal.*, 69:23-42.
FREUD, S. (1892-1893). A case of successful treatment by hypnotism. *S.E.*, 1.
——— (1905). Fragment of an analysis of a case of hysteria. *S.E.*, 7.
——— (1910). The antithetical meaning of primal words. *S.E.*, 11.
——— (1911). The handling of dream-interpretation in psycho-analysis. *S.E.*, 12.
——— (1912). The dynamics of transference. *S.E.*, 12.
——— (1915). Observations on transference-love. (Further recommendations on the technique of psycho-analysis III.) *S.E.*, 12.
GILL, M. M. (1982). *Analysis of Transference, Vol. 1. Theory and Technique.* New York: Int. Univ. Press.
HEGEL, G. W. F. (1821). *The Philosophy of Right.* Britannica Great Books, Vol. 46, ed. R. M. Hutchins. Chicago/London: Encyclop. Britannica, 1952.
MCLAUGHLIN, J. T. (1978). Primary and secondary process in the context of cerebral hemispheric specialization. *Psychoanal. Q.*, 47:237-266.
——— (1981). Transference, psychic reality, and countertransference. *Psychoanal. Q.*, 50:639-664.
——— (1989). Relevance for the understanding of adult patients' non-verbal behaviors. In *The Significance of Infant Observational Research for Clinical Work with Children, Adolescents, and Adults*, ed. S. Dowling & A. Rothstein. Madison, CT: Int. Univ. Press, pp. 109-122.
——— (1992). Nonverbal behavior in the analytic situation: the search for meaning in nonverbal cues. In *When the Body Speaks. Psychological Meanings in Kinetic Cues*, ed. S. Kramer & S. Akhtar. Northvale, NJ/London: Aronson, pp. 131-162.

MODELL, A. H. (1990). *Other Times, Other Realities. Toward a Theory of Psychoanalytic Treatment*. Cambridge, MA/London: Harvard Univ. Press.

SAMPSON, H. & WEISS, J. (1986). *The Psychoanalytic Process: Theory, Clinical Observation, and Empirical Research*. New York: Guilford.

SCHAFER, R. (1983). *The Analytic Attitude*. New York: Basic Books.

SCHWABER, E. (1983). Psychoanalytic listening and psychic reality. *Int. Rev. Psychoanal.*, 10:379-392.

——— (1986). Reconstruction and perceptual experience: further thoughts on psychoanalytic listening. *J. Amer. Psychoanal. Assn.*, 34:911-932.

——— (1990). Interpretation and the therapeutic action of psychoanalysis. *Int. J. Psychoanal.*, 71:229-240.

SMITH, H. F. (1990). Cues: the perceptual edge of the transference. *Int. J. Psychoanal.*, 71:219-228.

STERN, D. N. (1985). *The Interpersonal World of the Infant. A View from Psychoanalysis and Developmental Psychology*. New York: Basic Books.

Webster's New International Dictionary of the English Language. Second Edition. Unabridged. Springfield, MA: Merriam Co., 1959.

WEGNER, D. (1994). Ironic processes of mental control. *Psychol. Rev.*, 101:34-52.

WHITEHEAD, A. N. (1949). *Adventures of Ideas*. New York: Macmillan.

WINNICOTT, D. W. (1960). Ego distortion in terms of true and false self. In *The Maturational Process and the Facilitating Environment*. New York: Int. Univ. Press, 1965, Chapter 12.

10

Authority, Evidence, and Knowledge in the Psychoanalytic Relationship

AUTHORITY, EVIDENCE, AND KNOWLEDGE IN THE PSYCHOANALYTIC RELATIONSHIP

BY ROY SCHAFER, PH.D.

INTRODUCTION

This discussion traces the complex interplay of transference and countertransference in the clinical construction of evidence and knowledge and the establishing of *analytic* authority in the psychoanalytic relationship. Both participants are variably reliable sources of evidence on their own subjective experiences and on those of the other. By reliable demonstrations of understanding, responsibility, capacity for containment, openness, and flexibility, the analyst not only earns analytic authority but contributes to the analysand's development toward authority in co-authoring the analysis. The discussion closes with comments on the epistemological controversy concerning evidence and truth within a perspective that is narrativistic and pluralistic.

Who Is To Be Believed?

Complex transference-countertransference processes play major roles in determining the availability, communication, and consequences of clinical psychoanalytic evidence. To a large extent, these processes decide which evidence will be regarded as convincing and why that is so. Consequently, it can only be the slow, arduous analysis of transference and countertransference that will lead the co-participants to durable, rational, and useful agreements on evidential matters. The alternatives are confu-

sion, controversy, or the analysand's submissive compliance—
though sometimes, in subtle ways, it is the analyst's submissive
compliance with the analysand. In these instances of compliance
we deal not so much with knowledge as with new compromise
formations based on distributions of power that can fall outside
the analytic frame.

Often, analysts unreflectively package their role in these re-
distributions of power in claims of invariably superior psychological understanding and clinical experience. On their part,
analysands often claim that they are the final authorities on
their own subjectivities: after all, they assert, who can know
better than they what they think, feel, wish, and intend? As a
rule, it is exceptionally difficult for both participants to sort out
what is legitimate and what is illegitimate in these controversial
claims, or, if legitimacy is not the issue, then it is difficult to sort
out what will be most useful to reflect on at the moment. This
difficulty exists in part because, in the heat of emotion, there can
be no guarantee that even the best-grounded assertions will be
accepted by the other participant, or, if accepted, be used to
move ahead. For example, an analysand may use potentially
liberating insight into a difficult-to-accept unconscious motive to
reinforce habitual self-recrimination. In another instance, an
analysand may use the analyst's help in achieving an integrative
insight to reinforce an existing counterproductive idealization
of the analyst. On the analyst's part, he or she may use stabiliz-
ing insight into a countertransference enactment only to retal-
iate against the enactment-provoking analysand.

Thus, the questions concerning knowledge that it might be
best to address are these: On each occasion, who is to be believed
and why? And what are the consequences of doing so? In analysis, much time and effort are spent on these questions, although they may be put in other terms entirely. At their best,
analysts do not stint in this regard and do not regret that necessary expenditure of time and effort, for they understand that
fundamentally they are then engaged in analytic work of the
utmost importance.

Authoritative Rhetoric

In order to develop the points I have just made, I shall have to bypass other significant areas of potential confusion and controversy: the roles of authority, evidence, and knowledge in analysts' discussions with each other orally and in their writings and readings, and, relatedly, what they use in their teachings. I believe, however, that so much of what can be said about the clinical relationship applies as well to these other areas of psychoanalytic discourse—transference and countertransference being ubiquitous—that it should not prove difficult to extrapolate to those areas any conclusions reached here about the clinical dialogue.

It would, however, be wrong to leave only to extrapolation a few observations about confusing rhetoric that I should like to mention before moving ahead. How commonly we encounter in all forms of professional discourse such locutions as "Freud himself said . . . ," "As I have repeatedly emphasized . . . ," "Everyone knows that . . . ," and "In fact . . . ," none of which constitutes adequate support for any new theses being put forward. Citation alone never guarantees new knowledge. In addition, there are all those frequently used really's only's, obviously's, certainly's, clearly's, always's, and never's that, most of the time and until proved otherwise, are best taken as warning signs that a speaker or writer feels on thin ice and may be reassuringly encouraging a suspension of critical listening or reading in favor of an idealizing transference, a masochistic surrender, or a yielding to affiliative needs. The reassurance may be mostly self-directed in order to retain courage while developing a new point of view. Freud was a master of these rhetorical ploys, and while many of them paid off in the long run, some have created lasting problems in the realm of psychoanalytic knowledge.

These brief comments on rhetoric belong here, in my opinion, because the analyst's sense of authority in clinical work often derives in significant measure from all these other non-clinical engagements in psychoanalytic discourse. Consequently, we cannot afford to look into authority, evidence, and knowledge in the psychoanalytic relationship without at least making some reference to our other discursive ventures and exposures.

Unconscious Fantasy and Reality Testing

When working effectively, analysts steadily maintain a two-sided view of their authority on the matter of evidence in the analytic process itself. On the one hand, they must assume that, ultimately, they bear the responsibility that comes with claiming expertise in constructing evidence bearing on unconscious conflicts and fantasy. In this context, they must assume that their patients cannot speak as authoritatively as they; otherwise, they would be forfeiting the right to use the traditional name for what they are practicing, namely, psychoanalysis. Their claim of expertise is grounded in their relative neutrality regarding the constituents of their patients' unconscious conflicts and fantasies, their own didactic and technical education in detecting clues and constructing evidence bearing on disturbing unconscious mental processes, and whatever other qualifications they may have in the realm of personal sensitivity, experience, psychological-mindedness, analytic knowledge of themselves gained through personal analysis and supervision, and scholarship. In trying to understand the human beings in subjective distress with whom they consult, they have prepared minds.

In assuming this role and this responsibility, analysts provisionally take for granted that they can count on some support from their patients. They count on their having retained some capacity to remain aware of, and responsive to, the analysis as a treatment relationship. If this will not be so all the time in a clear and decisive way, then it will be so enough of the time, or it will be recoverable should it get lost during periods of stress; at least, it is a deeply buried potential that will become accessible in due time. Analysts count on this awareness or potential on the basis of their initial assessments of their patients' "ego strength." This is a flexible term that pertains both to more or less convincing evidence in their patients' life histories and to the observations analysts can make during initial interviews that seem to promise a reasonably steady capacity to be realistic, focused, in contact with others, and adaptive even when under stress—or, if not quite that, as in some so-called borderline conditions, then the availability of some sizable fragments of this capacity, enough to promise a starting point for a treatment relationship, however tenuous.

Also, when analysts begin their treatments, they assume that in their patients are sufficient glimmers of hope and yearning for something better in their lives to contribute to their siding with the treatment, enough to be able to counteract those frequent and inevitable waves of destructiveness and despair. From this more benign aspect of their orientation there flows from the patients some willingness, however meager, to grant that their analysts are knowledgeable and deserve authority with respect to analytic evidence. The analysts count on their interventions *also* being registered as constructive efforts to understand and help. All will not be seen through a glass darkly.

All of which is on the one hand—the facilitating one. On the other hand—the manifestly hampering one—are a host of considerations. For one thing, analysts have well-grounded expectations that, unconsciously, no patient is altogether ready to grant them the authority I have just described. Unconsciously, patients more or less fear, mistrust, despise, hate, rebel against, and aim to seduce in various ways these figures to whom, consciously, they have turned for help with their problems and whom they may even respect, depend on, and adore. In this regard, analysts anticipate that their patients frequently, perhaps even regularly and for a long time, will take their understanding interventions and evidential claims as confirmations of their (the patients') own worst fears. To judge by their emotional reactions on so many occasions, the patients' own best reality testing and their respect for their analysts' reality testing are frequently overruled by those authorities in the inner world which we have traditionally designated as superego, ego ideal, hostile introjects, ego defenses, self-destructiveness, and dominant fixations on narcissistic and omnipotent infantile wishes.

For example, those analysts who act in a kindly manner may well be regarded in very large part as feeling guilty, frightened of aggression (their own, their patients', or both), frightened of madness (their own, their patients', or both), or acting under their patients' omnipotent control. When analysts feel that threatened or controlled, it becomes "understandable" that they feel compelled to offer their patients support through reassurance. Or it may be supposed that these analysts are being kindly because they are dependent on their patients' affection, duped by their patients' defensive misrepresentations, are stupid dolts, or something else of a disqualifying nature. Likewise, those analysts who adhere firmly to a disciplined, judicious analytic mode of work may well be regarded as showing indifference, rigidity, or sadism, while those who maintain a somewhat informal manner may be taken to be seductive and to encourage acting out. And if, in their expertise, these analysts recognize the signs of these latent reactions and interpret them, they are likely to find that, at least initially, their patients will take any such follow-through as proving only how dogmatic, defensive, relentless, or overexcited their analysts are. Furthermore, their analysts' careful marshaling of evidence, when conveyed to the patients, may well be taken as betraying either a prosecutorial attitude or a good deal of insecurity.

In these ways analysts are often made to feel up against a closed system. Patients may sugarcoat these adverse and aversive reactions with shows of compliance and gratitude. But even the patients' sincere, rational agreement may be limited to conscious attitudes. It is not at all rare, however, that instead of sugarcoating, all these negative responses are shown openly, even triumphantly, and in a way that puts the patients in the role of prosecutor.

Still on the manifestly difficult second hand, the problems may take other forms. The reactions to the style and the content of the analyst's interventions may not be adverse or aversive in the ways I have just described. For example, a patient may idealize or romanticize the analytic relationship, in which case he or she may take a kindly manner as an artificially (technically) restrained show of love or desire or some other profound attachment of that sort that violates the bounds of analytic decorum. It is not unusual to encounter patients who think of their analysts as naturally warm but artificially confined and even frustrated by their dutiful attempts to observe the rules of "correct" technique. And, again, the patients may take their analysts' further interpretations of this kind of transference fantasy as evidence that supports their own eroticized interpretation of what is going on—for example, merely as instances of defensively protesting too much. Thus, once cast in a positive oedipal-parental role, the analyst will be seen as confirming that fantasy by interpreting ("sexually aggressive") or remaining silent ("anxiously inhibited"). Also, analysts have learned to watch for signs that one major function of these idealizations, romanticizings, and eroticizations is to block the way to analysis of suspicion, fear, guilt, envy, and hatred in the transference.

However it may develop in these respects, the patients' major unconscious fantasies serve to limit or block their accepting in any reliable way that they are in an analytic treatment relationship. For unconscious reasons, they must believe that they are in a predominantly social or familial context or, one step removed from that, in a clandestine affair. They do not believe that interpretation is that and no more. Consequently, the analyst's claims to authority and possession of valid evidence and knowledge remain contestable for a long time.

All of these on-the-other-hand factors are anticipated and, to the extent possible, dealt with patiently by analysts who retain sufficient poise in the stress and strain of the clinical relationship. How they deal with them will vary according to each analyst's individualized version of his or her school of thought, plus his or her best judgment about each patient's readiness for intervention or nonintervention. I emphasize *individualized* versions of schools of thought because it is these versions that determine differential weighting and selective presentation of evidence and differential sensitivity to the varied forms of transference.

It is in analysts' individualities that temporary and lasting characterological countertransferences come into play (Reich, 1951). The analysts' own neurotic and narcissistic countertransferences may intrude. Then they may assume or relinquish authority over evidence inappropriately, or they may misjudge evidence, seeing it when most others of their persuasion would not, or missing it when others would consider it conspicuous. They may decide to emphasize evidence that is of less moment, for example, switching to reconstruction when hints of hostility begin to fill the air. Of the temporary, situational-bound countertransferences, one must say that their inevitability has been recognized as providing important information or reasonable conjectures about undercurrents in the analytic relationship. In the interplay of transference and countertransference those undercurrents may eventuate in mutual enactments of the patient's unconscious fantasies. But no matter whether the countertransference intrusions are characterological and generalized or temporary and situation-bound, they create a huge realm of potential ambiguity and confusion on the matter of authority, evidence, and knowledge in the analytic relationship. It is as important as it is difficult to develop an analysis in which, so far as possible, these various influences can be sorted out. The required self-analysis of countertransference may be helped by scanning earlier dialogue for signs of helpful "supervision" by the patient, followed perhaps by further dialogue to bring the patient's evidence to the surface.

My reference to this "supervision" is meant to emphasize the value of taking into account those aspects of effective reality testing that have been retained by patients. These aspects may yield some very keen perceptions of their analysts' countertransferences. In this respect, patients can be acknowledged authorities on evidence concerning certain aspects of the analytic relationship, thus on what is going on in the room. Those analysts who respect this potential ability will also pay close attention to what their patients do with the fruits of their reality testing of countertransference. Useful analytic evidence may emerge concerning the problems of both participants and how these have shaped the analytic process as a whole. For example, a patient who sees quite a lot may give signs of feeling frightened or too protective of the analyst ever to mention it; and the analyst who picks up those signs is likely to find that they are keys to large areas of conflict involving not only the patient's guilt and persecutory fantasies but also the analyst's tendency to back off from analyzing frankly sexual and hostile features of the transference. The analyst who cannot recognize this protectiveness may have a smooth but unproductive time of it. On a deeper level, however, that analyst will be seen as confirming unconscious fantasies that it is the analyst who is ruthless, fragile, frightened, or under the patient's control.

To summarize the points I have made on this second, ostensibly hampering hand: Analysts must realize that they regularly confront an exceptionally tangled situation. In this tangle, only some of the time is the analyst regarded as a reliable and knowledgeable authority on analytic evidence. Sometimes the patient claims independent authority on evidence pertaining to the analyst's claims, and the claims made some of those times may be realistic and to the point. At other times, the analyst engages in a follow-through effort and uses as further analytic evidence how the patient has constructed evidence about the analyst as abuser or seducer and what the patient has then done with that "evidence" or "knowledge." Sometimes the patient then uses that analytic follow-through to doubly confirm her or his negative or positive views; and there are times when, finally, the patient gets the point and moves ahead, though it may have to be the analyst who first gets the point and then puts it to good use.

In my view, one would have to be an exceedingly dogmatic analyst to insist that this sense of a tangle needlessly complicates an already complex picture of what it is like to do analysis. For myself, I would say that the tangle is even more complex than I have so far described. So much goes on in the analytic dialogue that there is always a need for further and finer sorting out of the variables. Closure must be permanently deferred, even though there are many times when decisiveness of intervention is appropriate and effective.

Earning Respect

For the most part, I have been describing the two parties to the analytic relationship as they are in the early stages of analysis. In terms of absolute time these "early" stages may last for quite a while. I want now to discuss briefly how and why things may change for the better or change in the direction of shared authority and collaboration on matters of evidence—in that direction, because the analytic pair never altogether arrives at that end point in an irreversible way. The "early" stages often return, even if in modified form; their recurrence during termination periods is a phenomenon well known to analysts.

The particular factor I want to emphasize here, however, is the analyst's steadily, if not absolutely continuously, *earning respect* for his or her authority. I mean earning that respect *analytically*. How this comes about is itself a complex question that has stimulated various answers in the literature—far too many and various to be reviewed here. I shall limit myself to mentioning some of the main factors that I think help effect this change. Ideally, each analyst approaches each patient in as individualized a way as possible. To maintain this approach requires not only the prepared mind that I described before, but a capacity on the analyst's part to keep that preparation in the background. Only when it is in the background is ample room left for hunches, novelty, surprise, definition of unfamiliar angles on old problems, and entertaining not-well-understood connections and impressions. This capacity is the analyst's counterpart to the patient's increasing freedom to associate on the couch.

It is not easy to describe or explain the analyst's fluid balance in this regard. Ernst Kris (1952) and his followers have written about a temporary, readily reversible, creative regression in the service of the analyst's ego. Earlier, Freud (1912) had written of the analyst's bending his unconscious to that of the patient with an evenly hovering attention. And Bion (1967) wrote of approaching each patient without memory or desire. Although I do not believe that any of these ways of putting it stands up well when subjected to close conceptual scrutiny and careful introspection of how one changes while at work oneself, being descriptively incomplete and too dependent on rhetorical forcefulness, I do credit each with giving some sense of the analyst's flexible-fluid relationship to his or her own preparedness.

Along with this individualization and manifestations of this flexible-fluid position, the analyst earns some respect and authority within the relationship by continuously giving signs of a kind of openness, adventurousness, and curiosity as to both players in the process. I am thinking here of an old story told about Ernst Kris (few analysts, if any, were more knowledgeable than Kris in his time): Between appointments he would sometimes rush into the private rooms of the apartment in which he and his wife practiced, find her, and say in astonishment, "It's true! It's all true!" Frequently, one can sense that very attitude in his stimulating writings. In a more measured way, Betty Joseph (1988) has emphasized that the analyst must always "rediscover" with each patient the soundness of the principles guiding the treatment. This spontaneity in self-awareness shows in the analyst's voice, tempo of intervention, use of language, postural changes, and other nonverbal manifestations, as well as in the analyst's range in being both a reliable noninterventionist container and an animated participant in dialogue.

One can say that analysts establish their credentials by showing repeatedly and reliably that *they are better prepared than their patients to be unprepared.* In effective analyses, the patients, too, slowly begin to give signs of realizing and accepting that that way self-knowledge lies. These changes add to their willingness to trust the analysts as authorities on how to construct therapeutically useful evidence. They also add to patients' desires to become genuine co-authorities and *to feel free to show it*. At this point the patients give signs of knowing that, in the past, they were usually far too anxious, guilty, defensive, omnipotent in fantasy, and envious to have been qualified for this collaborative role. They also acknowledge their continuing, even if now more regulated, susceptibility to regression, and they are better observers of that susceptibility.

The end of it all is not idyllic. Not all conflicts have been fully resolved, not all hardships dissolved, not all mysteries solved, and not all disappointments and dissatisfactions done away with persuasively. The usual great pain involved in leaving a meaningful, beneficial analytic relationship testifies both to the gains that have been made, the continuing influence of conflict in the forever active unconscious mind, and the imperfectibility of any one analyst's analytic work. That the analyst can, in his or her own way, accept this ending without significant disappointment, resentment, shame, or guilt testifies to the kind of respect and individualization that I have emphasized as crucial to the analyst's knowledge of unconscious fantasy and her or his authority regarding evidence in the analytic process.

Last, but not least, there is the analyst's capacity for containing whatever projections emanate from the patient, whether they be persecutory fantasies, guilty suffering, or idealization. "Containing" implies being able to tolerate the patient's use of the analyst as a repository of feelings that are too painful to bear, too fragile to sustain, or too precious to be kept within the turmoil of the patient's inner life. That tolerance will be manifest in a capacity to listen empathically, explore patiently, and defer and dose interpretation until the patient seems ready to take on the challenge of further understanding. Only then, after it has been gently modified by the analyst's understanding, will the patient re-experience as his or her own what has been projected.

The Narrativity of Knowledge

We are left finally with some large, basically epistemological questions concerning knowledge, authority, and evidence. These questions are brought out forcefully by the introduction into psychoanalysis of the narrational point of view—specifically, the narrativity of knowledge (Schafer, 1983, 1992). According to this point of view, the clinical psychoanalytic dialogue is best understood as a series of tellings and retellings by both parties to the dialogue. In addition, the interpretive lines followed by the analyst in his or her interventions and increasingly accepted, assimilated, and used by the analysand may be understood as derived from master narratives. These master narratives make up the so-called general theory and major concepts of the analyst's school of psychoanalytic thought. The analyst's detailed interpretive efforts may then be regarded as story lines that are manifestations of these master narratives.

There are, of course, many different ways to talk about human development and suffering. That this is so within psychoanalysis itself is evidenced by the existence today of a number of different schools of thought (Kleinian, Freudian, Jungian, self psychological, etc.). Each of these schools may be characterized as operating within the horizons of its own master narratives: for example, for the Freudian, the instinctual and the tripartite mental organization, or structural theory, with object relatedness regarded as a developmental attainment; for the Kleinian, the primacy of the object relatedness within this Freudian scheme, etc.

The narrativity of knowledge—its being subject to different tellings—is what is in question in the context of the general topic of authority, evidence, and knowledge. For this point of view has been misunderstood in two important ways, and each of these ways has been used to discredit the narrational conceptualization. The two ways spring, in my view, from a common source.

In one way, exemplified by Spence (1982), psychoanalysis is built on two kinds of truth: narrative truth and historical truth. Narrative truth is the explanatory life story worked out during treatment that has more or less beneficial results, but, owing to its having been arrived at by the extremely approximate and ambiguous method of present-day dialogue in the analyst's office, has no sure truth value. Historical truth is what truly happened, that is to say, the actual facts or events as they would have been recorded by objective observers present at the time of their happening or by mechanical devices; historical truth is the only one with real truth value and is not necessarily congruent with the narrative truth of the treatment itself.

The misunderstanding exemplified by this way of handling the narrativity issue is this: that it assumes an ideal observer who adheres to no point of view at all, has no shaping and selective preconceptions, values, and methods of observation, and so is in a position of total disinterestedness and is invulnerable to critique from any other point of view. Implicitly, this hypothetical observer then speaks with the authority of God to all of us who are now cast in the role of firmly monotheistic believers. This figure is part of the scene even when mechanical recording is involved, because the recording itself has no relevance until examined by this hypothetical observer. The position described has been labeled variously as objectivism, realism, and empiricism. It is the position adopted by the school of logical positivism, a school that is just that—a school, a point of view—and one which, in its most dogmatic form, has lost most of its philosophical following in the present world of critical thought. In the world of psychoanalysis, however, which has in this respect lagged behind the times, the logical-positivist orientation still prevails, each psychoanalytic school claiming to be the only one that has got the facts "right."

The second way of misunderstanding the narrativity of knowledge has already been introduced in the immediately preceding remarks. In psychoanalysis, this view has been championed most recently by Hanly (1990). It is the direct assertion of the positivist view and does not posit narrative truth at all; at least it does not concern itself with that. Within this view, it is proposed that there is, finally, a knowable reality, an ascertainable truth that is our steady and only goal. This is a truth we can arrive at provided that we apply objective methods carefully and for long enough to eliminate uncertainties. Here again is the proposition of the godlike, totally disinterested observer, free of preconceptions and values. This would be the observer whose authority is such as to stifle critiques that are based on other epistemological assumptions. Presumably, this observer (or set of observers) is free of any constraints imposed by language, historical context, ideology, and so on.

As I understand them, both misunderstandings state or imply the idea, and may even be motivated by the fear, that without objective, nonnarrative truth there must result a chaos of unrestricted relativism or pluralism, in other words, a final babble of voices, a state in which "anything goes." To this idea or fear there are, however, several further narrativistic responses to be made. First, the narrativity of knowledge is not a cause or a prescription; it is an observation of what has always been the case and is obviously the case today in psychoanalysis; for there are and always have been more or less different versions of what psychoanalysis is (its principles, its methods, its findings), and there are and always have been different interpretations at case conferences of the same material made even by analysts who belong to the same school of thought. Sometimes these variations come about because there are individual differences in comprehension, sometimes differences in scholarship or intelligence or experience, sometimes differences in sheer temperament.

To all of which the realist/objectivist/empiricist might respond: Yes, but all that variance can be reduced, if not eliminated, by careful control of criteria, method, language, and so on. To this, then, the narrativist would have to ask: But who adjudicates the instituting of such control when, inevitably, there would again be differences of opinion as to the best way of getting at and formulating "the real truth"? Would it be, as one critic has put it, "the voice from nowhere," which is to say, the voice of someone with total authority, power, and infallibility? Who else could it be?

If to this the answer were made that today there are ongoing objectivist research projects producing statistically reliable results, the narrativist could reply that not every analyst accepts the relevance of this research to the clinical process. These clinicians are particularly attentive to the necessary artificialities of method, the simplification of variables, the probabilistic nature of the findings as regards reliability and validity, and often the banality of the findings themselves. Nonacceptance of this research may be based also on its not having been demonstrated that all types of research can be integrated within one conceptual and methodological system. And finally, the narrative aspects of the data collection and reporting inevitably reintroduce the narrativity that presumably has been eliminated. Thus, the research findings may be regarded as of interest primarily to the research-minded and very skeptical. It is, I believe, arbitrary and begs the question to impute naïveté or rigidity to clinicians who are not impressed by the research, for there do seem to be good grounds to question whether such research is essential to clinical work and its betterment. For these clinicians, psychoanalytic objectivist research is best regarded as no more than another discipline, a neighboring field, perhaps even an interesting or suggestive stimulus to further thought.

To return now to the narrativist thesis, the point being made and defended here is that any concept of knowledge must imply its verbal formulation and its communicability. These implications necessarily open up an examination of how the knowledge is being told to oneself and to others, within which tradition, with which set of aims, to which audience, and much else besides. This point of view does not deny truth. There is plenty of truth. It is just that truth comes in different versions. It always has. In this regard, the entire matter may be formulated as one of giving up denials. There is a greater likelihood of chaos de-

veloping on the psychoanalytic information highway from denial than from some reflective thought.

The reason for remaining calm is that we analysts all live in
one general culture with its limited supply of metanarrative possibilities or interpretive communities, as they have been called.
We live with the ever-present experience that we can understand one another, even if not perfectly, if only we try. We need
not agree. If pluralistic narrativity meant that we could not understand one another, there would be no point to meetings in
which we discuss common problems, and there never would
have existed the possibility of psychoanalytic debate or journals
with their readership.

Conclusion

I have surveyed many of the issues raised by the complexities
of authority, evidence, and knowledge in clinical psychoanalysis.
I have pointed to the place of rhetorical manipulation, arbitrary
claims of power and purity, the inevitability of a constructivist,
pluralistic, and narrative understanding of the therapeutic process, and some common misunderstandings of these various aspects of the issues raised. If, at the end of my methodological
and epistemological deliberations, nothing has been settled, I
take satisfaction in that outcome as it is intrinsic to my point of
view that, in the realm we are discussing, nothing can ever be
settled. That unsettledness is in the nature of a science or, as I
prefer in our present context, an exploratory discipline such as
psychoanalysis is.

REFERENCES

BION, W. R. (1967). Notes on memory and desires. *Psychoanal. Forum*, 3:272-273,
    279-280.
FREUD, S. (1912). Recommendations to physicians practising psycho-analysis. *S.E.*,
    12.
HANLY, C. (1990). The concept of truth in psychoanalysis. *Int. J. Psychoanal.*, 71:
    375-383.

JOSEPH, B. (1988). Object relations in clinical practice. *Psychoanal. Q.*, 57:626-642.
KRIS, E. (1952). *Psychoanalytic Explorations in Art*. New York: Int. Univ. Press.
REICH, A. (1951). On counter-transference. *Int. J. Psychoanal.*, 32:25-31.
SCHAFER, R. (1983). *The Analytic Attitude*. New York: Basic Books.
——— (1992). *Retelling a Life: Narration and Dialogue in Psychoanalysis*. New York: Basic Books.
SPENCE, D. P. (1982). *Narrative Truth and Historical Truth. Meaning and Interpretation in Psychoanalysis*. New York: Norton.

INDEX

ABOUT THE EDITORS

Sander M. Abend, M.D., [series editor] is former Editor-in-Chief of *The Psychoanalytic Quarterly* and is currently an Associate Editor. He is a Training and Supervising Analyst on the faculty of the New York Psychoanalytic Institute. He is a past President of the New York Psychoanalytic Institute, and has also served as Secretary of the American Psychoanalytic Association.

Owen Renik, M.D., [volume editor] is Training and Supervising Analyst at the San Francisco Psychoanalytic Institute. He is currently Editor-in-Chief of *The Psychoanalytic Quarterly*, Chair of the Program Committee of the American Psychoanalytic Association, and former Secretary of the Board on Professional Standards of the American Psychoanalytic Association.